Hope for the Adoption Journey

28 True Post-Adoption Stories to Comfort and Encourage

With blessings and
hope for your journey.

Love,
Rachel (ch. 3)

Katherine Piper

While the stories are true, to protect the children's privacy the children's names were changed (except those who passed away) and the authors used only their first name and last initial. The authors for Chapters 4, 7, 15, 20, 21 and 24 used pseudonyms for further privacy.

The information provided in this book is intended for your general knowledge only and is not a substitute for professional medical advice or treatment for specific medical or psychological conditions. You should not use this information to diagnose or treat a health problem or any condition without consulting with a qualified healthcare provider. Please consult your healthcare provider with any questions or concerns you may have.

Book cover design by BEAUTeBOOK.
Original Photography by Justcallmegertie.
Illustration by Trail Drawing.

For Diane
You were the trailblazer for this book.
Thank you for sharing your story.

Table of Contents

Acknowledgments

Thank you to the beautiful women who wrote and shared their stories. This book would not have been possible without your desire to encourage other moms. It's truly been an honor to work with you.

Thank you, Susanna, for helping to find additional authors.

This book richly benefited from the copyediting and consulting services of Linda Nathan at *Logos Word Designs*. Her experience and thoroughness were an answer to prayer.

Thank you, Maria Novillo-Saravia, at *Beautebook* for the cover, interior design, and formatting work. Your creativity and diligence to this project are commendable.

Thank you to my husband for all the encouragement, not only for this book but for all of life's endeavors. Thank you for all the evenings you watched a movie alone so I could finish this project, and for bringing me chocolate chip cookies while I worked. You are such a blessing.

May God be glorified through our testimonies.

Note to the Reader

While in China, I could hear the Body of Christ's heartbeat.

I heard it when our tour guide said she was curious why people would come to adopt special-needs children, the blind, the deaf, and others. She said, many Chinese people do not understand and they want to know why. Her question gave me the opportunity to share about God's adoption of His own children. Her question was only asked because I came on the heels of many others.

I heard it when I looked around the hotel dining room and saw families. Parents who had traveled so far to adopt, because they felt called by God.

I then realized it had been beating the whole time through folks back at home who had been helping us to prepare for our journey.

It beats when women choose to adopt from their own neighborhoods, through domestic adoption.

Christ's heart for the orphan beats through His bride, steady and rhythmic. It pulses each time another woman makes a commitment to love an orphan.

Its cadence can be heard in many places around the world. A beat means nothing unless there is another beat. And one woman alone doesn't send a steady message, but rather the collective whole.

We all, together, send out a rhythmic thumping of Christ's love.

When I returned home, I stumbled in my calling. I didn't understand it, and I felt so lonely in it. Later, I discovered many women have the same feelings. We have such great expectations and can be surprised by our own feelings of inadequacy, and by the struggle of it all. In this way, the heartbeat that is so strong and true can develop arrhythmias. The stress of the situation can create an irregular beat, a burden which can be so difficult to manage alone.

The members of Christ's body were never meant to operate alone and separated. We are meant to work together. We are strengthened by intertwining relationships, with other adopting mothers.

So here is a book with that quest in mind. Twenty-eight different women with different stories. May you, our reader, feel at home hearing their stories. May you pour yourself a warm beverage and cozy up with this group of friends. We don't judge your struggles, sweet mama. We understand the road ahead can seem daunting. This book was written just for you.

Our stories probably won't be the same as yours. You are writing your own story. The goal isn't to instruct, or to cause any guilt. The goal of this book is to remind you that you are not alone. The journey is well-traveled by the feet of many women who have gone before.

In the spirit of friendship, we share our hearts, our lives, and our stories. And our testimonies of God's goodness, even when sometimes it was difficult to understand.

May God bless you, dear reader. And may God bless His heart, which beats through the body of His Bride.

May her heart grow stronger still.

With love,

Katherine Piper

P.S. Some people choose to adopt a child in need, not because they are led by God, but because they decided to. In fact, they may not follow God at all.

If this is you, may I tell you I am truly impressed? I never would have considered adoption, except I felt God calling me into it. And the fact that you adopted, on your own initiative, is beautiful. I hope you feel comfortable here, and that you will find encouragement on your journey.

Finding Joy

God gifted me with both optimism and naiveté. As long as I can remember, I've also had a passion for anyone broken and hurting. Of course, this is not all that unusual in the adoption world.

I have three early memories I believe God used to dramatically shape my life. First, I remember watching footage of the famine in Ethiopia on the evening news in the early 1980s. I had never seen bodies so thin or bellies so swollen. I was about five and I don't have words to connect to that memory, but I know there was a deep emotional reaction.

The second memory was of when the U.S. news began reporting on the crisis of baby girls being killed or abandoned in China. I picked up a magazine in a doctor's waiting room, read the article, and promised myself, "One day, I'll adopt one of those babies."

Third, for about six years, I was convinced I had been secretly adopted and waited every week for my parents to tell me "the truth" about where I "really came from." I do realize this was a pretty ridiculous assumption, and it even became a family joke. But it felt very real to me as a child and looking back at it later I realized I lived for many years with an orphan mentality, feeling "less than"—less loved, less accepted. On the outside.

The more I have gotten to know adoptive parents, the more I notice many of us have this in common—a desire to meet the needs of a hurting world, and a deep emotional loss or pain somewhere in our story that allows us to identify with the specific hurts of the orphaned child. When I was dating Joe, I told him about this desire I had, to adopt one day. Of course, as my boyfriend, he was totally a fan of this plan. As well as any other plan I had. Just so I would say yes to his proposal! After we had been married a few years, I gave birth to our first child, a beautifully healthy and vocal baby boy. *Vocal* and *angry*. Our baby cried for hours and hours every day, and as I paced the hallways, the yard, and the neighborhood streets, trying to calm him, I thought, "I cannot do this again. I cannot have another baby anytime soon." As I sobbed on the phone to my OB, making an appointment to talk about postpartum depression, I thought, "I really, *really cannot* have another baby."

As Joseph grew and the crying stopped, and my emotions and hormones regulated, we started thinking about having another child, but I remembered his first year with a bit of horror. "Remember when I told you that I wanted to adopt, Joe? I think maybe we should adopt sooner rather than later. We can still have another baby in a few years, but for right now I think adopting would just be so much easier."

So much easier.

Remember I told you about the optimistic naiveté God had gifted me with? I wasn't lying. I was optimistic. And so naive that now I just want to reach back and hug my former self, pat her on the back with a "Bless your little heart." But it was that outlook on life that allowed me to happily jump into many of the hardest things I've ever done—college, grad school, marriage, parenting, adoption, missions work—and these have all turned out to be the very best things, which I never would have tried had I known how very hard those journeys would be.

Surprisingly, once we were comfortably married, Joe was not actually as much of a fan of the adoption plan as he had been when it was just the romantic talk of starry-eyed college students. He was honestly a little apprehensive about his ability to love a child that was not "his own." He had signed up for a mission trip to Mexico with our church, and when he left, the question was still unsettled. We didn't talk for the whole week he was gone (in the ancient days before texting, Facebook, and WhatsApp). As soon as he got back, he was so excited to show me pictures of the orphanage they had been working with, and as he scrolled through pictures of precious little dark-haired kids, he gushed, "I loved those kids—I could love one of those kids as mine. Let's adopt." And we were off.

Our first adoption journey started off smoothly. Because of country requirements and timelines, and our close connection with a family that was adopting from Ethiopia, the decision to adopt from Ethiopia came quickly. From paperwork submission to homecoming was just one year, nearly to the day. *Easy peasy.* Except once the process was done, and it was time to just do life together, nothing was easy at all.

Our bald little Isaiah, with his doe eyes and mile-long eyelashes, came home like a hurricane at fourteen months old. He was sick from the start, with snot everywhere and a racking cough, and as I lay in bed one of the first nights back at home I thought, "Why has it never occurred to me this kid could have tuberculosis? Did they even test him? I don't remember! What if he infects Joseph?" Joseph was two and a half by then and although generally happy to have a new playmate, a little overwhelmed to have this little firecracker suddenly into his stuff all the time and taking up his parents' attention. As they played together and figured out the new normal of being brothers, there were a few times Isaiah bit

Joseph, hard enough to leave tooth marks.

The second time I saw him bite Joseph's face I smacked Isaiah right across his face. Hard. I went to Bible study that day and, as my friend opened her door, I burst into tears. I held out my hands and confessed, "I hit him today. I hit my kid."

For the next five years, I lived in a cycle of anger, shame, depression, helplessness, and hopelessness. Joe and I had read all the recommended adoption books and gone through the parent training offered by our agency, but I just did not know what to do with the feelings I had towards this child who was so beautiful but, as it turned out, difficult for me to love. I had written a blog post on *joy* just before we brought Isaiah home and I remember thinking I had wrecked our joy. That it was gone forever. My inner protective tiger momma came out when Isaiah was sick and when he was biting, and I started holding him at a distance, emotionally and sometimes even physically, to protect Joseph. My protective instincts turned out to be very hard to overcome.

Joe's love for Isaiah came simply and easily. I envied this and felt the weight of something terribly wrong with me, because I could not feel loving towards this child. I did care for him, and did everything love does as an action, but his behaviors continued to bother me and embarrass me so much I could rarely *feel* loving. I dreaded the frequent tantrums, huge crocodile tears, and throwing himself on the ground just because he got the wrong color bowl for his mac n' cheese. I dreaded naptime, when I would wrestle him into his crib and he would not go to sleep no matter how long I rocked by his crib, held his hand, sang to him. Eventually I'd just put him in and let him cry. He'd poop his pants and scream.

It felt like we were constantly locked in battle mode and I could not see a way out. Even the things he did to be sweet bothered me. He sat super close during story time and licked my arm as I read.

He hugged everybody, including his great-grandmother, with a full-body cling, hanging and lifting his feet up until the person nearly toppled over. I knew we both had love to give and wanted to receive, but honestly, I could not figure out how to make those connections.

I hid my feelings. One time I tried to reach out to a friend who had adopted at the same time we had. I asked her, "Do you ever feel like you made a mistake?" Her reply was quick. "No! Never!" Oops. I shut up quickly. Changed the subject.

How overwhelmingly shameful to be a mother who cannot love her child. Especially when I had been told all my life, "Oh, you are going to be such a good mother one day. You'll be a natural." Especially when so many people who saw our new family gushed about what a beautiful family we were, what a wonderful thing we had done, how adoption was so beautiful. I felt like a phony all the time. Our smiling family was in the church magazine's adoption article. *Fake.* Our friends were so inspired by our family they decided to adopt from Ethiopia as well and I tried to be excited for them. *Phony.* I smiled when we were out in public, held little Isaiah close, proclaiming to the world, "Yes! You can love a child from another country, another ethnicity!" *Failure.*

Fake. Phony. Failure. Clueless. Idiot. Jerk. Unloving. Incapable. Wrong choice. The enemy had a pretty tight grip on my feelings for those five years and I had no idea. Would Jesus ever say those condemning words over me? Absolutely not. And yet I never asked that question. I accepted the assessments without a fight. I loved God as much as I was able to through all those dry years, but I very rarely felt His love for me and never experienced the forgiveness, freedom, and most of all, the fresh start that He was always holding out to me.

During that season, when Joseph was four and Isaiah was

three, we had another little boy. I gave birth to Adam, and he was a sweet, quiet, little baby. His presence in our family during those years was a reminder I could be a loving mother, overall, but then I was really conflicted with feeling *less than* an ideal mother for our adopted child. At the same time, I struggled again with postpartum depression. This time it was somewhat freeing, and I could recognize and own the fact that no matter who or what, it wasn't the personality of the child but the huge life change that accounted, more than anything, for my emotional troubles. I could admit I just really had a hard time with big life changes.

Eventually I couldn't hold it in any longer. I started sharing little bits of my struggles at Bible study, which seemed like a safe place, with a group of moms who had known us for a few years. They accepted my prayer requests without judgment and really prayed for us. One mom, who has now become one of my most beloved forever friends, shared she had even felt some of the same struggles in attachment and bonding with her own adopted child. *"Wait, you too?"*

That day was a major turning point in our family's journey. To be able to share my ugliest junk and to still be loved and prayed for was huge. To hear *"Me too"* was life-changing. You mean, I am not alone in this? You have struggled through this too? There may be something different on the other side?

I started hoping again. Joe and I attended a conference and discovered the work of Karyn Purvis, attachment guru and God's gift to adoptive parents. We realized Isaiah's challenging behaviors were normal for adopted children and we came home with new parenting tools. We shifted our focus from compliant behavior to stable attachment and bonding. I started seeing my beautiful son in a whole new light, his behaviors not as attacks against me but as messages communicating his basic needs. I was able to have compassion for him again and see him for who he really was. I remembered he was just a very hurt, scared little boy.

Our family life, and my inner thoughts, changed quickly. We prayed, our friends prayed, and we practiced different parenting methods we had learned at *Empowered to Connect*, Purvis's conference. I heard her syrupy-sweet voice in my head always, replaying the tapes of "Oops! try that again!" and "Help them see how precious they are." Those overwhelming surges of love a mother feels for her newborn babe? I began to feel *those* … towards Isaiah! I saw him working to connect and express his needs and we were able to meet in the middle. Joe and I learned so much about sensory needs and learning differences I was finally able to find compassion and connect with Isaiah on deeper levels. I could tell him I loved him and really *feel* it, not just say the words. Our family had experienced a miracle. We were a miracle.

Joe and I had always said we wanted to have four children. Two by birth, and two through adoption. We still didn't want Isaiah to be the only black child in our family. But after all we had been through with his adoption, we hadn't exactly felt called or capable to adopt again. As things began to change in our family, we started praying and asking God again about what He would have for us. It wasn't long before we both felt like we should adopt from Ethiopia again.

The process at that time was a little longer, but we were okay with waiting and had fallen in love with the Ethiopian culture. We loved the idea of our two adopted children having such a cultural bond. We did as much research as we could, endured the disagreements and hesitations from friends and family who thought we were crazy to adopt again and risk our family's new-found happiness and security. We sent in an application and a check to our new adoption agency. This time, we were prepared for a longer wait. This time, we knew all the typical orphaned-child behaviors, what to look for, how to deal with it. We had counselors on our radar. Our praying friends were on call. We read and reread Purvis's *Connected Child* so we could be better prepared for whatever our new child would bring to our family. We prepared for the worst, as far as adoption behaviors go.

After a long wait we brought our little girl home. We introduced Ayana to her three big brothers. The shy, petrified girl we met in Ethiopia blossomed into a girl who would jump onto a pile of wrestling brothers without a second thought. Her kisses and sweet voice had them all wrapped around her finger from the very beginning.

Ayana adapted to our family very quickly. She picked up words, phrases, and nuances without a hitch. She quickly learned how to use her sweet little girly voice to communicate her needs. But for me, a big life change, even after the biggest struggle had ended, equaled a period of depression. It was hard for me to settle into the new normal. I could easily feel love for this little girl, and all three of her big brothers (praise God), but still the dark days came.

At the start of 2016, I was in a dark place, depressed and feeling beaten by circumstances and the realities of our new life as a homeschooling family of six. I knew I had so much to be thankful for. God had done miracles in bringing her home when many said it would never happen. But still, I was overwhelmed, tired, and often sad. Teaching three boys at home and working at bonding and connection with a new toddler was *hard*. One day one of my sweet boys excitedly exclaimed, "Mom! You smiled! I forgot what it looked like when you smile!"

So.

That was an eye opener.

As part of *Legacy Principles*, a mentoring class I signed up for, Linda Werner had been leading us in a journey of increasing intentionality. I remember one night she spoke rather harshly about women who keep asking for help and keep cycling through the same issues but never actually take the steps needed for growth and change. I thought Linda's words were maybe too strong at the time, but they jolted me out of my own rut. I thought, "Oh that sounds like such a waste! This can't be me." So, I slowly started to wrestle more with my own junk and really try to move towards healing.

I was deep in the trench and fighting every day to even want to get out bed. I knew there were some good options to walk through for healing but just the thought of making all the phone calls and appointments necessary was incredibly daunting, on top of juggling family, church, and full-time homeschooling. And washing my hair. And making eighteen meals a day plus fourteen million snacks. Because at that point *everything* was Just. Too. Much.

Linda shared a podcast that January that encouraged us to choose a word for the year. Instead of just choosing any word, it was a teaching that focused on asking God to develop in you a greater capacity to experience and live out a certain fruit of the Spirit. After praying for a short time, I knew I needed to ask God to teach me about *joy*.

It seemed like a big ask. I felt so far from joy, it seemed nearly impossible to ask God to bring me that far in one little year. But I knew in my head that our God is the God of the immeasurably more. So I asked for joy. I also resolved to take advantage of *any* opportunity that God put in front of me that might bring me closer to this new goal.

When Katherine invited me to a Bible study called "Joyful Journey," I joined. Lindsey gave me the number for a new counselor. I made the call. I talked to a new friend about her own depression. I made an appointment with my doctor. I listened to podcasts. I prayed and journaled and blasted worship music. I made myself go to girls' night out and ladies' prayer nights. I went walking with Bryn. I said yes to missions' opportunities at church. I took naps. I watched *America's Funniest Home videos* to laugh with my kids. I went to concerts. We went on vacation with new family friends and intentionally practiced relaxing and unwinding. I started tagging all my Facebook and Instagram posts with #JoyYear so I could look back and celebrate the blessings.

And bit by bit, moment by moment, with each deep breath and smile and connection, God grew in me a new capacity for joy. I learned how to feel joy, recognize it, anticipate it, make room for it, value it, prioritize it, and celebrate it. I learned how to say yes to joy-growers and say no to joy-killers. I learned about guarding my inputs. And I messed up a lot. I blew up at my kids and got mad at Joe and said yes to way too much. But it didn't send me into the black spiral anymore. After a taste of joy, I knew I wanted more, and it was always worth retooling and reworking whatever was broken to get closer to what God really had for me.

Sounds rosy, doesn't it? It was. Often. But I learned one more important lesson about joy. I don't think you can experience and appreciate the fullness of joy if you have not walked through its opposite experience. And so, while 2016 was a year of joy, it was also a year of desperate sorrow. We said goodbye to Joe's sweet grandma after watching her slowly decline in a nursing home.

It was a heavy season. There were moments of hurt, misunderstanding, and silence from family members. Old patterns of broken relationships played themselves out over and over. We left behind the house and neighborhood we had loved for nearly a decade. We dealt with all the normal fighting you'd expect from three brothers, as well as the added burden of attachment struggles, hearts broken by early loss, and the dynamics of adoption and race relations in this volatile society. We homeschooled and fought the good fight against the dyslexia and ADHD monsters.

But hardest of all, we began the walk with a dear friend through her husband's suicide and the long aftermath of rebuilding a family. All I can say now, which is crucial for this Joystory, is that sitting in that deep, dark place and fully engaging in it made the sweet moments, small victories, and baby steps out of the pit so much sweeter. It was the real-life illustration of how much brighter a pinpoint of light is in the deepest dark. It takes the darkest nights to see the most stars and I think it's the same with grief and joy. If we surround ourselves with too many fake lights and distractions from the world, it is so much harder to see the real lights that are there. Distractions dim the light. Joy is richer after sorrow.

As 2017 dawned, I found myself unwilling to wipe the slate and leave my Joyyear behind. I felt like God was whispering this verse to my spirit, "Therefore, since we are surrounded by such a great cloud of witnesses, let us throw off everything that hinders and the sin that so easily entangles. And let us run with perseverance the race marked out for us, fixing our eyes on Jesus, the pioneer and perfecter of faith. For the joy set before him he endured the cross, scorning its shame, and sat down at the right hand of the throne of God" (Heb. 12:1–2, NIV).

After a few weeks of praying around this verse, I realized it was okay to not let my Joyyear be done. Jesus had *endured* for the *joy* set before Him. In the same way, I'd have to learn how to endure: through discovering the joy in raising four children, homeschooling with learning differences, battling my own physical and mental tendencies towards depression and anxiety, and even enduring to find the *joy* in fixing eighteen meals and fourteen billion snacks every day. When my gaze shifts to Jesus, it is a *joy* to be surrounded by the chaos of young, living, healthy children and a husband who may be hungry but he's here for us, praise God. And even though we wake up most mornings to cereal on the floor and bikes left overnight in the rain, it is a *joy* to be allowed to raise these four precious souls. Even the dyslexia and the ADHD become *joy* when we finish a new chapter book, or someone remembers to brush their teeth without a reminder, or that crazy creative energy works to build an amazing invention and the giggles are loud and true.

So now, the Joyyear continues and I take the time to celebrate the light in the dark and *joy endures.*

Leah W. and her husband Joe have four children; two by birth and two through the privilege of international adoption. Leah homeschools the children and makes three meals and fourteen kajillion snacks every day. Leah blogs infrequently at http://thecolorbeautiful.blogspot.com and works with sheismorethan.org to eradicate teen sex trafficking in Uganda and Orlando, Florida. She loves quiet moments and blasting worship music.

Grace Found

Before adoption, I thought I had parenting figured out. I knew how to meet my children's needs. They received the love I gave them, and they enjoyed life. I remember feeling tired with busy boys (five and two years old); but, in just a few short months, I would look back with such a deep aching desire to be that kind of tired again. Adopting Kelly was the beginning of breaking down flimsy ideas I held about what faith and love are.

The day we walked into her orphanage and realized the little girl waiting for us was very sick, my heart broke. Soon after though, a trembling hit me that brought shame. Immediately, we recognized she had fetal alcohol syndrome, and every fiber of my being was already looking to run out the door. Her stiffened body was unable to rest and conform to me when she was placed in my lap. She screeched and looked for anything she could begin stimming on. At seventeen months, she was wearing loose 0-3 months clothing. Her only nutrition came through the cut-off nipple of a bottle that she choked down. A few minutes later, most of it was soaking her as she lay rocking her tiny body back and forth in the bed.

"Have you made up your mind? We need to begin the paperwork." Our facilitator pressed.

We looked at each other and knew the decision we would make would change every aspect of our family life together forever. This wasn't supposed to be how it would all go down. Instead of feeling great joy, grief was already creeping in.

"Give us a few minutes alone," I replied. Standing in a back alley, we prayed and quickly went through the checklist in our minds about what had brought us here and to her. She is not a mistake. She has been created for love. She was wasting away, and we were given access to peek into her life. We would never be the same again. Now we knew what orphaned children with special needs were living like. We held one another tight and felt the shift begin from our old life to the new one as we gave our "yes."

I came home feeling like a fake. While I was grateful for the new life that awaited Kelly and truly wanted to be a part of pouring love into her, she only viewed me as her enemy. Unable to reason with her, I could only be viewed in her eyes as the inflictor of pain. I was constantly pulling her hands away from her face, because she would cram her fingers into her eyes and up her nose until she was bleeding. My time was spent trying to intervene as she slammed her head against the metal legs to our chairs or figuring out how to get nutrition into a girl who was in so much pain from reflux.

"Congratulations! Kelly is so sweet! We are so happy for you guys!" Those celebratory words hit me like a wave and I wanted to die of the guilt I was holding onto. "I don't want to do this anymore. I don't know who I am! I can't help her! She hates me! I want to sleep again! I want to play with my boys who I can actually benefit!" Those are the replies that screamed in my head, while I uttered, "Thank you! It's been challenging."

How can I feel this way? I am selfish and ungrateful. I am not who I thought I was. Where was my compassion? One day about six months later, I fell into a heap on the living room floor. "I am not strong! I can't do this, God!" I looked over at her, numb as she sat oblivious to me. She didn't care if it was me or anyone else there.

I didn't realize it then but that was the beginning of a long journey to healing. My heart began hearing heavenly words that day, which couldn't have come from my own mind. The peace of God fell on my soul as I heard, "When will you give this to me?" For the next hour, I was bawling on the floor letting out the deepest sobs I had been holding in for so long while I was trying to be strong, capable, and compassionate.

The moment I let Jesus back in to take my overwhelming shame, disappointment, and guilt, I could breathe again, knowing this was going to be about the minute-to-minute, maybe even the second-to-second, journey of receiving and extending grace. I didn't realize when we adopted Kelly that it wasn't about the grace upon her life, but about the grace God was about to pour out all over our family.

As the years passed, we prayed for milestones to be reached and we rejoiced when they came, no matter how long we waited.

We changed. Our priorities changed. What we thought we needed before was replaced with a desire to hear and see God at work in our lives. Holding to faith now means that in every situation, we are pressing in to see God's movement.

He began moving us to create places of healing. Growing gardens, bringing in therapy pets, becoming focused on integrating God's Word into our teaching and spending our lives to minister the grace God was giving us to more orphaned children with special needs. We went on to adopt four more gifts.

Our freedom came in understanding we never had to pretend we had it all together. We just needed to gain the revelation that relationship with our Heavenly Father was the safest place to be. We needed to truly comprehend that giving up what we thought was ideal, and going through the hard, was our only way towards finding what was going to be the best for us.

Kelly is fifteen now and developmentally a seven-year-old. She loves her animals and takes care of our rabbit and turtle. She plays Legos and puzzles and is my partner in the flower garden. She dreams of a job caring for animals on a farm one day, and nothing would bring us more joy than to see her worship God as she rides her own horse in the pasture. We are free to dream big again, fetal alcohol syndrome or not. In good days and in bad. There is joy and beauty to be found in the treasure of a moment.

"Jesus looked at them and said, 'With man this is impossible, but with God all things are possible." (Matt. 19:26, NIV).

Tina K., founder and director of ministries to adoptive families at Grace Haven Ministries, is a homeschooling mom to eight precious gifts, five adopted internationally with special needs, whom she raises with her husband Randy of twenty-one years. She and her family live in beautiful northwest Arkansas with their trove of family pets.

Learning to Love my Son with Special Needs

We had two young biological children when God led us to adopt a two-and-a-half-year-old boy from Europe with Down syndrome. I became pregnant the month he arrived home, and the following years were the most grueling of my life.

We were in a foreign place when we adopted our special needs son from Bulgaria, and it had nothing to do with the location halfway around the world. The experience of Down syndrome was only vaguely familiar to us. The fact that we had left our cozy, untraveled life to adopt a child internationally was unexpected. And the little boy we wrapped carefully, joyfully, and hopefully into our family was absolutely the most unexpected.

We loved him, valued him, and fought for him. But when we finally had him in our family, it wasn't easy to be near him … and it took a long time to fall in love with him.

Ethan became my son at the tender age of two and a half. He had been placed in a state-run orphanage at birth, because he has Down syndrome. By the behaviors and lack of behaviors we observed after we got him home, we realized he had not been touched, moved, or spoken to much for those precious first months and years of his life. He had no experience eating from anything except a bottle, probably propped up, with a giant hole cut in the giant nipple on his recycled glass bottle. He completely lacked any awareness of positive human interaction. With understanding less than a newborn, he didn't know that people respond when you need them. He didn't know about exploring. He only knew *need* and his own capacity and incapacity to meet that need, spending his time turned internally, stimming and silent with his back to the world.

We knew it would probably take a while for him to recognize us as something more than caregivers. We knew he had a lot of simple life experiences to catch up on. We had seen other families adopt children from similar orphanages with the same diagnosis and they thrived in their families and developed wonderful, silly, spunky attitudes. We entered the relationship with patience and hope.

However, we didn't realize what it would be like to be the parents of a little boy who absolutely shut us out of his life. He received no touch calmly. I tried and tried to hold, rock, or even carry him on my back in a carrier. He screamed and screamed! In retrospect, I wish I would had known I could move more slowly, to move into his world step-by-step instead of jumping to actual and prolonged touch. He did not look at our faces either. He preferred to be physically distant from us. When we (or anybody) initiated face-to-face contact, he stared over our shoulders, above our heads, anywhere else.

He struggled to eat, eating only a spoonful of each meal sometimes, panicking if anything other than a completely smooth, sweet texture entered his mouth. He had no emotional control, no awareness of interaction or play, did not seek help when distressed, and spent all his energy drowning out his awareness of the world outside of his own lap. At the beginning, he assumed he couldn't move if there was any obstacle. If there was something like a thin rope laying on the floor, he couldn't comprehend that he could cross it. We tried spanking his hand when he got into the dog food, and a confused and upset crying proceeded. He had no understanding of cause and effect, and we had better success blocking and baby-gating all the no-no's because he was unable to learn yet. In retrospect, I might have praised him for exploring and just washed his hands. Also, in retrospect, I'm glad I blocked things instead of fighting to teach him about no-no's. He genuinely wasn't ready.

His hands were constantly in his mouth. He was chronically dehydrated because he didn't drink any liquids besides his soupy meals, so his hands were perpetually stringy, sticky, stinky, and soggy up to his wrists. We had to use a towel constantly when interacting to combat a very real feeling of nausea because of his hands. Those gut-level disgust reactions really impacted our relationship. There was guilt for these feelings, despite our best rationalizations. This was a time when our positive internal mantras became important. "I love him, because he is my son." "He is doing well, and I am doing well." "Yes, spit is gross and it's okay to towel your son before touching."

Comparing to other people and other parenting during this years-long, lifelong season is *deadly*. I am not other people. Despite what I thought about my inadequacies, I really was and am the person who knows this little boy best. Despite not being able to understand much, despite not being able to meet all his needs, despite everything, I know him best, and my efforts are what he needs. Depression and discouragement love to sit on the shoulders of those struggling and suffering. They came for me and I carried them a long time. And it is okay. But let me show you more than I could see then: You are doing a good job, your life will change, you will see many successes, you will have beautiful seasons, and there are easier days ahead.

For years, we couldn't go out because he became so easily

overwhelmed. We couldn't go out in the yard very often, because the stress of new things interfered with his eating. Between that and a new baby who didn't sleep, I was very isolated. There was ear-splitting screeching. Developing awareness and interest in the world meant getting into stuff, throwing and slapping. It is tough to put a positive spin on those behaviors, but we did. Physical terror at hair-cuts and eating strikes left Brian and me feeling our helplessness.

Ethan didn't cry when he got hurt. At one point, he fell out of his crib onto his head. We only knew because we heard the thunk onto the hardwood floor. We were careful to watch for him hurting himself so that we could be close to him immediately. It was confusing, because he was distressed by physical closeness. We weren't sure we were actually doing the comforting thing! Years later, I do know that he desires us to be close and sometimes desires our touch when he is distressed. Some physical response and closeness is a good idea.

For months, and then off and on ever since, he was unable to fall asleep until late, late hours, screeching and hysterically laughing for hours before sleep finally came. We could not hold him to comfort him; that immediately made it worse. Our hearts groaned when we had to sit outside his door rather than holding him while he struggled through out-of-control emotions. We eventually found sleep aids to help him—low doses of liquid melatonin at first and then clonidine for several years after. He still has spells of easy sleep and difficult sleep.

Not long after adopting Ethan, my husband and I sat by each other on the couch, looking at our son who was sitting with his back towards us, scooted into the far corner, hands slurping endlessly, and we came to the realization: "He has special needs." We didn't mean the Down syndrome, a simple developmental delay. We weren't experiencing the curious, fearful, tentative relationship we planned to protect and nurture. There was nothing. Less than nothing, as his inborn instincts had been ineffective in the orphanage. A newborn who wasn't held. A toddler who wasn't spoken to. The hundreds of injection scars from dull needles likely from sedatives given day and night. He had no awareness of relationship, no awareness of other human beings as something more than furniture—furniture that might hurt him. He was like a newborn who didn't cry when he was hungry or hurt. We longed to love him. He could not receive it. There were neurological impacts from all the neglect.

We reached for him, we held him, we did all the things in the books and classes. We rocked him, we fed him, we spoke to him and kept him close. As much as we could, that is. The more we did, the more distressed he became. I experienced the personal trauma of *causing* my son to disassociate. By rocking him when he couldn't tolerate it. There was no guidebook for this combination of neglect and what we began to accurately call institutional autism and sensory processing disorder. I put my emotions on hold, waiting for the time when our relationship could become something more. Patience was important. But as the years passed, I needed to develop something additional: an acceptance for our new normal, whatever it became.

Somewhere around four years home, all the waiting and patience and guilt and fatigue crashed down on me. The waiting for love that wasn't coming. The answering of well-intentioned questions from guests, "When did he bond to you?" when he hadn't yet acknowledged me. The attempts at trying to be close to somebody who could not tolerate my nearness. The deep feelings of guilt and shame for what I could not provide my son. I could not feed him so that he wouldn't have fear-triggered food meltdowns. I couldn't even tell when he was hungry. I couldn't tell when he was sick. I couldn't comfort my own son. I couldn't do *any* of the roles that I hold so dear as my role, my job, my *purpose* as a mother. I felt like such failure.

Then followed my first ever experiences with antidepressants and counseling. I struggled with the idea of trusting God when He'd so personally led me into such a long season of suffering. (During all of this, I'd given birth, moved twice, and my baby had struggled particularly with not sleeping.) I had recovered from childbirth and nursing and was still unable to keep up with tasks. There was a lot of mental fog and fatigue. And pain. Such guilt and shame. Such feelings of failure. The other adopted kids I compared us to seemed to like their parents. The other adopted kids with Down syndrome learned how to play. The other adopted kids learned to talk. I couldn't even … even … anything.

I was struggling through providing his basic needs and was even struggling with that. I couldn't recognize when he had strep throat recurring regularly—only noticing when one of his siblings caught it days later. Mealtimes were more about calming anxiety than providing nurturing. Travel (from grocery store trips to visiting family) was all built around trying to keep Ethan okay. Ethan stayed home while the rest of us went to Disneyland. It was perhaps no surprise that I needed counseling.

Here are the words from my turning point. The thing that started me towards health again:

My counselor asked me, "Can you accept your relationship with Ethan is limited?"

My relationship with Ethan is limited.

If you have been in my shoes, then you may understand the power of this statement already. It means so much. It means our relationship does not, at least currently, have the capacity to be more. It means I'm not failing. *Not failing.* It is like the term "special needs." It means something is different. I *could* attempt to accept the limitations. To accept my limitations in caring for Ethan?

Self-acceptance in my weakness and my limitations was far more difficult for me than accepting Ethan's limitations.

My relationship with Ethan is limited. It's different. And it's not something I caused. Wow. Ethan has trouble processing sensory information, has limited emotional control, and is too afraid to trust, because of his years of neglect. Ethan's brain development was altered and has become like an autistic brain because of those years of neglect. If I consider all of that, I am not a failure as a mother and our relationship is not a failure either. Those little things, those little successes, they count. They matter.

The pureed chicken noodle soup Ethan chows down without hesitation is worth celebrating. The way he cries and grabs at me (Ow! New development challenges!) when he's unhappy or hurt is huge progress. The way he plays on the piano and has mastered the swing in his play-room show his development. His huge range of expression and the glint of mischief in his eye—what freedom and growth he has experienced. No, he is not particularly bonded to me. No, he cannot do and does not experience life like the average person. Yes, a lot of things are harder for him. But we aren't failing him. We are meeting him where he is. And we are loving him just where he is. No failure.

Oh, hope, how I'd missed you! Oh, gentle love, where had you been hiding? Oh, acceptance, you are a tricky one, but you held the key to peace.

I talked to God about the trust thing. I talked with Him long and hard. Because the suffering bit was genuine. The hurt Ethan experienced was real. The pain of the years of his rejection of me is real. And the loss of the relationship and life we expected is real. I found a curious thing when I looked into Scripture about suffering. It's portrayed hand in hand with joy. Suffering. Joy. Suffering/Joy. Suffering and joy. Suffering with joy. Joy in suffering. I can't say I understand it, or that I felt joy during my suffering. But I kept talking to God about trusting Him and He kept being faithful.

I'd like to tell you more about the very big things that came about in our family and in our extended family because of Ethan. Like how my parents became missionaries. About how several of our friends up and adopted children with special needs. About the truth shed and relationships built between our family and others experiencing "limited" lives. And the truth about what's important, which we learned as we became Ethan's whole-hearted, accepting family.

But that would take too long.

God is faithful. It's been almost six years since we adopted Ethan. He's eight years old. He is nonverbal, not potty-trained, has control issues and big anxiety issues. And we want him. We love him. He is our son. Somewhere along the way, the pain and the awkwardness melted away. I am now proud of him, pleased with him, laugh at his antics, and am anticipating the future with as much joy as trepidation, just like my other kids. And just like my other kids, I become frustrated and don't know what to do. Our new normal is feeling refreshingly "normal" no matter how different it is from other people's lives. We are home.

If you are considering adopting a child with significant autism and/or a history of neglect mixed with developmental delay, I encourage you to:

- Be patient with your feelings and your spouse's feelings.
- *Don't compare yourself or your child to others.*

- Get a support team—for yourself.
- Consider what your, and your child's, limitations are, and don't blame yourself for these. Limitations *include* those things you hope will develop with time, like trust.

Rachel D. lives in the Pacific Northwest with her four, soon to be five children. When her first two daughters by birth were three and one years old, she and her husband Brian adopted their son Ethan from a Bulgarian orphanage. He has Down syndrome. She immediately became pregnant with their third daughter. Between normal adoption issues, severe feeding challenges, fears, sleep issues, and the complete withdrawn behaviors of Ethan ... and pregnancy and a baby who didn't sleep, they went through several years of "fire" before emerging into stability again a few years later. Strengthened (and with less naiveté), they are adopting again from the same orphanage, six years later. She blogs in fits and spurts at breezysunday.com/blog.

Look Back: Brokenness Reveals Hope

"I think of God, and I moan,
overwhelmed with longing for his help....
But then I recall (look back on)
all you have done..."
(Psalm 77:3 & 11, NLT, parentheses added)

This is hard. No. It feels impossible. Tears fall. My sobs are ugly and pathetic in this hiding place.

Parenting beloved children who seem to resist connection with all their might is deeply painful. How? How do we keep on keeping on?

How can I endure two-hour tantrums, hateful glares, raging screaming fits that seem unending when my heart is broken, and discouragement floods into those cracks like liquid steel, making it hard to breathe under the weight?

This time I'm crying in the van, and hiding from my children while writing these words on my iPhone just to re-group before jumping back in. I cry loud, ugly, and broken to the One who shepherds my heart, begging for wisdom on how to shepherd my lamb's heart when mine is horribly weary. And I beg Him to redeem my frustrated words and actions. Again.

Through this heavy cloud, I sense my Shepherd's voice soft and clear:

"Look back..."

My sobs stop as one of our other children approaches my hiding place with an iced drink she made me (how do they always find me?). She has been in the kitchen washing dishes out of love for me—this child who now daily receives my love and showers me with hers—also once resisted my love with a powerful vengeance.

"Look back..."

She's a miracle, this one offering me a cold diet soda on ice. Her beautiful, sweet attachment to me and her dad is a gift I once was too discouraged to imagine. We were broken in that season when "the call" came.

My mind trails back eight years prior. Edward and I had three young children and I was struggling to learn the balancing act of working and loving. My career as a social worker had slaughtered my heart for vulnerable children.

Our business had failed in the crash of 2008. We'd lost our home and relocated out to a rural community, and were living in a rented double-wide trailer. In that season as we healed from failure, Edward came to me one night and said, "I can think of no reason to not adopt that is not selfish. Let's start the foster-adoption process." In that moment, I felt our Shepherd's faithfulness as if He were saying, "I've directed his heart towards adoption, now trust Me." For years my heart had longed to adopt children, yet Edward's heart had not been ready. Now his heart was changed, now that our material resources and large home had been replaced with an empty bank account, a double-wide trailer, and surrender.

The following week we stepped out onto the ocean of Foster Adoption with trembling faith. The classes, trainings, mountains of paperwork, and invasive interviews began. It felt like an unfolding miracle coming out of the valley we'd been traversing. I had no idea how much deeper into the valley our Shepherd planned to take us.

Nine months later, my iPhone rang. The social worker's number on caller ID caused a million butterflies to flip in my stomach. We'd been told the wait would be two years, but it had only been two months since we'd submitted our final documents to the Foster Adoption department. "Rochelle, your family has been matched with a baby girl!" Two weeks later, Edward and I became foster parents to our daughter Neveah, with the plan to adopt her. She was nine months old.

I recall sitting in her foster home meeting her for the first time. We were each taken back by her fragile size and the beauty of her angelic, innocent face. She was placed into Edward's arms first. I caught my breath watching her being held for the first time by the strong, loving arms of her father. Her large, gentle, dark eyes framed by long, curled lashes looked up into Edward's face revealing, tentative curiosity. As she was held, enveloped by the protective, strong, loving, arms of her father, her young and broken heart was unaware of the protecting love that surrounded her. Not only was Edward a stranger to her, his tender, safe, committed love was something she'd never known.

I noticed dark strands of un-kept hair strung down each side of her beautiful face and longed to care for her. This tiny angel-faced beauty looked up at Edward's face again, this time reaching up with her sweet hand; she cautiously dared to touch his cheek, melting both of our hearts. We had loved her and committed to be her parents, without ever seeing a photo or knowing her history. Yet now we were forever changed by the touch of her vulnerable innocence.

Gently, Edward placed her into my waiting arms. Her precious little body felt fragile and stiff. We were strangers and safety was not something we represented to her in that moment. Felt-safety was a rare condition for this precious one. After years of praying and waiting for this child, she was here. We would lay our hearts down for her, yet the vacuum of loneliness and pain of rejection from her precious broken young heart would blindside me in the months to follow. Although we'd trained, and I was even a social worker who knew what to expect, the intensity created by attachment dysfunction, along with the cruel uncertainty created by a typical foster-adoption process, threw me into the darkest pit of my life. My breath would be caught by this stark reality—to take a child out of a dark place, we must journey into the darkest places to reach them.

Neveah was instantly adored by our first three children Rose—age nine, Elyse—seven, and David—six. Daily, they held, fed, and played with their new little sister. They'd cheer, screaming loudly at each new sound when she began to finally babble. She was our princess. Yet, perhaps that was the biggest part of our problem— she wasn't really ours. As we treasured her heart, and as she would slowly show a slight evidence of beginning to trust, we received unexpected news.

Neveah was twelve months old when she said her first word as Edward walked in from work that afternoon. *"Dada!"* she squealed, and her three young fans and I all cheered crazy loud. She was beginning to heal. The next morning as the kids played, my iPhone rang. The familiar number of Neveah's social worker on the screen caused me to take a breath as I answered. Although we were willing to take a risk, although I strongly advocate for the rights of birthmothers to parent whenever it is safe for their children, this was close to home and I was blindsided again.

"Rochelle, the judge has changed Neveah's plan from adoption to reunification to her biological mother." Memories from my career as a social worker of children abused by the drug culture pierced through deeply, causing me to feel nausea.

A month later, we sat in the courthouse waiting room in anxious anticipation. Although foster parents have *no rights* in court, Edward and I had come. Sitting in the waiting area, we watched each woman who came in, wondering "Is she Neveah's mother?" Women and hurting children filled the dirty waiting area. The heavy brokenness felt outside the doors of juvenile court is beyond description. Edward nudged me. I looked up. A woman who looked like an angel sat across the room. Her lips, eyes, features were clearly the same DNA as the child we loved as our own. My heart ached and broke with love for this broken angel who God loved and blessed with the honor of creating Neveah. If only she'd been spared the pain that brought this kind of heart ripping.

"The case for baby Neveah." The bailiff's voice broke my thoughts and he ushered us into the back of the courtroom.

Sitting in court, my heart felt suffocated as the judge declared reunification visits would begin the following week. Fear over what another separation could do to Neveah, along with panic over my inability to protect her, felt like a roaring ocean wave crashing me breathless under the water we'd dared to step out onto. God seemed oceans away. I exited the courtroom quickly, trying to hold back tears.

Sleep did not come to me that night. I watched Neveah breathe peacefully in her crib next to our bed and pleaded with God to please spare her further pain. Early the next morning her social worker called and scheduled the visit in her office for the following week.

The first visit Neveah had with her beautiful, precious birthmother was painful. As I sat next to her social worker in a dirty, gray CPS waiting room, something within pushed me to break the silence and ask a question that had been weighing on my heart for months. "Is her mother pregnant? I have a feeling." Her response was "No, I don't think she is." Silence continued as Neveah played contently on my lap, unsuspecting. Finally, a door opened revealing the arrival of the angel face I'd fallen in love with at court. She nervously joined us in the stale waiting room.

Although Neveah had no memory of her birthmother, she was placed without invitation into her arms, as her social worker quickly led them away to the visitation room. I was instructed to remain in the waiting area. Neveah was out of my sight and, again, in the presence of people she did not know. My heart ached. An excruciating hour later, they returned. Neveah saw me and began to cry desperately, leaning towards me, pushing herself away from her birthmother's body, reaching for me. Her birthmother's eyes revealed horrific pain. Neveah clung to me with all her might, pressing her face into my chest. Her angel-faced mother left in tears. The room was again silent as her social worker turned to me and declared, "Rochelle, you were right. Neveah's mother is expecting a baby. The child is due in ten weeks." This news of a child we'd suspected and prayed over opened a floodgate of tears. My emotions were raw. My heart pleaded with God to protect the unborn treasure we'd already been praying for.

The parking lot was hot, warming my tears and further suffocating my breath as I lifted Neveah into her car seat. As I fumbled to fasten the straps, she vomited. Our precious foster daughter was clearly anxious and horribly affected by the visit. She hardly slept that night. Neither of us did. By 2 a.m., I was beginning to experience the first panic attack of my life. With a racing heart, I ran outside and stared up at the stars in a weak attempt to find hope and breath. In that season, panic attacks began to plague my life several times each night. The depression that clung heavy made it difficult to be emotionally available to our children. Neveah and our other children needed me more than ever, yet it felt difficult on some days to breathe. God seemed out of reach, yet, in that season, a miracle was silently unfolding— Neveah began to reach for our hearts. The protective walls surrounding her young heart were beginning to open and, slowly, she was learning to be loved.

We somehow endured the next two months of emotional brokenness. Through a series of events, we learned that Neveah's social worker would be requesting termination of parental rights at the next court date. Nine weeks had passed since the last court date. I saw her beautiful angel-faced mother sitting alone and extremely pregnant. She knew this day she'd surrender her heart. Love propelled me to her. We embraced, strangers; perhaps I looked like an enemy, but love poured from me. Tears fell from her beautiful eyes spilling onto her dress. She held her swollen belly, loving her unborn child. I told her Neveah would always be her daughter too and she'd be honored in our home, encouraging her to contact us to visit when her heart felt ready. I told her Jesus loved her beyond description, that He'd given His life to adopt her as His own daughter. The bailiff interrupted, calling us into court. Within minutes, underscored by a startling strike of a judge's anvil, the angel-faced woman was no longer Neveah's legal mother. The tearing of her heart was clear. Never take for granted the bloody tearing of a birthmother's heart.

Ten days later, my iPhone rang. The Child Protective Services phone number on the screen instantly triggered feelings of anxiety. Looking at Edward and taking a deep breath, I answered.

"Rochelle, we have a newborn baby in our custody at the hospital ready to be picked up. Can you come for her?"

I replied, "We are not expecting a foster child at this time unless the child is related to Neveah."

The reply, "This is her sister, can you come for her?"

Muting my iPhone, I looked up into Edward's concerned eyes. "What do you think?"

Together, we decided that another season of depression and panic attacks was nothing compared to the life of a child, especially this child, in need of security. Edward replied "Of course." I told the social worker, "We will come for her. What's the address?"

When we arrived at the hospital's NICU, they rolled her warmer towards us and invited us to look upon newborn Jewell for the first time. She was one of the most beautiful infants I'd ever seen—tiny, brown with dark eyelashes touching her pink cheeks as she slept.

Hours later, I sat alone in our living room holding Jewell's tiny body close to mine, amazed as I looked at her precious face. Somehow I felt stunned about how our day had unfolded and the miracle I held in my arms. At 2 a.m., it was my turn to feed this beautiful treasure. It did not seem right that I would have the honor of loving a child we'd not created nor pursued. We'd prayed for her long before anyone knew she even existed and now she was here, beautiful, healthy, and peacefully nursing a bottle as she contently nestled close to my heart. This child, a foster baby, was likely to be in our loving arms for only a few weeks. I adored her and longed to love her fully without fear of losing her. Panic attacks threatened to return as I held this vulnerable angel baby.

Closing my eyes to pray, my mind's eye saw black darkness like the blackest night in space without stars. Throughout the enveloping eternal blackness I saw clay pots—visible from light that shown from broken cracks. I realized that inside of each pot was God's light. Yet, His light could only shine out of the broken pots. The most broken pots were the greatest vessels of light. Perfect vessels without cracks were as dark as the surrounding atmosphere—even though they held the same light within—that light was unseen. My heart sang "Lord, I get it. So, break me!" Fear of having my heart broken was replaced by love. A love that was willing to be broken for Him, and for this child. Broken vessels are vessels that shine bright with His hope. Our dark world is desperate for His hope. Our dark world is desperate for broken vessels (2 Cor. 4:7).

"I get it." As 1 John 4:18 (NASB) says, "... perfect love casts out fear." In the weeks and months that followed, I continued to feel fear often, yet it did not have a hold on me because I was willing to be broken out of love for Him, and out of love for these ones so close to His heart. The panic attacks never returned. This time, my heart was available to love our children. Surrendered. This time I was free to love with abandon, whether or not that love could be returned. This time I was also free to reveal my brokenness, weakness, and fears to others, resulting in more support and love than I'd dared to ever imagine. This time, when fear came in I could learn to look with understanding at the Cross. Out of love for me, "He was despised and rejected—a man of sorrows, acquainted with deepest grief" (Isa. 53:3, NLT). His love led Him to the cross to be broken to death as payment to adopt me as His own child. And then, He said "... take up your cross and follow me" (Matt. 16:24, NLT).

So, break me.

Over the next year, with a newly surrendered heart, I began to slowly learn how to fearlessly love our children within the depths of their scars. With a new freedom, we loved our daughters' biological family and social workers and attorneys and all who we could have feared. Fourteen months later, our family was sitting in that courtroom again, but this time the judge declared "Neveah and Jewell are now the legal daughters of Rochelle and Edward. They are *adopted*."

During that season, our oldest children came to me and Edward holding their pony-fund jar. Rose spoke for the others. "Mom and Dad, we've been talking. We've decided that kids need homes more than we need a pony. Could you take our pony-fund and use it to adopt again?" The kids began to pray we could adopt two more children.

Through a series of miracles, we walked out onto the raging stormy ocean of adoption two more times. Three years later we adopted Cobin (the biological brother of Neveah and Jewell), and then a year later, Tsepo, our son from Lesotho, Africa. Through each of those adoption valleys, there were many tears, and feelings of panic were frequent. And now, as we continue learning how to uniquely parent each of our children, I cry often. It's hard. Yet, as I sit in this van, remembering to remember, my heart *knows* that *hope* prevails. Discouragement has again been dismantled by renewed hope.

I didn't think it was possible to find healing in that five-year season as we stumbled along, clumsily learning to parent our beloved Neveah's broken, unattached heart, fighting suffocating discouragement as seasons passed without evidence of connection. How many buckets of discouraged tears did we cry? Only He knows, He who holds every tear.

But now—She loves *big* like a shining, warm light every day.

"Look back..."

Glancing back, my mind's eye sees another one of our children who raged daily tantrums, intense beyond description. I'd struggled emotional and physical exhaustion with trembling arms, holding him for hours each morning, trying to keep him from self-harm or harming another. Tears would flow as my heart of love would ache for him to find peace, and fear for what his future could hold. Discouragement seemed to cloud all hope in that season, and loneliness bit deep.

Now daily he instead runs to my arms just to be held. "I love you" are words he says often while touching my face with his little hands. This one who stole my heart before we even knew his name has not had a single tantrum in two entire months.

I'd never dreamed we'd make it this far this year.

"Look back..."

I hear His voice. I know His gentle touch. He who runs to the darkest and most broken places out of love, redeems all.

Now I take a deep breath. This month has been especially intense, but somehow finding hope in the storm is easier than it once was. It's time to leave my hiding place and get back in there to painfully love our other powerful little world-changer through another episode of frightening behavior while clinging to this truth: His kindness, when I'm a mess, is what changes my heart and life. By His grace I'll go back in there and show His love in that same way this evening to the treasure who is screaming out her broken cries today. Because a connected heart longs to listen to the one who she's connected to, and these broken places will someday, be a radiant source of hope.

His love is kind and unimaginably patient and long-suffering. Hope will someday shine from this broken place. Hope will even shine through the mistakes we make along the way. Beauty always arises from ashes—when spring comes. We just need to hold onto His hope through the winter.

Mamas who are in the trenches too, aching with steel-weighted, discouraged hearts:

Look back at His faithfulness. Remember, He's loving you through this and redeeming your every mistake. His loving arms are gently leading you as He holds your children close (Isa. 40:11). *He loves you.* Breathe.

Friends who have stepped out, or perhaps found yourself on a journey into the Valley of Hard, where discouragement suffocates hope:

"Look back..."

If you are new to the journey where *hard* sucks life from your heart and you see nothing behind you, then let me assure you—

He's now writing the story you will *look back* upon.

He's got this. You are not alone.

Remember and breathe.

> *"I cry out to God; yes, I shout.*
> *Oh, that God would listen to me!*
> *When I was in deep trouble,*
> *I searched for the Lord.*
> *All night long I prayed, with hands lifted toward heaven,*
> *but my soul was not comforted.*
> *I think of God, and I moan,*
> *overwhelmed with longing for his help....*
> *But then I recall (look back on) all you have done, O LORD;*
> *I remember your wonderful deeds of long ago."*
> (Psalm 77:1–3 and 11, NLT, parenthesis added)

Rochelle R.'s childhood was spent in two countries. Brokenness in her own life and the lives of others near and far propelled her into a career as social worker. Adoption and the brokenness surrounding it pushed her into a season of panic and depression. In that valley, her Shepherd whispered hope and a greater passion for broken hearts. Her heart is to offer hope and encouragement by allowing His redemptive love to pour through our brokenness, breathing purpose into the painful parts of life. It is through brokenness that we give His love and freedom away. In that place, we can laugh at mistakes, heal, grow together, and receive encouragement as we step out towards the unique calls within our hearts—as we dare to accept His invitation to follow Him into the darkness where His greatest treasures await.

5

Hope at Home

My adoption story starts where all the best stories do, with God interrupting, surprising, and empowering. It starts where I catch a glimpse of something far beyond my experience, something that smacks of adventure, healing, hope, destiny, and change, lots and lots of change! For one thing is clear to me looking back, adoption changes us all. I used to think adoption was all about the child—all about God's extravagant healing love for the orphan. But now I realize it is all about us parents too—the Father's extravagant healing love for me, and for you, dear reader.

It was back in the spring of 1999 when my husband Stephen and I said "yes" to adoption. Stephen and I were sitting in a parent meeting at our three biological children's small Christian school when a woman (Susan H. whose story you can read in this book too) stood up to speak. The meeting itself was actually over, but she had asked if she could share about an opportunity to have Russian orphans spend a summer in your home. I didn't know Susan at the time and I was busy filling out a form the school required; I had no interest at all, to tell you the truth. Adoption was nowhere on my life radar. As my head was bent over the form I was completing, I had this sensation of someone lifting my head, kind of like a marionette string being gently pulled. At the same time, five words dropped into my spirit, "You need to do this." I did not hear with my ears, but I will tell you, it was as clear to me as if

I had heard it with my ears. I turned to Stephen and said, "I really think we are supposed to do this," to which he responded, "I know."

As with many of you reading this book, our story progressed from that simple "yes" to many complicated twists and turns. We experienced the disappointment and loss of an adoption that fell through after a year of paperwork, prayer, and expense. We experienced the privilege and joy of bringing home our first two children, a son (five) and his big sister (ten) from Russia. We experienced the surprise and challenge of going back to the same orphanage to bring home two more brothers (seven and ten), expanding us into a family of nine.

As we went through the process of making the huge adjustments demanded by adoption, changes to our schedules, budgets, bedrooms, purchases, prayer lives, friends ... God was busy changing me from the inside out. I found that the added weight of adoption, its new structure and building materials, required a sturdier foundation for my marriage, parenting, devotional life, and so on.

Love comes in a package, and adoption is one of the most beautiful packages God uses to encase His radical love. It is a package not only meant for the orphan. We parents also must unwrap the package of adoption and learn to enjoy this gift of love. I have discovered it is a lifelong process. Like Mary Poppins' carpet bag, we reach our hand in to pull out one thing (what we thought adoption was) and discover there is so much more in there. Many times, Stephen and I have said, we really didn't know what we were getting into when we said yes to adoption. But we have found out that is okay, since we did know Who we were saying yes to. Mary Poppins pulled out a floor lamp and potted plant from her bag. How did that fit? What else is in there? What other expression of the love of God might we find, even many years after that first yes?

For adoption is not a one-time event marked by a judge's decision and a joyful homecoming. It is the occupation of transformation, the life-long journey of an orphan becoming a true son or daughter.

Not long after bringing our first two Russian children home, we were enjoying a typical day in our "new normal" of post adoption when our five-year-old son asked if he could watch a movie. This request was common—really common. When I answered "No, not now, my son," (my "really common" response) our son was devastated. We had begun to see that disappointment was a trigger for this child and that his response to it was often extreme, far out of context for the normal disappointment every child feels when he doesn't get his way.

This time he declared in his broken English, he was "not going to live here anymore." He preferred the orphanage and was leaving, never to return. I am still full of thanks to the Holy Spirit for the whisper of His voice at that moment, showing me a life-giving response to this new, but soon to be commonplace, rage.

"My son, mommies don't leave their children, so if you are going to run away, I will have to run away with you." He looked up at me in anger and stormed out the door.

Following him, both of us barefoot in the heat of the Atlanta summer, I asked, "I wonder where we will sleep tonight?"

"On the side of the road" was his response.

"Wow, that will be uncomfortable, but mommies always stay with their children."

Just like the "Runaway Bunny," this mama was going where her son went. Our conversation continued like this for about a quarter of a mile.

And then our precious son said, "Let's go home," all of his anger and pain drained.

I have found the Lord to be "a very present help in trouble" (Psalm 46:1, NASB) as we have faced countless moments like these over the years. Not all of our crisis moments have resolved themselves so nicely, but what a strength and help Jesus has been to me. I have found when I fix my eyes on His eyes rather than on the problem at hand, I always receive hope and peace. His love for me fills me so that I have love to give my child when mine has dried up. I am by far the best mother when I am first a daughter of God.

I have discovered that included in this role of adoptive parenting is a call to be spiritual shock absorbers; the shock of their trauma and pain reverberates into my life. And I have the opportunity, which sometimes I have not made the most of I confess, to release hope, love, and faith into that vulnerable place.

We have had, and continue to have, many opportunities to demonstrate what love looks like to our children. Moving to America was not the only thing foreign, and therefore suspect, in their eyes. The simple culture of family, love, connection, discipline ... have provoked both positive and negative responses from them.

I've tried to describe the difference between parenting our adopted children and our birth children over the years. My friends who have not adopted will often say what we are dealing with is no different than their situations. It is hard to explain, because on the surface it doesn't sound that different. But for me it is as if someone has taken a situation and put it down on paper, and then come along with a bright yellow highlighter and colored over the words.

There is something different—it is accentuated, more intense, more urgent. It stands out and draws my parental attention in a more alarming way. And I realize my feelings, my reactions, are also highlighted. They are more intense, more loaded with fear for this child's future, and a deep awareness of the healing work that has yet to be completed. Maybe it is because I see that my biological children have, underneath whatever difficult issue we are facing together, a solid foundation of unshakable truth—they know they are loved, they are safe, they are accepted. But when our adopted children are in the midst of a similar life-issue, I sense a vulnerability that simply does not exist in our birth children. It may be a behavior that in one is simply an immature expression of a desire, or a character trait that needs some direction, or a season of testing, but in the other is an expression of the residual fear of being rejected, of being unsafe, or of an illogical drive to remain in survival mode long after the need to do so is over.

So, I have had to change my parenting, and also my mode of defining what is beautiful and good.

I remember in the early days after our second adoption the sweetest thing—a simple picture of adoption. It happened almost every weekday around 6:30 p.m. and it was one of the most deeply moving, truly beautiful things I have had the privilege to witness.

Our three boys, all recently home from a Russian orphanage, would climb up on the wooden fence in front of our house and just look down the road. I remember the first time they did it, I wondered what they were up to.

And the oldest, still speaking only Russian, pointed down the road and said something about "Papa." And I recognized "waiting," a Russian word I had learned. Over the years there have been many moments like that one, the kind of moments that compel you to reach for your camera in hopes that you can somehow hold onto the warmth and beauty of it all. I didn't get a photo of my boys waiting for their papa back then, but I see them still and think, "That right there is what adoption is all about—that child has a daddy to wait for at the end of the day."

But my understanding about what is beautiful has changed, or more accurately has expanded, since those early days of the papa-lookout. God has been teaching me to see the beauty and power of adoption in what at first look (and even second and third look) appears to be only ugly.

Let me explain by telling you another adoption story, although if you are like me you may not recognize it as beautiful.

A few years ago, my husband and I traveled to Texas to be with his mother, who was having surgery. Leaving our seven children, all older teens and young adults by this time, made us a bit nervous since a few of them were not doing too well. Just as Stephen's mother was being wheeled back into her hospital room after surgery his phone rang.

As soon as I saw his face I knew two things: it was one of our children, and it wasn't good.

"Dad, it looks like I've gotten myself into a little bit of trouble," he says.

He was making this call from jail.

The details aren't necessary, but I will tell you I was so angry. I felt deeply disappointed, deeply discouraged, and deeply weary of the battle.

And I could only see the ugly in this.

A few hours later, I was able to take the time to pray, which began with me complaining to the Lord, and then asking Him once again to please tell us what to do to help our son heal and live in the freedom of sonship.

And as is always the way with God, He answered my desperate question with a life-giving response, so different from what I was looking for.

"But Beth, this is a *son* who has a *daddy* to call when he has 'gotten himself into a little bit of trouble.'" Just that.

One sentence that completely changed my perspective and transformed what was ugly into something beautiful.

What felt like yet another failure, of my son and of our parenting, became a powerful picture of adoption.

For this was no orphan.

This was a *son*.

Who had a *father*.

This was simple, deeply moving, and truly beautiful.

This, my fellow adopters, is what adoption is all about. It isn't what I had dreamed of when we brought our children home seventeen years ago, and it has cost us more than we ever imagined, but it is the work of the Father's love played out in all of our lives.

It is what adoption is all about.

Adoption has been a precious gift in my life. To be a part of God's redeeming and extravagant love for children, to be a part of the eternal work of an orphan's transformation into a son or daughter—*Wow!* This is the ride of a life-time, and it only gets better with time—not always easier (sometimes, but not always), but definitely more powerful as the work of adoption reaches the deepest places in all of our lives.

Many of us who have adopted children from "hard places" know the realities of out-of-control rages, complete shut-downs, compulsive or destructive behaviors, or many other manifestations of grief, rejection, pain, and fear from our child's past. If you are like me, your first response is quite naturally to see the behavior as a problem to be dealt with. To this day I have yet to have my initial reaction to my child's rage, for instance, be, "How exciting. Here is a wonderful opportunity to see the power of the Gospel on display in my own home. Let me press right into the middle of this raging child's life and reveal the love of God to him."

No, I'm afraid to say that every time we are faced with a difficult situation, I have to overcome my own bit of anger or offense or hurt or discouragement, or fear, or weariness ... Have I covered most of your reactions too?

But I will say that I am learning to quickly and even instinctively embrace the opportunity inherent in each manifestation of some past hurt in our adopted children. I see the tender mercy of God in the exposure of what at the moment is something ugly and off-putting. When my child pushes me away, rejecting my love, I am able to recognize the opportunity, and I am honored that once again I get to be the one to pour out the unconditional love of God on my hurting child.

Think of it, friends! It is for such a time as this that God brought our children into our homes. All those years ago when God called us to adopt, He saw the day when my child would be safe enough, surrounded and embraced by years of the love, care, and safety that can only come from a family, to let out into the open this next layer of pain, fear, or anger. It is for such a time as this that Stephen and I were called, that you, my dear friends, are called to love your child.

Where else could your sweet daughter or son let that deep sense of rejection or that swirling anger, or those wordless fears and anxieties be laid bare? God looked ahead and saw a time and a place right there in your home, under the covering of your love, and said, "Right there—I see it. That is where this precious child of mine will be safe enough to be known. There I see my servants, who have opened their hearts to love big, will not turn from this need that looks so irritating or ugly. No, they will love. They will lead. They will hope."

This is our time, dear parent. As Esther was in the right place at the right time to be available for God to use in the saving of the Jews, you and I are uniquely placed for God to use us in His amazing plans of healing and freedom for our children, "... for such a time as this..." (Esther 4:14, NASB). God brought these children out of their relinquished state and into your home. Let us not pull away from the hard issues to avoid the discomfort, or try to quickly cover it over to keep them hidden. Rather, let us tap into the very love of our Father God and see the amazing opportunity He is giving us to love as He loves. Indeed, to love as He has loved us. For He has never turned away from the ugliness and need in you or me, has He? Oh, how good He is! How wonderful is this Gospel. It is indeed Good News for us parents, and for our children.

I want to end with one more story. I was praying for our children one morning telling the Lord, "What are the chances that out of seven children, they will all walk closely with you? That none of them will get into some big trouble? Lord, I just do not want to accept that any of my children will become one of the statistics. I am going to have to find faith in you for this God—it will be a sign and a wonder." As I was talking with Him about my concerns and grappling with my fears in the face of the odds, I heard two words in my spirit, "Not one." These words dropped with a weight into my heart and my spirit, filling my mind. It was as clear to me as if I had heard it with my ears. And as soon as I "heard" these words I knew a few other things as well. I knew God wanted me to pray into this—it was more a call to prayer than it was a "done deal." It was a solid promise from Almighty God and He wanted me to partner with Him in it. It's funny how two words can carry so much information and weight, but God is pretty amazing that way.

So, I had a weapon in my hand (1 Tim. 1:18). "Not one" of my children was going to become a statistic. This call to prayer gave me faith to believe that our family could beat the trend, faith to fight the fears of a mother. As excited as I was by this word from God, I didn't have time to tell Stephen about it that night. It sometimes takes us days before we can really sit down to a proper conversation (another reality of having seven children). I did call my friend Susan and shared it with her since the two of us have prayed for each other's children for years. I thought the Lord would not mind at all if I included her eleven children in this "Not one" prayer. I figured that if He could do this saving and keeping work for seven, He could surely do it for eleven more. That next night something extraordinary happened.

I went to our church to attend a meeting. It was the only meeting in a series on the presence of God that I was able to attend. As I sat in this meeting, the man who was speaking went over to the piano and began to play. Then he began to pray over people, singing and speaking what he felt the Lord was saying. He asked me to stand. At this point I was not at all prepared for what came next. I knew the Lord was about to bless me and I was excited to be prayed for by this man of God, so up I stood.

Then something so precious and powerful happened. Something I will never forget. This man began to sing, "Not one, not one, not one of your children will fall away from me. They will *all know my heart.*" Yes. Three times he repeated the very phrase God had spoken to me the day before as I was walking and praying. Three times God had this prophetic man sing those words I had only spoken to one other person. And then He added that all of my children would know His heart. There is nothing Stephen and I desire more than this for our children. Nothing. We have come to know the heart of God is so kind, so good, so full of love. That they would each know His heart is the bottom line, isn't it? He didn't promise that none of them would struggle, that they would all behave perfectly, or that they would never make a bad choice. But He did tell me, in no uncertain terms, that they would not fall away from Him and that they would know His heart.

I cannot tell you how many times I have reminded the Lord of this promise, how many times I have prayed it, or how many times Stephen and I have reminded each other of it. I cannot tell you because there have been seasons when it has been literally my constant daily payer. I believe it. And when the facts don't seem to match up to the promise, I am bold to remind God that He promised it and confirmed it supernaturally.

I share this with you my dear fellow mamas because I believe that this "Not one" call to prayer and promise is for you too. I believe that you have permission in the Lord to receive "Not one" for your children. Let us stand in faithful intercession for our children, believing God to do what only He can do. That not one, not one, not one of our children will fall away from Him; that they would *all* know His heart. Amen

Beth T. is the mother of seven children, four of whom were adopted from Russia. With all seven children now in their twenties, Beth has many stories to tell of the faithfulness of our God in her home, in her children, and in her heart. Cofounder of Hope at Home based in Atlanta, GA (http://hopeathomeblog.blogspot.com/), she is passionate to come alongside adoptive and foster parents as they co-labor with God in the transformation of orphans into sons and daughters.

6

The Beautiful Ugly

It was a hot day, just like every day in the Amazon jungle. Flies swarmed around me as I started washing the dishes from our typical breakfast of scrambled eggs and bread from the little stand down the road. My baby girl, only five months old at the time, was down for her morning nap, and my energetic boy-child, then three, was playing quietly in the living area. My husband was out running errands or saving the day, one of the two or maybe both.

I walked across the kitchen to put the plates away in the new cabinets my husband had tediously and lovingly built for me since our home was basically a big wooden box with minimal storage space. As I turned back to the sink, I caught a glimpse of two big, brown eyes peering back at me from the bottom of the porch railing. Every afternoon our home was filled with little street kids, curious about the new white family with the bald baby girl and blond-headed, blue-eyed boy who had recently moved in. But it was unexpected to have a morning visitor. A smile crossed my lips as I peeked back from the doorway. My Portuguese at the time was less than perfect, but I knew enough to get by. I called to the little scraggly-dressed girl staring at me and she slowly meandered up onto the porch.

And that is what it looked like the day my life was turned upside down.

It was not some big event, nothing catastrophic or even

particularly memorable. But from that moment on, this little brown-eyed, small-for-her-age girl would be woven into our family in a most painful and yet supernatural way.

As the weeks and months went on, we learned her story and began caring for both her and her younger siblings, though somehow she herself held a peculiar place in our hearts from the start. From breakfast on our front porch every morning to treating for lice and teaching how to bathe and use a toothbrush, she moved us and challenged us. In less than a year's time and through a series of unexpected and challenging events, she bore our own last name, the first foreign adoption in the history of this tiny jungle town on the banks of the Amazon.

Just like that we were parents of an almost seven-year-old girl with a story that would slowly unravel and come to light, beginning for all of us a journey of learning what it really means to love selflessly and sacrificially.

"I don't even know what to talk to her about," I said to my mom during a phone call in those first weeks of her joining our family. "She just follows me around and answers in one word when I ask questions. What do I say to her? How am I supposed to get to know her?" They were really rhetorical questions. Just me grasping in the dark at what it was supposed to look like to mother this child who I knew very little about aside from the pain of her past. And even in that, my knowledge at the time only scratched the surface of the deep wounds we would unearth in the years ahead.

Those early days were confusing for me. I had wept and pleaded for the Lord to bring her into our home. I could not bear the thought of her living in the conditions of her previous house and I constantly worried about her safety and well-being when she wasn't under our roof.

Now, here she was in our home, with her own bed, her own

clothes, and our name printed on her birth certificate as though she were born to us. Prayers answered. Yet somehow, I felt like a wall had been constructed in both of our hearts, seemingly overnight.

The bricks that laid the foundation of that wall were the lies she told. She would lie about everything. From homework to the color of the sky, it was almost humorous the way she thought she could deceive us in every aspect of daily life.

Except it was not funny at all. We were already heavily burdened with the isolation of our location on the map, the difficulty of mastering our third language with a child who spoke not a word in our first, the climate of the Amazon weighing heavily on us along with sickness, a nursing baby, and a highly energetic three-year-old. These of course were all in addition to the realities of our whole purpose in being there: to show the Love of Christ to those He brought along our path. And they were many. Indigenous families showing up at all hours of the day and night with heavy needs like malaria and gaping wounds. Neighbors in need of necessities like clean water and clothing. Fellow national missionaries desperately needing encouragement while we ourselves felt like the weight of the world was on our shoulders.

Our days were spent serving, sacrificing, listening; and now our evenings were spent deciphering truth from lies, mostly unsuccessfully, with our newest addition. We were ill-equipped for the challenge before us, all the while with no idea that there was a whole community of fellow adoptive parents out there in the same boat, fighting this same battle, because we were in Nowhereville, Brazil with little communication to the outside world.

We soon moved to another small town about a thirty-minute boat ride away after recognizing the oppression we were facing living on the same street where much of our daughter's pain had been inflicted.

This brought a bit of relief but also propelled us into more confusion. We longed to just be a family. To spend time together without the deception, stealing, and lies. It seemed the more we loved, the worse the behavior progressed. We disciplined. We talked. We practically begged. While we had progressed from the yelling, biting, and hitting, we were now on the other end of the spectrum with hiding and manipulating and I still don't know which is worse.

You don't raise yourself on the street for six and a half years with no consequence. So, the lies, manipulation, and disobedience flow so naturally to her that at times she doesn't even perceive it. She resists our love. She has yet to grasp the fact that she no longer has to protect herself; she is safe here. So, she hides behind the walls she built so long ago of self-preservation and self-focus and replaces each brick as we attempt to take the walls down.

Just the other day I was scrolling through Facebook, something I try to avoid mostly as I know it can be a trigger to bring me back to my insecurities and doubts. And there it was, staring back at me. The long, heartfelt and beautiful post about that adoptive mom. About their journey with their daughter and all the emotions, pain, and hardship, but then how there is bonding now. How their daughter couldn't be near the mom in those first weeks, but now she can't leave the room without her. How they are living their dream and so on.

After just three months.

And I sit there once again mulling over the mom-guilt as I think back through my day. How it was hard for me to be in the same room. How I answered swiftly and emotionless to her questions throughout the day. How I stiffly hugged her goodnight. How I can't trust her words or actions because it seems like every single time I let my guard down, I'm deceived again.

After almost four years.

So often I wish I could go back to the me on the porch from what seems like a lifetime ago. I would take me aside and hug me really tight and tell me to sit down. Then I would share the trials ahead, not to scare me away, but to prepare me. I would tell me that I am not crazy like I will feel so many days. That these emotions are normal. That there is hope. But that my life is never to be what I imagined it would be. That our story, at least as far as we have come until now, will not be the one for the Pinterest boards and adoption brochures. I would pass myself a tissue and give myself another hug right about then. I would go on to tell me to seek out community. It is out there! These things would have changed so much about our path in those first two years, if we had just known that there were others out there. If we had only known.

I would tell me to love gently. To believe more. To forgive myself and my daughter. To be gracious, too. To cling tightly to my spouse. To relish the moments with my other two children, too, because I don't want to miss their little years in the wake of this painful storm.

There is a common perception out there that implies that adoption, because it is a concept based on the Gospel and because it is redeeming a child from their orphan status, is simple. Of course, we may be quick to admit that the process is complicated. The attorney and the judge and the biological parents or the orphanage and the paperwork and the waiting and the waiting and the waiting, that part is hard, but then—*then*—it's smooth sailing.

"All we need is love." Right?

Adoption is far from simple.

I see heart-warming adoption quotes on social media all the time. In fact, not long ago I stumbled across my own "Adoption" board on my Pinterest and couldn't help but laugh out loud at what my picture of adoption looked like back then. Back before the long nights and tears and confusion and calling out to God.

Because once the Facebook pictures are posted and the excitement dies down over this new addition, you may find yourself face to face alone with a reality you did not stop to consider before:

Yes, the Gospel is a picture of adoption into the family of Christ. Beautiful indeed. But also, the Gospel includes immense amounts of suffering. Without death, there is no redemption. Without pain, there is no joy in victory.

If it were not for the fact that something went terribly wrong, adoption would not be necessary. Be it death or abuse or abandonment, intentional or otherwise, there is a tragic reason this child needs a different family from the one that shares the same bloodline and facial features. There is a broken past with every single adopted child out there and it leaves a mark. Sometimes that mark is a faded scar that is barely noticeable to the untrained eye.

Other times, it is a gaping flesh wound that needs constant attention and care.

God chose to give us the latter.

So, we move forward in faith, day by day. Because we believe God is molding us through this process. Refining us to make us a little bit more into His image. Slowly we learn to die to ourselves for the sake of this one beautiful gift God has given us. Yes, she has turned our lives upside down. Yes, we have had to die to many dreams to live out the plan God has for our family. But we have always found it to be true that His plan is better than our wildest imaginations. Always. She is worth it because she is made in God's image. And we are made better because she was made ours.

I told my daughter once that adopting her has taught me more about True Love than any other single thing in my life. She was clearly confused by my statement and I fumbled to explain because words just don't seem to suffice to convey all that the Lord has done these last four years.

I hope one day she understands. I hope one day I understand. And that is exactly what pushes me on to try again tomorrow to live out the beauty in the midst of the ugly.

Ashley W. is the wife, of ten years, to her pilot husband, Richard, and a disorganized homeschool mom to three, two biological and one adopted from the Amazon jungle in Brazil, where they lived for four years and founded Grace House Amazon, a home and day program for at-risk children. They currently live in South Texas and travel frequently back to their jungle home where they are a part of The Amazon Network, a group of Christ followers committed to using their gifts for the glory of God and the edification of His Body (www.theamazonnetwork.com). She loves coffee and writing and she blogs infrequently over at www.onthebeautifuljourney.blog-spot.com about life in the jungle and loving without limits.

7

Set Free

"Katherine, choose something!" My mom repeated. We were at a souvenir shop full of trinkets, and once again I could not make a choice.

"Choose now, we have to leave," I heard. I stood there, looking, I still couldn't make up my mind.

"Okay, it's time to go." I left without anything.

I always had a hard time making decisions. My family disliked shopping with me, as I stood perplexed by all the options. As a teenager, I read James 1:5, which says to ask God for wisdom about decisions. I was set free from my indecisiveness, and I started praying prior to making almost every decision. My weakness became my strength. I started to make decisions faster, and I made really good ones. I consulted His wisdom while shopping, regarding college, as a sales manager, and so on. Through this experience, He taught me how to listen to Him.

I'd like to share the rest of my story using horses as an illustration.

I was like a mare, married to a big-hearted stallion named Cyrus. I had a sweet foal named Clover, who grew up close by my side. I lived on a ranch owned by a Rider who tamed me. I loved my Rider. He was very good to me and always helped me. He called me by name and would spend time with me.

My Rider was gentle, and I loved to interact with Him. He

would teach me and feed me. He was incredibly light to carry. He never used a bit, bridle, or whip. He would just quietly talk in my ear to direct my steps.

My Rider began to call to me more often, telling me I needed to take in a new foal. One who wasn't born from me. One who didn't have a family. He told me I was well taken care of, but there were horses who were hungry. I felt intimidated by this new journey. We had been on other journeys together, but never one this encompassing. He continued to visit, while encouraging me to adopt this new little foal.

Choices are so hard. "Which one should I choose?" I would ask my Rider. One day, He told me to choose a one-year-old foal in China, who was blind in both eyes. I didn't see a picture of her nor did I have any special feelings towards her when I did. He just told me she was His choice.

I shared with Cyrus, and he was ready to go. His big heart always wants to help. I shared with my two-year-old Clover, and she danced around for a new playmate. I shared with my horse relatives and friends in the stalls near mine. Some were really excited. They wanted me to follow the Rider wherever He led.

Some horses were not happy and shared their doubts. "A blind foal? How can you take care of her? What will your future hold?" They didn't want us to go. One older mare even cried over the decision.

Most of the ranch horses lived in stalls. They liked their stalls, which they felt would keep danger out. They liked the comfort and security of being within the same dimensions. They liked the regular feeding schedule, and the sense of well-being that any horse feels being close to familiar others. Sometimes they would take a walk to eat in well-known green pastures, or use the recognizable paths. They loved the Rider, but they preferred to stay together and work on the ranch. They definitely didn't want to leave their comfortable situation to go into the unknown, which made some of them barn-sour.

The Rider had moved new horses closer to us during this season. Horses are social creatures, and He knew we would need the encouragement that comes through like-minded friends. Some of these horses had been on various journeys with the Rider before, and they encouraged us to trust Him no matter where He led. Some of them had adopted, and they encouraged us to see the importance of helping little orphan foals.

One day while out to pasture, I met up with some wild horses I knew. Wild horses are beautiful, but they don't have the Rider to help them. They nickered their approval about my upcoming journey to get the new foal. They had never nickered about my barn work; they always ignored what they considered busywork. This new journey resonated with them in a way I hadn't expected. Perhaps wild horses don't understand the need for a Rider until a horse goes on a journey.

Our journey to China began long before we actually arrived in China. Many kind-hearted horses helped us to prepare. We arrived one year after we started. We met the little filly, Lively. She was very thin and her hair was in poor condition due to protein-deficiency. She had a rounded bump on her forehead from where her brain had grown, since she had been on her back so much as a newborn foal. She did actually have a little bit of sight. We were told she started to be able to see a little around her first birthday, which coincided with the time prayer began for her.

She clung to one good-natured, black-haired stallion, but gave the rest of her orphanage group dirty looks. She cried when he gave her to us. She immediately clung to Cyrus in desperation. She didn't care for mares and wouldn't let me near her unless Cyrus was around. If we were eating, and Cyrus left for a few minutes, she would shriek until he returned.

Although Lively was smaller, she attacked Clover constantly. She was aggressive and would bite and scratch her, especially if Clover went near Cyrus. She would pin her down and not let her up. Cyrus and Clover had always been close, and so it was painful to watch Clover take a step back in silence, while Lively fought to keep Cyrus to herself.

While we were in China, I became sick and needed antibiotics. I was scared to be so sick in a foreign land, far from my country where reliable medicine was available. I implored the Rider for help. The next day I happened to get into a conversation with two mares from my land and mentioned my illness. One happened to be a doctor, and the other happened to bring antibiotics with her. The doctor told me those antibiotics were exactly what I needed, and the other mare gave them to me. I was on the mend before the day was over. I knew my Rider was looking out for me, even while I was far from home.

We returned to our old stall, but nothing was the same. I thought I was done, but another journey of learning the Rider's sovereignty was just beginning. Lively didn't care for me, except to take care of her needs. Lively and Clover fought constantly, and I learned to trim their hooves so they wouldn't scratch each other so badly. I used a gate to keep them separated while they played.

Lively would be over-the-moon excited whenever she met another horse, big or small. She would run in circles, vying for attention. When she was given attention, she would chummy-up, as close as possible to them, and give me a sneer. She was looking for a really fun horse who would play with her all the time, and who wouldn't try to teach her. I felt sick in my stomach watching her act this way around others, but Cyrus thought she would grow to love her family in time.

A few months after our return, I became pregnant. I was delighted. However, when my hormones increased, my feelings towards Lively became stronger and more negative. I desperately wanted to protect little Clover from the attacks, the bite marks, the scratching. And also, from Lively's constant pull on Cyrus, which kept him from Clover.

As the months continued to roll by, it became apparent Lively had cognitive problems. She was unable to learn language, but just made one sound she used as a "word" repeatedly. She damaged property and sucked on anything she could get her mouth on. She was very hyper and spun in circles constantly, while yelling her "word." She ran into us because of her visual limitations. Lively hurt all of us when we would lean to hug her, as she would accidentally snap her head into ours. She was impossible to teach.

I never expected Lively would have cognitive issues coupled with her visual limitations. One day, I felt my unintentional expectations for Lively and our relationship shatter. After this realization, I felt like a dark cloud moved over my heart. I felt numb. My heart felt so heavy. It was an effort just to walk. I had never felt depression before.

I didn't visit with my Rider anymore. Oh, I knew He was there, but I would just walk by uttering snarky or sad comments. My head hung low in discouragement. I looked out from my dark stall through bars of discouragement, hopelessness, and resentment. I felt hamstrung. How can I follow a Rider like this? How could I go on journeys with Him?

I had never intended to be a permanent caregiver. Visually-impaired adults can live independent lives, but the addition of cognitive challenges would make that impossible. My life as I knew it was over. I was now a permanent caretaker of a foal who was unable to learn, did gross things, hurt my Clover, and—to top it off—we didn't even like each other.

I did not want to get up in the mornings. I only got up for little Clover. I tried to avoid Lively, so I might forget for a few minutes that I was now trapped with her. I was nauseated and sick for seven months of the pregnancy.

I struggled as I read about other horses rejoicing over how well their new adoptees were doing. Clover had a hard time with her, and I had no advice to give her. We would kneel down next to her bed and tell the Rider we were sorry and ask Him to help us love Lively.

I became Lively's caretaker only. I fed her lots of protein and made sure she had her needs met, but I didn't go any further. I felt like a different mare would be a better mom for her. I talked to Cyrus about disrupting the adoption, but his big heart was appalled at the idea. Sometimes, I would imagine we were going to disrupt the adoption, to take the edge off my disappointment.

We took Lively to the best eye specialist. After looking at her eyes, he said a cornea transplant would help some, but since she had so many complex eyesight issues, she would likely lose the little eyesight she had if her eyes were tampered with.

About seven months after Lively's adoption, I read a blog where another adoptive mare shared her struggles, and I mentioned my own. She immediately responded and said she would pray for me. That morning was particularly bad, and I felt so discouraged. My heart felt so very dark and heavy with its lack of love, and I asked the Rider again to help me with Lively. I put the fillies down for their naps and went to lay down.

I heard Lively wake up a little early, but I still wanted to save the last few minutes to rest. I felt the Rider's pressure on my heart to go and get her instead. After a little hesitation, I went to get her.

I tried to keep her skin from touching me as I walked. I put her down next to me, thinking "Okay, I've done what You've asked."

The next thing I knew, my tiny small heart started to fill up with the Rider's love like a balloon. It swelled larger and larger and was so intense I started crying. I hugged little Lively and could not let her go. She wasn't hyper like usual, she just hugged me back. I could not stop crying. I saw a picture in my mind of when she was dropped off at the orphanage. And *I knew* from the day she was dropped off, and every single day she was at the orphanage, she was mine. She had been mine the whole time. I suppose since the Rider is outside of time, He knows these things.

Over the next couple of days my heart shrank back down. However, I always had this little seed of love left over from that day, way down deep inside. From that time on, I could look at her and tell her I loved her. I could not do that before. As time moved on, I knew I loved her, but I still didn't like her.

About eight months after her adoption, we went to a party. Lively hugged every male in the room. When we got home, she would not go to Cyrus. She wasn't actually attached to him like we had thought. I showed Cyrus a Facebook page of two daughters smiling and hugging. The other family had "cocooned" their daughter. I said, "This is what I want, can we cocoon her?" He said yes.

Desperate for improvement, we intensely cocooned Lively for six months. Much to our familial horses' dismay, we did not allow them over until she was already in bed. We didn't go to parks because she would chase the other foals to hug them and hurt Clover afterwards. We didn't go to barn services anymore because she would cling to her teacher and not return to me (even if I stayed in the class). It didn't work to take them into the main service. So, I quit attending services and only went to a small home fellowship with them.

We had constant struggles with familial horses after we started cocooning. Thankfully, some helped us by heeding our requests, but others were against our decision and sought to circumvent our attachment strategies. They weren't able to recognize that the affection she dished out on them was indiscriminately given to everyone she met.

I read an article somewhere online about attachment disorders that recommended keeping Lively in the same area with me for a month. This solved a lot of problems as I knew exactly what she was doing all the time. The fillies could not fight, and things were not misused. I wish I had done this from the beginning.

After my new little foal, Spirit, was born, the darkness over my heart lifted. However, I still didn't like Lively. She continued to run in circles while yelling her one "word," and would now topple into my new foal. She was truly chaotic. I finally gave up trying to teach her to talk and would just pray every day for the Rider to help her speak.

Spirit had severe allergies, and about a year after she was born we took her to a NAET specialist. She noticed Lively and talked to us about NeurOptimal Neurofeedback. The training was done on both sides of her head. We signed up for fifteen sessions. The first night, after dinner, she said, "Thank you for food." I could not believe it. She could talk.

Previously I had wondered why I had gotten pregnant so soon after we adopted Lively. It made things so tough. In hindsight, I can see how Spirit's birth and subsequent allergies were the avenue we needed to discover neurofeedback.

During the cocooning, I became more attached and protective of Lively. We slowly lifted Lively's cocoon. At the beginning, we didn't let her hug horses until she knew them. Then after a few visits, they could give her a quick hug only when they were leaving. After a few more visits, we would let them hug her when they arrived and when they left, but her hooves always remained on the ground. This is still our rule. We also don't let them horse around or tickle her.

We still try to avoid big gatherings, or the overstimulation will make Lively regress. She has to eat in between her immediate family members or she will regress. These new rules have created some separation between us and our families. Many horses have been displeased because we don't fit in our previous stall like we used to. As the conflict grew, I kept hoping Lively would be "fixed" so we could return to "normal." At that time, the disagreements we had over her attachment struggles became another strain in my faith over the Rider's decision.

It had been six months since neurofeedback, and Lively was four years old, but she seemed stuck again, as she could only link two words together. She wasn't progressing anymore. We wanted more neurofeedback, as this seemed to be our only solution.

I asked the Rider for help with Lively and a neurofeedback solution. I wanted a system we could keep at home and use more often. Soon after, through various internet searches, I was on the phone with Pete from brain-trainer.com. Pete had experience with neurofeedback and adopted horses. The brain-trainer also focuses on the whole brain, not just the sides. After more prayer, we purchased the system.

After the first session of HEG, which focuses on the front part of the brain, Lively turned to me and said, "Mommy sweet and beautiful" and gave me a hug. That was the first time she had said anything nice to me. After five sessions she daytime potty-trained herself (I had tried to teach her unsuccessfully for six months). She stood taller and seemed more self-aware. Somewhere along the way she stopped colliding her head into us.

Our relationship took off after brain-training. She started to hug me all day long. She can still pull away if she gets too much attention from other horses, but she is usually fine if they respect our social boundaries. Recently, I tried an EEG program designed to "train down excess activity" (called FRE1C). She now sits in a chair rather than rocking back and forth in it, and she seems more mature. There are other EEG programs that I look forward to trying.

Lively's forehead receded to normal, and we also started growing her mane out. (We had previously cut her hair short because of its strange texture.) She grew a pretty black mane that flowed around her face.

Some horses came to visit our home fellowship. They had been on a long journey to Africa with the Rider. They asked Him if He would help Lively with her eyes. A couple of days later, Lively mentioned seeing the playground, which was a good hundred feet away. Afterwards, she asked me what the red in the sky was. I told her it was the sunset. We took her back to the eye specialist, and he was surprised at how her previously cloudy corneas had become clear. She is still visually impaired, but she can see better than she used to.

I wasn't sure how to educate a little filly like Lively. She needed special teachers because of her vision impairment combined with learning disabilities. Yet, she would quickly lose the attachment we had gained by being in a school with other horses. I asked the Rider and He led me to a home-school charter. Lively stays with me all day, and they send a speech therapist and a Braille teacher to my house during the week. They also send mobility and technology teachers for her. The school has been such a blessing.

It seemed like we were on the right track until one day I

became furious over something Lively did that had upset me since we first got her. I was shocked at my strong reaction and finally realized the only reason I could be so mad, so quickly, was because I hadn't forgiven her.

Later on, I walked by Clover and Lively playing happily in the field. They play together peacefully for hours, and snuggle together to read. When one of them is hurt, the other rushes over to help the hurt one back up. They have no resentment over their past. It's all gone. They live in the present.

I prayed to forgive Lively, and the next week the same issue arose. This time I fixed the problem and moved on. I wasn't angry anymore. Seeing the difference, I methodically went through our past and forgave her for everything that had upset me (intentional or unintentional).

I hadn't realized I had built bars of resentment between Lively and myself. Resentment ignites anger. Unforgiveness keeps the embers burning. Forgiveness puts the fire out. With the bars of resentment broken down, my relationship with Lively became much more peaceful. Sometimes, something happens that will make me upset, but I pray to forgive, and my emotions calm down.

I had repetitious, negative self-talk about Lively that had developed during my depression season, and I didn't realize it for a long time. When it finally dawned on me, I started countering those thoughts with something positive. Usually I countered with, "Yes, but she's trying so hard" or "She's come so far." Those negative thoughts disappeared. They can make a reappearance, but I try to "talk back" to myself with something positive right after, and they go away again.

It took me months to realize I had developed unreasonable, continual anxiety that lasted all day long. One day, I asked the Rider to please help me with my intense anxiety. I went outside, and a honey bee flew in my mane, got tangled, and stung me on the right side of my head. It hurt, but I finally felt perfectly calm inside. I thought clearly and had no anxiety at all. I went to the internet and read that depression and anxiety look like brain inflammation on brain scans. Perhaps the prior depression and later anxiety were connected? I didn't know if the bee sting would be a permanent solution, so I started taking curcumin (for inflammation) hoping it would help; either way the unprovoked anxiety hasn't returned[1].

Little Lively is still hyper, but she has her calm moments. She is the calmest when she is by my side. My other two can be tired and fussing, but Lively will remain even-tempered. Lively tries to keep Spirit from misbehaving. She runs to find me if Spirit is up to mischief. When she is not by my side, I am looking for her. She lifts her little hoof up and says, "What the heck?" just like I do.

We've found a barn service that has a family room where Lively can come with us during services. She lays her head down on me, and I stroke her mane. We have peace in our relationship. I am learning to enjoy who she is, rather than who she is not. She has become the daughter whom I love and like.

The other day it was pouring rain, and we all went to walk down to the creek to see how high it was. On the way back, Lively was walking up the hill ahead of us. She always wants to lead the way. Her hoof got stuck in the mud and she pulled it out and continued to plow up the hill. She got scratched by some hard-to-see branches, moved aside, and continued climbing in the pouring rain. My heart swelled with pride watching my resilient, tough, little filly. Originally I did not understand her strength and resented the way it manifested itself. I have discovered she is

---

[1] I don't recommend getting a bee sting in the head, without talking to your physician first!

stronger than me.

I've learned the Rider doesn't build stalls for horses. The horses build their stalls. These stalls can keep horses back from going on journeys with the Rider. The Rider loves all His horses, whether they stay back at the barn or go out on the trail with Him. The greatest difference is the horse who goes out on a journey gets to experience the Rider.

On a journey, a horse can understand more about the Rider. The Rider can bandage up the horse's leg after an injury. The Rider is urging the wide-eyed horse to trust and move forward as she struggles through a rushing river. The Rider is pleading for the thirsty horse to cross the wide, dry desert, especially when she desires to stop. The Rider always goes with His horse. The horse may have scars from her journeys, but the Rider has more. Through everything they go through together, they develop a special sort of bond. A deeper level of trust.

I've learned Lively didn't come "as is." The Rider had plans to change both of us. I ask Him daily for many things pertaining to Lively. Cyrus and I now have prayer and fasting times, which has proven beneficial. Lively's adoption wasn't the end, it was just part of the process. *And, even though the path is challenging at times, it is the path He wants me on, and He is with me on it.*

Some days, the journey ahead can look daunting. She can regress, and I can too; but it's short term. I've learned when I focus on Lively and her struggles that it makes my head hang low. I can't look over at the other horses because they may not approve. I have to look up, towards the Rider's face. I have to listen for His voice.

One day, He showed me how He has used the controversies surrounding Lively to set me free to follow Him completely. He wants me to follow His voice and to be about His business. The social expectations I could never meet after adopting Lively prevented me from going back to my old stall. Even though I love the familiar horses, I've had to take a step away. I need to be His horse. He must be my focus. He used Lively, whom I thought had trapped me, in order to set me free. I've been set free. "Now the Lord is the Spirit, and where the Spirit of the Lord is, there is freedom" (2 Cor. 3:17, NIV).

Journeys are preparation. The Rider strengthens horses so they can go on more difficult, and longer journeys. "If you have raced with men on foot and they have worn you out, how can you compete with horses? If you stumble in safe country, how will you manage in the thickets by the Jordan?" (Jer. 12:5, NIV).

He wants to guide us on winding paths, around thorny bushes, and over slippery rocks. He wants us to trust His voice in our ears, whispering which way to go so we can be stronger and go further. He wants to take us to places where we can run. When horses gallop, they are so fast their hooves barely touch the ground before they stretch out again in another leap forward. He wants us to run free with Him like that. Pulling forward. Never looking back. Straining with all our might towards what is ahead. Maybe, someday, we can race like that with Him ... so fast that it will feel like we're flying.

Katherine P. worked as a sales manager until she had her first child. She lives in the country with her husband, three children, eight chickens, and two cats. The dog died. She homeschools the two oldest, while chasing around her adorable, but strong-willed two-year-old. Her own happy place is an action movie accompanied with dark chocolate.

8

The Silent Months

This is a story of adoption, its pain and its joys. It's a story of the overwhelming guilt and shame that consumed me as I struggled to remain faithful to God's calling to mother two older girls with special needs (Anna and Claire) who had grown up in separate orphanages. It is a story of God's faithfulness in our lives as we walked a difficult path. And most importantly, it is a story of redemption in the lives of our precious daughters and in the life of our family. Following God's calling in our lives is hard sometimes, and we fall beneath the weight of it. And it is okay. Jesus fell beneath the weight of the cross, and Simon carried it for Him. Was His falling enshrouded in shame? There is no place for shame and secrecy in doing God's work and in sometimes falling beneath its weight.

We felt so alone in our pain. The shame and guilt that consumed us was far too heavy a load to carry. No one should ever have to feel shame because they have stepped out in faith to meet the needs of the broken, abandoned, and abused children of society and found it to be beyond their ability to meet all the needs alone, or to produce the warm fuzzy feelings of motherly and fatherly love. Loving these children is not about the feelings. It's about the work of it. It is about God calling people to care for His damaged children. It's about choosing to be faithful to love when the feelings don't come. So, come along with me on a journey of love and loss, of pain and redemption, of sacrifice and blessing, and may you find a fellow sojourner for your pilgrimage.

* * *

I suppose it started the day I met her, that long awaited, momentous day when the clouds would part and I'd first lay eyes on the precious child for whom I'd prayed for over a year.

I had been warned to keep my expectations low, even to not have any at all. I felt I had no expectations, other than a desire to love a child who had never known a mother's love. My family life with nine biological children was wonderful and overflowing with love, and we had something to share.

The first time I saw her, her head was enshrouded in short, raven black hair that hung low on her shoulders in a way that struck me as different, as remarkably low. She peeked up at us from beneath her deeply bowed head with a shy, sweet smile. We walked over to her and sat down next to her.

I felt a fear in my stomach. There was something about her that scared me. Was it her mannerisms, the way she hung her head so low, the way it seemed small for her tiny shoulders?

The director said, "She's quiet now, but she's one of the hyper ones in the orphanage."

Neurological issues, I thought, and my anxiety grew. My mind was suddenly filled with pictures I had seen of her on other people's blogs. She was always off somewhere, throwing a ball, sitting with children much younger than herself, jumping, not involved with the other teens who were being adopted.

And here I was, with this child sitting beside me. The awkwardness was painful, and anxiety rippled through my body as the pieces came together in my mind. She was different from what we had been told, and I felt a distance, a separateness, a fear that gripped me.

I can't do this, I thought.

And yet, there was that ever-present awareness that this was the child God had chosen for me. I was called to be her mother. He would make a way. So, I ignored my feelings and went and signed the papers. She came in with us and sat on my lap.

Where were the motherly feelings? I was numb and stunned and afraid.

"Are you happy with your child?" The man asked.

"Yes," we answered.

We said "yes" over and over again. I'm saying yes to God, I thought, void of the feelings I'd thought I'd feel.

Soon the signing of the papers was over and it was time to go. I didn't know how to be her mother. I held her hand and walked out of the office, wishing with all of my heart the feelings of dread and estrangement would end.

After returning to the hotel, we walked to an Italian restaurant. Anna sat awkwardly on the chair, her head bowed low, refusing to look at the menu. She couldn't decide on anything, so I chose for her. She sat beside me, disengaged, sulking, sad. She lifted her legs and put her feet on the seat of her chair and buried her head between her knees. I looked at Mark, and his eyes met mine. "There's something wrong," he said in a quiet voice.

The sick feeling burned inside of me like the sting of a jelly fish. We finished our meal, all of us that is except Anna, who had eaten nothing. We stood up and pushed in our chairs. Anna sat there, not moving, her head tucked between her knees. I pulled her chair out and took her hand. She quickly pulled her hand from mine, but she stood up and followed us.

We walked out of the restaurant, but as soon as we were on the sidewalk, she walked as far away from us as she could. If you've ever been to China, you'll understand how concerning this was on the over-crowded streets. We insisted that she hold our hand. She hated that and continued to pull away.

I didn't want to be her mother. But how could I not be her mother? She would turn fourteen in two days. God had moved Heaven and earth to get us there on time to adopt her before she aged out of the adoption program and could no longer be adopted. If I couldn't be her mother, then she would never have one. How could I judge this child in the first moments I'd met her? I knew, deep within me, I was called to mother this precious child who felt so foreign to me.

And she was lovely, beautiful, strikingly so, yet somehow she repelled me. It didn't make sense. I, who had never met a child I couldn't love, felt nothing for our clearly lovely new daughter. That was when the guilt began to invade the peace I'd known before we traveled. And who could I tell? I was so ashamed of my feelings. I don't think I even admitted them to myself.

The first two months we were home, Anna barely tolerated me. Her face would light up when she saw Mark, and she followed him around like a puppy dog. She adored him. When she would hear his car drive in the garage, she'd run to meet him.

The rest of the time she withdrew from all of us, especially from me. There was *nothing* I could engage her in. She didn't play or do school work, and she made no relationships with anyone in the home other than Mark. The deep sadness was pervasive. It affected everything we did. We tried to be happy and jovial and include her, but she often sat in a chair as far away from us as we would allow her to, with her head hung in a deep pout, while we tried to maintain some sense of normalcy in our home.

I chose to be very intentional about loving Anna with my

actions and my words, even when I didn't feel it. I've always loved children and acting out my choice to love her wasn't really what I had difficulty with. I had difficulty with the feelings.

In the midst of Anna's difficult adjustment, our other new daughter, Claire, was sick and had five long hospital stays the first year we were home. This was very hard on Anna and my ability to bond with her.

The girls' presence in our home affected everything. Our evenings had been structured. Mark would come home from work and begin family devotions. The girls acted out, giggled and tried to interrupt in any way they could. I didn't want to put them to bed early, or put them in any way away from us, so eventually the reading in the evenings stopped, be it right or wrong or just out of necessity.

Likewise, our homeschool was difficult. In the beginning, the girls constantly called me. Then I set it up so that the girls had a child helper who they had to ask for help. And during the long hospital stays, our older children maintained our homeschool, *for a while*. But then, eventually it began to fall apart. They just needed their mom, and I was in the hospital.

During Claire's first hospital stay, which was merely three weeks home from China, Anna was so sad and withdrawn when Mark would bring her to the hospital that I felt I could not be her mother. I wasn't home, and Claire's needs looked bigger around every corner. I felt she needed a mom who could be more present.

Emotionally, I *really* felt that I could not mother her. I was growing more and more aware of some significant cognitive needs that were presenting themselves with Anna. I felt I couldn't do both, and I didn't feel it with Anna. Not only did I not feel it, I was beginning to resent the constant shadow her dark mood casted over every activity our family shared.

Within a couple of months, both girls were in love with me, and so desperate was their love and need for me that there seemed not one moment when they were not either calling my name, interrupting the other children, following me around the house, hugging me, hovering over me when I sat down for a moment, or fighting with our little children in an attempt to get my attention.

Anna loved me with a fervor that exhausted me and repelled me at the same time. She was precious and lovely and desired to please me. She longed to be loved. I know now that I did love her, but I couldn't feel that love the way I wanted to. Anna was attaching just fine. It was I who had trouble attaching to Anna.

I loved her in deed and in truth. Yet I found it so difficult to get to know her. And one cannot have the feelings we all long for when we don't know someone. In so many ways, she was a puzzle to us.

As we began to build a history together, the feelings did begin to come. I did grow to know her, but I couldn't see our progress amidst the guilt and exhaustion I tortured myself with. That's because this precious child I rocked and held and loved with my actions, also pushed me away from her with her endless demands on me.

Our teenagers needed help being launched. The little ones longed for me. Anna wanted constant physical touch and attention. The weight of all the needs, and the guilt about not being able to feel the feelings I expected myself to feel for Anna, just kept eating away at me, and eventually, it became just too heavy a load to carry.

I remember the day I broke. I was standing in one of the halls of Children's Hospital. Claire had had a bone spur removed from her spine and had lost the function of her legs in the process. She was healing, but she'd already been in the hospital six weeks straight, and she'd had three other hospital stays before that.

The children were tumbling over themselves in the halls. Anna was bored and fussing that she wanted to go home, and as much as I tried to be at the hospital daily, it seemed Claire was bonding more with the nurses than she was with me.

So, I stood there, amidst the littles, with Anna and Claire, trembling. Pictures from some faraway place in my childhood flashed across my mind in strobe-like fashion, like a movie I didn't want to watch yet that couldn't be paused. My hands shook. My knees felt weak beneath me. The hall spun in circles, and I lost my balance.

The nurses helped me to a chair. "Here, sit down. Are you okay?"

I told them I was okay, that I had just lost my balance, and we were on our way to the cafeteria. I'd be fine. That was the day I stopped eating.

It was like something snapped inside of me that day. My stomach tied up in a knot, and my throat felt like I was being choked to death slowly. The irony of it all was that I was so loved, loved by my precious husband, loved by each one of our dear children, even by our newly adopted ones. Yet the needs weighed so heavily that I felt like I was suffocating and that no amount of love I could give would ever be enough.

I woke up every morning and felt a mounting anxiety about seeing Anna. She was hyper vigilant, and I could not open my bedroom door without her standing there waiting for me outside of it. Or if she was still asleep when I woke, as soon as my foot hit the top of the stairs, she would bound out of her room and almost knock me over with her hugs. My heart would sink, and I'd force myself to hug this dear soul who loved me with an intensity that was beautiful and lovely and yet so very painful for me. I bristled when she touched me.

A big problem to have, eh? I thought to myself, a child who adored her mother, her mother whom she had longed for all of her life and now had, yet a mother who recoiled from her love and need for her. And the guilt would rise in my throat.

Always we worked it out, and she knew she was loved, but the intensity of her need for me was constant. She was by my side every moment until I would retreat into my room in the afternoon and lock out my family for a couple hours each day.

Then the spring days turned into summer days, and nothing changed, except for the amount of time I was spending in my room. The pain and anxiety kept growing until I felt I couldn't leave my room without Mark.

Claire came home from the hospital in May, and most days I'd take the kids to a pool, come home and feed them, put the littles to bed, and close my door to my precious family. In the mornings, I no longer left my room. I'd wait until Mark was ready for work and then I'd come downstairs with him.

I felt as though my home was no longer my haven, but some foreign place I feared and was compelled to withdraw from. One day our son John came up to my room and asked me if I was trying to starve myself to death. I had lost fifty pounds.

That was when I knew something was really wrong. Yet I couldn't do anything about my feelings, and I was so very ashamed that I couldn't feel the feelings of love for my precious daughter that I felt I should have. I felt so bereft and so terribly guilty, and so totally alone.

And then one day in August, I got a message on Facebook from a friend who'd also adopted an aging-out child, sharing her feelings of how hard it was, and asking me how I was doing. I wrote her back.

Somewhere between the lines of my message, my friend saw a desperation and a need beyond what I had intended to express. She immediately began looking for a way to help. Within a couple of days, she and another friend had found a precious loving family who offered to take the girls for a couple of weeks to give us a break. I was shocked at first.

Yet, I had my friends encouraging me to take a break, and deep inside I knew I needed something to change. So, we told the girls they were going. We presented it in a positive light, but I knew they were afraid. Within two days, we were driving halfway to meet the family who had so graciously offered to take the girls and give our family a rest.

When I hugged Anna and told her I loved her, she just said, "I love you too Mommy." She didn't ask me if I'd be back. And I didn't bring it up. I think she expected me to come back. We had talked of this as only being a visit.

"Of course I'll hurt you. Of course you'll hurt me. Of course we will hurt each other. But this is the very condition of existence. To become spring, means accepting the risk of winter. To become presence, means accepting the risk of absence" (Antoine de Saint-Exupéry, *The Little Prince*).

The ride home felt strange and lonely, and we were riddled with guilt. We'd worked so hard to bond with the girls, to cocoon them, to keep them with us and to care for them, to love them, and now we were leaving them in the hands of another.

During those first couple of weeks home, I did feel a lightness to my days. I felt like I had my home back again, and I could leave my room and feel comfortable again. We were all able to talk about our feelings. I had an overwhelming sense of relief from the responsibility. And, I was beginning to be able to eat again.

I began to miss Claire. I did not miss Anna. The weight that was lifted off of me along with not having her in the house was huge. It feels cruel to say it, and it felt terrible to feel it, but that's how I felt. For ten months, I had given all I had, and I felt no closer to having peace in my home than I did when I came home, except I was now exhausted.

It was an awful way to feel. I felt the painful inequity of it all. My friends were telling me how good Anna was doing, and while I was relieved to hear it, I also began to feel more and more that I didn't have what Anna needed. And even as all these thoughts jumbled together in my mind, I felt a guilt and a pain so deep it really incapacitated me.

The family that was taking care of the girls was growing attached to Anna and felt that we needed to come and get Claire and leave Anna and *let her go*. She was doing well, and the general consensus among the people involved was to make a decision to let her go sooner than later so that she could begin to heal and move on.

That all made sense to me, and somehow felt all wrong at the same time. And then there was the blatant fact that I had begun eating again and felt no desire to bring her back. Could I sacrifice my health for one child when ten others needed me? And every report I got from my friends was that Anna was doing well and was happy, which further reinforced my feelings that I must have been doing something wrong, and that I just could not be her mother.

We had to get Claire home for an appointment and we had two days to make the decision about what to tell Anna. Did we tell her I still needed time to heal and further drag her along? Or did we make the decision to look for a new family for Anna, to let her go and allow her to begin to heal from the new hurt that now we ourselves would cause?

We were beginning to think that perhaps God was showing us that someone else could be better parents to her than we could. Looking back, I think we walk such a narrow line between God's best for our lives and mediocrity. I think we were in a very vulnerable place and had lost sight of the conviction of what God had called us to do.

The support people in my life were extremely worried about me and could not see how I could bring Anna home. I felt weak inside and was carried along by those in my life who loved me. So, the decision was made to go and get Claire and to tell Anna that I was sorry, that I thought I could be her mother, that I wanted to, but I couldn't, and that I was so very very sorry.

I needed to do the unthinkable. The shame and horror I felt at what I was about to do was crippling. I was so terribly ashamed that I could not even call the social worker at our agency. To this day, I regret that decision. She could have told me my feelings were normal, and I could I have rested in her reassurance of my ability to love and parent Anna.

* * *

So, the very next day, on a Sunday, I was to go and tell my daughter Anna, for whom I had prayed and loved with my actions, and held and rocked and parented, and promised to love forever, that after ten months I couldn't keep those promises.

I didn't sleep that night for the agony I was about to cause. Deep inside I had lost sight of God's best for our lives. I had forgotten God's promise to finish what He starts and the deep calling we had to be Anna's parents. I was looking at the circumstances and not at God. I couldn't see any way to be better than I was. And right then, I didn't feel I could be very good for anyone.

I don't know how I got in the car that day. Somehow the drive ended far too soon, and we arrived at the meeting place. Both the girls came out to see us as we drove in. Claire hugged me, and I went over to Anna and hugged her too. She knew she wasn't coming home with us because I wasn't well enough and Claire had appointments.

Dear reader, I did the unthinkable.

I told her that I had to tell her something, that I couldn't be her mother, that I had tried so very hard and thought I could but that I can't, and that I'm so very, very sorry. She looked startled and shocked as she tried to process the horrible words I spoke.

Then I took the pearls I had bought for her in China out of my pocketbook and placed them in her hands. I wrapped her fingers around them and said, "Honey, I want you to have these. I bought them for you when we were in China." I told her I loved her. And I walked out.

She reached for me and ran for the door, but her respite mother grabbed her. Anna fell to the floor, and then I was gone. She cried, a horrible, agonizing, moaning, primal cry. We went outside and put her things in the car for her to take back to her new home, and I could still hear crying inside.

Then we left. We drove away from her. We left her there, crying, longing for us, in another mother's arms. And it hurt so terribly. I wished I could make it better. I wished I could undo it all. And the power to undo it all lay within my hands.

But the power to love her the way she needed to be loved eluded me, and I didn't understand that. I know the God of love. I know the One who loves perfectly, the giver of all love, and I asked Him over and over again to fill my heart with His love for her. I prayed He would hold her and love her and protect her precious heart.

The next days were filled with appointments and the busy schedule of a large family. There was an awareness that it was easier without Anna. I even felt like I had my family back again. Yet amidst the relief and rest Anna's absence provided, a deep sadness pervaded our home. We were constantly aware of a sense of the inequity of it all, of a feeling of loss, and even though frequent reports from our friends and the respite family told us how well Anna was doing, we never had peace that we had done the right thing, and it never really felt okay that she was gone.

Mark and I would come to the decision each night that we needed to go back and get her. Yet as soon as we followed that path through in our minds, my stomach would begin to churn and I would feel nauseous at the reality of what having her back with us looked like for me. So, we would clasp our hands together and pray for wisdom and grace, and for peace for sweet Anna.

There were a few times when I discussed the possibility of going back to get Anna with everyone involved, but they told us we couldn't go back, that the damage we had done was irreparable, and that we had no choice but to move forward, that moving forward was best for Anna. And move forward we did—

For two long weeks.

Towards the end of the two weeks, the pain became too great. The thought of looking for another family for *our daughter, our rose*, felt undeniably wrong.

Mark was convinced we had to go back and get Anna, and even though I had no confidence in my ability to be her mother, I felt a deep awareness that I *was* her mother, sick or well, healthy or broken. I was her mother, and she was our daughter. We needed to get through this together. Anna needed to come home, and we needed to bring her home.

I also knew, deep within my heart, that God would be with us, and that He would finish the work He had begun in our hearts and in our lives so long ago. Somehow, I felt that on the very day Anna's biological mother had abandoned her, God had known that He was sending me to go and get her to be her mother, and that all the days in between He was somehow leading us to each other. The fact that I was broken suddenly held no importance at all.

Sometimes moms are broken.

Up until this point, shame had kept me from calling the social worker from our agency. Finally, we did. The love and grace we received from our agency blessed us in ways I don't even know how to express. Suddenly, so many things felt okay again. Perhaps just the confirmation that our feelings were okay from the social worker changed everything for us. We expressed our desire to go and get Anna and our concern that we had hurt her too deeply, and our fear that we could never repair the damage we had done.

I can still hear the social worker's precious words to us. "There is no hurt that is too big for God to heal. She's your daughter. If you want to go get her, then go get her!"

* * *

The very next day, Mark and I drove all the way to get Anna. We had no idea exactly how it would all work out; we only knew deep in our hearts that we were called to be Anna's parents. I was filled with such a dichotomy of feelings. I longed for our family to be whole again. I knew it was right to bring her home. I did feel a dread in the pit of my stomach about how I would handle it all, and I couldn't see how anything would be any different now after only a month. I was strictly going to bring her home on faith that day, faith in God and faith in Mark's deep conviction that we could do this together.

I wasn't healed. The pain was still fresh, and I still felt so very broken.

As I look back on that day, I think of the verse that I kept in my mind every moment as we trusted God to bring the girls home: "for we walk by faith, not by sight" (2 Cor. 5:7, NASB).

The truth was that I was in no different position that day as we rode up to get Anna than I had been in before we'd traveled. I had flown to China trusting God that whatever we faced, we would face together, and that I could do none of it in my own strength. God hadn't called me to do anything on my own. He'd called me to trust Him, to step out in faith and follow Him. He was calling me now to trust His ability to blend our family together as only He can, and to heal the hurt we had caused Anna.

I think if we as the Body of Christ could fully grasp this concept of resting in God and allowing Him to move the mountains that lie before us in our lives, then the sky would be the limit of what God could and would do through us, and in us, on behalf of His precious children.

We pulled in the driveway and drove up to the house where Anna was staying. Then I saw her. She was standing in the doorway, smiling nervously at her daddy. She looked lovely. Her long bangs were pinned to the side, and her bright eyes searched me for answers. She looked at me, smiling, questioning. I walked over to her and hugged her, and she hugged me back. I stepped back from her, taking in her presence again after the long month she had been away. Mark was talking to the couple who had been taking care of her. They told us she was excited when she heard she was coming home to live with us again.

The pain and loss this precious child had experienced again in her life—and really so much of it at my hand—staggered me and filled me with an intensity of feeling I hadn't felt for a long time. It was sorrow and regret for the pain I'd caused along with admiration that she had made it through. Anna had survived, and I was amazed at how strong and grown up she seemed. We visited for a while and then we said goodbye.

Soon we pulled into the parking lot of Olive Garden and went into eat. I sat next to her on the bench. We chose our food, and then the questions came. Anna's face was serious, her eyes sad. "Why you say you not come back? Why you come back?"

There were no words to ease her pain, or to undo the hurt we had caused her in our biggest debacle of parenting ever, yet I answered honestly. "We came back because you're our daughter and we need you. We love you. I don't really know why we told you we couldn't be your parents. Somehow we thought someone else could be better for you, that you would be happier in another family. But then it hurt too much, we missed you too much, and we knew that we had to come and bring you home. We're so sorry that we hurt you."

Then Mark said, "Anna we love you. The kids love you and miss you. Everyone can't wait to see you."

Her eyes were wide and understanding, accepting. She was quiet a moment and then looked up at us again. "You miss me?"

Tears filled my eyes, tears of pure love and respect for this child I had hurt, for my daughter. "Oh yes! We missed you. We're so sorry Anna. We should have come sooner for you. We should never have left you at all. We were so confused and wanted what was best for you, and we didn't know what that was then, but we do now. No matter what happens ever again, you are our daughter, and we love you. Whatever happens in the future, we're going to get through it together, forever, no matter what. We're family. And we love you."

I was in awe of her ability to accept our words, at her bravery and willingness to try again with us. "I miss you. I miss my family."

Many times throughout the meal she asked if we really loved her. She asked us over and over again, as if with each confirmation, she could begin to trust the love a little more, as if each affirmation of our love thrilled her, and she couldn't hear it enough. Joy began to radiate through the tentative smile she had worn, and warmth and confidence began to spread across her face like the sun filling the sky as it rises slowly over the mountains.

We finished our meal and went to the ladies room together. It felt good to be together again, mother and daughter, doing simple mother and daughter things.

When we got in the car this time, I sat in the back with her. She sat in the middle, and I sat on the side. Within a few minutes, she was in my arms resting her head on my shoulder. I brushed her hair back from her face and kissed her forehead. We sat like that the whole way home, Anna in her mother's arms, and I, holding my daughter and feeling the love that I'd longed to feel for far too long. I had my daughter back with me, and it felt so very right.

Somehow amidst the pain of almost letting her go, my need to be forgiven by Anna, and her amazing ability to give me that forgiveness, a deep and special love began to grow in my heart and an acceptance of this precious young lady God had given me. An aching longing to mother her filled me once again, and a deep bond began to blossom within both of us because we had come through the winter together and had made it to the spring.

I'd like to say that all was well and easy after we brought Anna home. But that wouldn't be truth. It wasn't the end of the story. Things were better, but healing took time. I was reminded that love is not a feeling but a choice. Just as in a marriage, the feelings come and go, but the choice to keep on loving with our actions is what makes our marriages go the distance. It's no different with loving our children.

Sometimes it's in the darkness that we find our way. And it was that way for us. We can celebrate God on the mountaintops, but it's not on the mountains that we come to know Him. It's the awareness of our soul's thirst for something more that causes us to search for Him, to long to know Him as He is.

Dear reader, there is an eternal world that is far more real than this tangible temporary one in which we spend our days. If you are in the midst of a dark place attaching to your child, or in any area of your life, pray.

"For our struggle is not against flesh and blood, but against the rulers, against the powers, against the world forces of this darkness, against the spiritual forces of wickedness in the heavenly places" (Eph. 6:12, NASB).

The battle to love and heal these precious orphaned children is not won here in this natural temporal world. It's not won in our own strength, by working harder or expecting more of ourselves. It's won through prayer, and by resting in the confidence of what God will do if we trust Him. We cannot do this on our own. How can we expect to change the life of one precious child without the hand of our loving God picking up the pieces as we drop them?

He has dwelt among us, joined us in our home and in our hearts, and has brought us through the valley to the mountaintop. We stand in awe of His ability to work all the details out in our lives. And He can and will do the same for all of us after we get home with our children.

Diane M. is a mother to thirteen children, two who went straight to Jesus' arms, nine biological, and two who came home from China days before they turned fourteen and aged out of the China adoption program. Diane is a wife to the most wonderful man in the world, and daughter of the King, sister, by God's grace, to the Lord Jesus Christ, who has changed her life and helps her every day to be more like Him. She is a homeschooling mom and a writer who has chosen to share the story God is writing in their lives on http://mylifeingodsgarden.com/.

9
Healing Rain

This morning as I rode in the car with David he asked me, "Mama, is it morning or night? It's dark out."

I replied, "It's morning, D. The sun is still there, it's just hidden by the rain clouds."

He quickly shot back in confusion, "Why would God make rain?"

I replied through held-back tears, "because the rain will bring spring."

I remember the day David was conceived into our family. It was a cool, damp Wisconsin spring afternoon. Cameron looked at me with pleading eyes and shivering shoulders. "Mom, do I have to finish my last event?" We were cuddled together with his sister, Bethany, at a middle-school track meet.

We had three children then, our dynamic A, B, and C. I was a single mom with our oldest, Amy, until my husband, Shawn, and I married. She was four then. Little more than a year later we were picking out baby names, Keagan for a boy, Bethany for a girl. God graced us with another sweet girl. Several years later, we prepared again to welcome an addition to our family. Kennedy for a girl, Cameron for a boy. Cameron it was. I remember a friend saying, "You have the beginning of an alphabet." I hadn't even realized.

In some silly way, I think God did. Looking back now, I see evidence of God weaving our incredible "D," as we call him, into our framework. Somewhere in another land much different from our North American life, a woman carried my boy to life, a year and a half after we thought our family was done growing. He was given the name David.

We first learned of David that day at the track meet, as I snuggled my kiddos close and tried to tell myself that the "finish what you started" attribute I was building into Cameron was worth the ache in my bones from the chill of the spring rain. I pulled out my phone and began scrolling to pass time under our umbrella. Moments later, a man walked up and stopped in front of us. He paused for a moment and with a gentle smile asked, "May I take a picture of your family?" I hesitated. He quickly assured me that he wanted to use the camera on my phone and said, "I want you to see what I see."

Friends, truth be told, I am so proud of my tribe and I make them endure pictures far too often; but, this was not a photogenic moment and my attitude was looking a lot like my rain-soaked appearance. In the end, my desire to be polite won over and I handed over my phone. When he handed it back with a smile and a pause, we thanked him and he disappeared into the sea of tired athletes and dedicated parents. We giggled a bit when we looked at the crooked photo. It was hard to imagine what it was he saw that made him stop.

We resumed looking through pictures and posts on social media. An image of a ten-year-old boy filled the screen with kind, brown eyes. I smiled and knew immediately that he was a child without a family of his own. I had seen profiles of several children through missionary connections in West Africa. His smile was infectious and immediately Cameron asked who he was. I explained they were searching for a family for him and he said, "Why can't he be my brother?"

When we got home that evening, he ran to the house and asked my husband the same question. It only took moments for my husband to shoot that "You put him up to this" look in my direction. Friend, you know that look! I went into defense mode and before three words left my lips, he was asking me to see the profile. I watched my guarded, composed husband begin to weep. I remember asking God "What are you doing?" I knew at the very least he was stirring our hearts to advocate for this boy. I couldn't imagine how we would ever navigate the mountains of paperwork, finances, and, let's be honest, the tough stories we had heard about troubled kids. I knew nothing of what God was about to call us to, and I wasn't ready to go into it voluntarily.

I sent off an email to the contact listed and asked how we could advocate for him; what could we do to help? My inbox lit up quickly with a "Why not you?" I shared my concerns and all the reasons why we just couldn't see a way; but at every turn, we were offered one. We were drafted by God for a war of redemption. In the months ahead, it became clear that this season of training was about our redemption too; and I was going to have to apply that same "finish what you started" grit I had tried to instill into Cameron on that cold, spring day.

David's "birth photo" into our world had been taken by what I believe was a God-appointed photographer, and we were all in. Like many adoption stories, there were high highs and low lows. We were tested and stretched and asked to tighten our boot strings like never before. I can't count the number of times I asked God if He was certain of this calling on our lives. Time and again He assured us to press on.

Twenty-three months later, after brain surgery for me and the bankruptcy of our adoption agency, after the transition of our oldest leaving home and troubling stories of unsuccessful adoptions ... we boarded a plane with our hearts fuller than our suitcases. David was twelve then, and we were told he had significant vision impairment, keeping him from an education. We stepped into the unknown with raw faith and trust that our Father would equip us. And David did too.

I remember one of the first days we were with our son, my husband decided to walk to the bakery with him. We were quickly suspecting by that time that his vision impairment was not nearly as bad as we had originally thought or that David had really adapted well. Either way, Shawn felt confident that he could navigate the short walk down the side of the busy capital city road of Burkina Faso with him. David was excited to go with his papa, but once they were beyond the safety of the gates to our guest house, he froze. Traffic was heavy as his new daddy urged him on. He waved his hand to him saying "Come on, David." David stood in what looked like defiance.

This was the beginning of the first battle. We had prepared for this, but nothing we learned was coming to mind as my husband was filled with concern and frustration. Eventually, David followed with reluctance and they returned to the safety of a familiar guest house. David spoke no English at that point. He had no words and we had no point of reference to know where he was coming from. Many months after we were home and David had gained some language, he said to me one day, "I didn't want to go with Papa, I didn't know him." I wasn't sure what he was even saying until we put the pieces together, but he was referring to that day on the dry, busy streets of Ouaga. He went on to tell me, with the only words he could conjure up, that he didn't recognize his Papa with different skin and he questioned if he was safe.

As I held my boy for as long as he'd let me, my eyes filled with tears. I wanted to say to him, "I'm struggling to trust my Father right now too, Buddy. He looks different to me and I'm not sure I want to follow Him." We were in the throes of everything unfamiliar. Life had become isolated and hard at this point, and I was beginning to question if I wanted to step any further outside the gates of my safe faith.

I spent some time with a veteran soldier recently. As we sat across the table from each other, with him being thirty years my elder, and coming from different backgrounds and life experiences, we began to draw some parallels. We both had walked down a path in a foreign land. God had called each of us to a place we hadn't really signed up for voluntarily. Him to the battlefields of Vietnam, us to the battlefields of a broken past. I'm going to be a bit transparent here and tell you, I was in love with the idea of God using me. I had served on several mission teams and I always returned home encouraged by the faith of the missionaries and native brothers and sisters. It was hard to see the bigger purpose in my everyday life and I longed to be part of what God was doing on the continent of Africa. We knew there was room in our hearts and in our family, but I had no idea what that would look like. There was no amount of training and education that would parallel the experience of swinging our leg over the side of the boat in faith, as Peter had. I could sense the gentleness of Jesus urging me to keep my eyes on Him, but the waves rose quickly.

We had done a lot of life in our sleepy rural community with some amazing people. The kind of people who open your fridge without invitation because it's just that comfortable. People who show up for hard times and holidays and who had watched and cheered alongside of us as our family grew. It was no surprise when we announced our family was growing that this same love and support was there sometimes even before we asked. We had our armor. Whatever hurts needed to be healed in our brown-eyed boy were sure to be met with an abundance of compassion.

The night our plane landed, after thirty-six hours of travel home, we looked into the eyes of our loved ones and felt relief. These were the people who knew us. Everything about our lives was familiar to them and they believed in us. As I talked with my veteran mentor a few days ago, I imagined him coming home from war. I imagined that he too longed for his people, who had watched him grow from a young boy. But stepping off that plane was a different man. And for our family, we were about to learn it was much the same for us.

In the months to follow, life got hard. It became exhausting the day I explained to the school that I was showing up with a hug, a listening ear, and David's favorite ice cream snack after a few hours of him acting out. Grace. It didn't make sense when I explained to loved ones not to show too much affection because we needed to bond. Healing. It was confusing to friends who didn't understand that my son was not just "being a boy" when he was playing aggressively with their daughter. Culture. Nightfall fell in our camp and the reflection of the Son on the moon was hidden by dark storm clouds. Marriage became harder to navigate, relationships became strained, and the thrill of being the hands and feet of God faded fast.

The rain began to fall for months and I wondered if it was our new normal. Could it be that God had brought my son home to the physical safety of a home and a family but that he would never see healing on this side of heaven? There were several car rides and crying sessions during that season, and so much confusion. I couldn't muster up the courage to lift my eyes from the waves, but the very character of our Father offers a refuge. For us, it came in the form of counselors and community. I began to reach out and ask for help. It took energy I didn't have some days, it really did. Fear had to be put in its place as I rallied my troops. The rain began to slow, and I became filled with hope.

Holidays and special days can be hard for kids who come from hard places. If you are reading this and you are already an adoptive parent, you may be nodding your head in agreement. Some kids have a supernatural amount of resilience, but for our boy those days are just plain hard. This became apparent through our first year together as a family. As the second year came around, we braced for it. We were no longer green soldiers and we prepared. Maybe in some ways, it contributed to our success, but the greater likelihood is God was allowing our son to exhale and he began to trust. My husband and I looked at each other several times through that second Christmas with amazement as we sat in the front row of God's beautiful redemption.

The greatest gift we were given beyond our Savior was peace in our home. In the dead of a cold Wisconsin winter, the "rain" had ushered in "spring" and the promise of God's good, good grace shone once again. We are different people now, all of us. Mom, Dad, and our A,B,C,D. But, I want to encourage you that different is okay. If David were here, and already literate, he would roll his eyes in a typical fourteen-year-old way, because this has become our anthem. We don't all look the same and we don't all live the same, but we can strive together to love like Christ.

Dear friend, I don't live in the walls of your home and in the depths of your heart, but God does. He is with you in every battle, every trial, and He is with you in every victory. This very moment I am asking Him to send an army of angels to stand wing tip to wing tip around your family. I have prayed He will sustain you down every turn and that you would find joy in the midst of battle. Exod. 14:14 (NIV) hangs on my wall to serve as a reminder "The LORD will fight for you, you need only to be still." I pray this verse sows seeds of peace and confidence into your heart too.

Lisa S. is a lover of Jesus, wife, and partner to Shawn, and holds the title of mom to Amy, Bethany, Cameron, and David. She enjoys writing at https://deep-roots.blog/2018/01/19/roots. She is intentional about connecting with other adoptive families and doing life alongside them. In her "free time," she works as a real estate appraiser and embraces rural life with her family.

I Wish I Had Known

"Be careful what you ask for, you just might get it!"

Our Sunday School teacher chuckled as we walked in with our newest bundle of joy—our second child, our beloved first daughter, born on the heels of our oldest son's first birthday. Our hands were full, and our hearts overflowed. After four years of marriage, three years of infertility, countless tears and doctors' appointments, and prescriptions and desperate prayers, the Lord had given us two children within fifteen months of each other. A boy and a girl. Curly-headed, brown-skinned babies who filled our days from beginning to end and brought endless laughter and joy to every minute. These kids were a dream come true. My desire to get pregnant was gone, replaced by a passion for adoption and birthmothers, and encouraging others to build families like ours because our life was just so good. Our world had been turned sweetly upside down and we wouldn't have wanted it any other way.

When we were dating, my husband and I probably had the same conversations as most couples speculating about the future. Kids or no kids? How many and when? Would I work or stay at home? But sprinkled in amongst those exchanges was one more possibility: adoption. Both of us had the desire in our hearts. As we talked it through, we assumed we would have two or three biological children then pursue adoption. This sounded good and reasonable. We had no reason to expect any trouble getting pregnant.

A year after our wedding my clock started ticking. I stopped taking birth control and started logging dates on my calendar. One month went by. Nothing to fear. Two months went by, then three, then six, then a year. I could not believe it wasn't happening. I was on my face before God, begging for a baby, questioning why He would give me this insatiable desire for a child yet withhold this blessing from me. I wept.

I fought jealousy as friends announced pregnancy after pregnancy and forced myself to attend baby shower after baby shower. I despaired, wanting so much to know the wonder of a baby kicking me from within, dreaming of how I would tell my husband the big news, yet realizing that day might never come. We consulted with a doctor who ran tests, did exploratory surgery, and found nothing wrong. He prescribed Clomid then added progesterone. I went in for countless ultrasounds, yet continued throwing negative pregnancy tests in the trash month after month. My faith wavered, and my prayer life hit a wall. The medications took a toll and began to have unwanted side effects until, finally one day, I was done. *Done.*

I began making phone calls and researching adoption, despairing at the cost and knowing it would take years to save up enough money. But one day a small agency was brought to our attention. They only did a handful of adoptions each year, but the philosophy of how the adoptions were carried out was rooted in God's Word and prayer. The fees were based on our income, which gave us hope. Paperwork came in the mail, our first social worker did our home study, and we wrote letters and put together a scrapbook of "us," praying the right birthmother would see it and know we were "the ones."

Nine months later, our dream came true. We experienced the miracle of love beyond anything we thought possible when our son was placed in our arms. Then, our daughter. Three years after, another daughter, then another son. Finally, in 2010, we flew to Ethiopia to bring home our caboose ... a-three-year-old orphan whose sweet smile and spunky spirit would complete our family.

Life. Was. Good. So very good. Ask me about adoption and I would happily have filled your ears with every reason this was God's "Plan A" for us all along, how the love you have for a child is exactly the same no matter how they join your family. That the love of a family would overcome every hard question and every struggle, causing these kids to thrive and be healthy, God-fearing, and family-loving adults. I would fiercely defend our unique family, telling you we were blessed with the privilege of living a little slice of Heaven here on Earth, where every nation, tribe, and tongue gather under one roof as one family. Yes, God had put us here for such a time as this, and we loved every minute of it.

Then the hard season came. So many of us go into parenting in general, and adoption specifically, with a plan. We have been coached in attachment, cultural standards, how to discipline, whether or not to co-sleep, to bottle or breast-feed; there's verbiage regarding the relinquishment of our children and the circumstances surrounding that event, how to discuss their stories in an age-appropriate manner, and the importance of a perfectly straight part in our daughters' braided hair. We seek out diverse churches and adoption-friendly playgroups. We educate the adults in our children's lives on trauma and the behaviors that can result, and we fight to advocate for our children wherever necessary. We tell our babies every single day how much we love them and how thankful we are to have been chosen to be their parents, that they are a gift and fearfully and wonderfully made by their Heavenly

Father. We watch other parents and try to mimic the successful ones, hoping for the same good and healthy result. So, imagine my surprise when this was not enough. Put yourself in my shoes: a child I fought for, drove across the country or flew across the world for, suddenly began to reject me and everything I wanted to offer.

The dance of attachment can be a very difficult one. Whether a child came home at birth or much older, they have been through a huge loss and change that affects how they see everything. Their responses to this early trauma can vary greatly, which means there is no "correct" way to handle this, no single book with the answers, no "proven" parenting method that guarantees healing and attachment. Some children struggle daily from the first day home; others seem to be fine until the stress of puberty and the hormones associated with it take their toll on their bodies and minds and cause underlying fear, anxiety, anger, and a myriad of other possible troubles to surface and wreak havoc on the child and the entire family. You begin to expect the unexpected, to question everything, and constantly to wonder what the root of the behavior is ... is it adoption grief? Is it just normal childish behavior? Is it a combination of both? The guessing game can be incredibly draining and disheartening when everything you thought you knew turns out to be wrong.

As my children got older and the idyllic "little years" began to be a distant memory, fear and anger filled too many of my days. My expectations of what the years would look like as my kids grew up were shot down and destroyed. I was ashamed, embarrassed, and felt robbed. I questioned everything I had ever done as a mother, wondering what I could have done differently in order to have prevented what was now happening. My kids were *good* kids, so wonderful in many ways, but some of them were struggling more deeply than I knew how to help. My heart was broken. I began to realize one of the biggest struggles for an adopted child, especially in a transracial family like ours, is their identity. They just don't know who they are. Are they black? Are they white? Are they somewhere in between? In which friend group do they belong? And the questions ... they just get so tired of the questions ... so they try to get around them, often by staying distant from their parents. After all the Scripture I had taught my kids, all the prayers we had prayed together, all the sweet ceramic whatnots we had made to celebrate them and their place in our family, how in the world did they not know and grasp who they were in Christ? How were these kids so confused that they sought approval everywhere, it seemed, but from us and from God?

Because, like you and me, they are human. I made so many mistakes in those years. I looked to all the wrong places for advice (Google, Facebook, parents who only had biological children) and kept trying to find the answer, the one thing I was missing; the fix-all just had to be out there somewhere. I tried everything and my inconsistency only fed the chaos. And you know the worst part? I was embarrassed. I wanted to "represent" adoption in a way that made the whole world want to do it. I wanted my family to be living proof of the gospel in action, drawing parents to find and fight to bring their children home. I, I, I, me, me, me.

I was focused on all the wrong things and doing everything I did for all the wrong reasons. God had to do a major work in me to pry my eyelids apart and allow me to see my sin and to give my children the grace they so desperately needed. I was doing the best I could with what I knew, no doubt, but maybe I can help you start your journey with more knowledge and therefore to avoid some of the pitfalls I struggled (and still struggle) with.

What do I wish I had known when we began our journey with

our children? Bear with me. There are quite a few...

1. *My kids will sin.* Did you know you are raising a sinner? I didn't realize this fully until many years into my parenting journey. I remember my oldest two children when they were toddlers. I had our chosen system of training and discipline down pat and it seemed to be working very well. They got along wonderfully, were well-bonded to us as their parents, and joy filled our home. So, imagine my surprise the first time one of my innocent babes told a lie. Or the time my child called a kid they had just met a "loser" and almost got kicked out of the kids' club ... on a cruise. Yeah, that was fun. I was the mom standing in wide-mouthed shock. "What in the world made you think that was okay?" The answer to those questions really is simple. They knew it wasn't okay. They knew they shouldn't lie or call other people names. But they allowed sin to have its way and caved. Just like you. Just like me. Hence, my next point...

2. *I will sin as I parent my kids.* Yeah, my flesh sometimes wins and I allow it to take over, saying and doing things I know are wrong. Of course, this is not a news flash to anyone who knows me, but to realize how deeply sin influences my parenting when I am weak is truly humbling and disturbing if I'm completely honest. Confession: I have yelled at my kids. Often. I have disciplined in anger and turned away from a child when the connected response would be to take them in my arms.

But sometimes, when I am hurt, angry, or just plain weary, I don't *want* to be connected. Sometimes I want to be alone and I just want them to find a way to entertain themselves, take a nap, anything to give me peace and quiet. Selfish ... yeah, that's me on my bad days. Selfish and angry and not very motherly, I'll tell you that. This mom who begged for kids, and cradled those babies with tenderness, fails miserably and gets ridiculously annoyed by the childish behavior that is completely normal. I forget to give them grace and push them away, only deepening the chasm between us when they are angry and hurting. I've heard it said, hurt people hurt people. So, in order to effectively love and nurture my children I must seek healing for my own wounds, identify my own triggers, and fall at the feet of Jesus in repentance when I fail. I must learn who I am in Christ and allow that truth to permeate my very soul, becoming the driving force of how I love my family. The human love I try to tap into in order to raise my kids is faulty and limited. It is often conditional and easily dampened. But the love of God, of a Holy Father who gave everything to save me and bring me into relationship with Him, is endless in supply, unconditional in nature, and the perfect balm to heal broken hearts ... mine included.

3. *Anger is a part of their grief.* I had heard that adopted kids could be angry. I thought I could handle it, would be ready for it, but I couldn't imagine it being *that* bad. I mean, what would a kid who has been raised from birth or rescued from poverty and brought up in a fun, loving, and nurturing home have to be angry about? And even if they struggle, I'm going to love them through it, right? Wrong.

I did it all. Read all the books, listened to all the tapes and CD's, researched and questioned those parents who had raised their kids well, and my kids were going to grow up happy, well-adjusted, and thankful they had such a wonderful adoption story filled with love and God's hand of mercy. Unfortunately, my kids didn't get the memo. Despite all of my efforts to help them feel secure, wanted, and loved, they struggled. All of them. Now the degree to which they struggled has varied greatly from child-to-child, but at least some level of anger has been part of it for every one of them. I unconsciously minimized their loss when I thought telling the story sweetly throughout their lives would lessen the impact.

Do you remember being a kid and wishing you had a different family? I do. I remember thinking my aunt and her husband were so much more fun than my parents. They were outdoorsy, noisy, traveled, and seemed to enjoy family life every day. For adopted kids, they *did* have another family, even if only for a few hours. There *was* an alternative, and when they are frustrated with me, our rules, or our family in general, it is only natural to wish not only for a different family but to wish for their *first* family. They didn't have a say in where they ended up, and, well, sometimes that just makes them mad. Who can blame them?

4. *Each child will process their story in their own way.* I have already mentioned that my children have struggled with varying degrees of anger. Some of our kids seek to talk it through and understand why they are ours and what might have been if circumstances had been different. Others clam up, shut down, and shut us out. Some draw close, needing physical comfort in hugs and cuddles. Others reject us, pretend they don't know us in public, and hole up in their rooms with the door locked because they just don't want anything to do with us. This has been so difficult for me. I am a talker by nature so the kids who need that side of me are so much easier for me to deal with and understand. The ones who shut me out are an enigma to me and I struggle to connect. Hurtful words, slamming doors, and heated arguments trigger my insecurities and I become very afraid for what the future holds. My husband handles those things much better than I do, and I have often had to let him handle those situations because, honestly, I just make them worse.

Dealing with such a wide variety of grief reactions and needs is completely exhausting and causes my head to spin. It's one thing to have head knowledge of the varying ways people deal with grief, but the reality feels very different than what I foresaw when I imagined myself as a mother at this stage of life. In my weakness, all the research in the world flies out the window when I am triggered. Rejection hurts. Period. I am not good at steeling myself against taking it personally, though that is what I need to do. I am a work in progress, just like my children.

5. *I should stop wearing adoption t-shirts.* When my kids were young, we moved to Middle Tennessee where adoption was booming and there were no shortages of conferences, retreats, and conventions about adoption, fostering, and orphan care to attend. They all sold shirts and I was a faithful purchaser. I wanted to support the ministries involved and be a "good advertisement" for a cause so near and dear to my heart. "Adoption Rocks," "Love makes a family," and "Superman was adopted" were among many logos I wore proudly with my babies in tow. I even had them on bumper stickers.

As my oldest kids approached the tween years though, I noticed a difference in them when I wore those shirts. They seemed more distant towards me. I finally realized the shirts made them feel awkward. It made sense, of course, once I took the time to think about it. Most adolescents want to blend in, be part of the crowd, and not stand out unless they choose to do so. I will support organizations who advocate for adoption and orphan care wholeheartedly, but I no longer wear shirts that have logos specifically mentioning adoption.

6. *No amount of parenting methodology will guarantee any outcome.* I have said many times that I cannot take credit or blame for how my kids turn out. I mean it. I have read every book, blog, and article known to man and tried to implement the very best methods and policies in my parenting, casting a vision for the future and determining to mold and shape my children into sold-

out followers of Jesus. But, friends, *is it possible that this is not our job*? As parents, what has God asked us to do? Train up a child … yes, of course. Love and discipline … certainly. But who is the Author and Finisher of our faith? Jesus. Who brings conviction to the hearts of man and turns the hearts of children toward their Heavenly Father? The Holy Spirit. Who gifts every human being who seeks Him with the faith necessary to place their lives in the hand of a holy God? Well, that would be God. I have a huge role to play, many opportunities to point my kids to Christ and model living a vibrant Christian life in intimate relationship with the Lord, but the decision to follow Christ is ultimately one they must make *for themselves.*

And here is the hard part … they may fall hard into sin and rebellion before coming to their senses and crawling on their hands and knees before God for mercy. (Just like I did.) Even harder? They may not surrender to the Lord during my lifetime. I may be with the Lord before my kids fully embrace Him. And then there are the kids who reject God and faith and everything they are taught and will not be with their parents in eternity. Every Christian mama or daddy's worst nightmare.

We live in an era that blames parents for everything. We must stop listening to the lies that place the blame for our kids' behaviors and credit for their successes squarely on *our* shoulders. I would wager we are *all* doing the very best we can to raise our children, because we love them with every fiber of our beings. And even our perfect Father God's kids … every one of them … has rebelled.

From Adam and Eve in the sinless perfection of the Garden of Eden on down through all of human history, not one person has ever escaped this life without failing and allowing sin to separate them from their Creator. Not. One.

Save Jesus.

And, friends, we are not raising little Jesuses. We are raising kids with strong and determined sin natures that will only be tempered by the work of the Holy Spirit. It can be done; their lives can come into alignment with the will of God and receive healing from any trauma they have experienced ... but not in our power. Only in full cooperation with God can we even begin to hope for our children to grow into adulthood with a healthy walk with Christ.

7. *I cannot look to people successfully raising biological kids for my parenting model.* This is probably the single largest source of frustration I have had as a mother. We were the first in our circle of influence to adopt, so I had no model for how to parent aside from my friends who were raising their kids alongside me. I had a few "older" mom friends who had successfully raised their children into young adulthood, and, liking what I saw, I determined to mimic their parenting methods. At the time, I knew nothing about in utero trauma and how it affects the brain of a developing baby. I believed my kids, just like everyone else's, only needed firm boundaries and a solid swat on the behind when they misbehaved. As they grew up, I couldn't understand why it wasn't working and all the discipline they had been taught was falling to the wayside. And I compared them to their peers. *Huge* mistake. How unfair of me. How wrong I was to expect my kids to be like anyone else, but especially like kids who had known nothing but unbroken security from the moment of conception. Comparison kills relationship. I was guilty, so terribly guilty, of this, and it was toxic to my relationships with my children as they struggled. Did I want the best for them? Absolutely. That is why I worked so hard and researched like crazy. But the best for them is just that ... *what is best for them.* And the best for my kids is certainly not the best

for the other adopted kids whose stories are their own, unique in joy and pain, unique in success and failure. I have absolutely no right to expect my kids to be like anyone else but who God created them to be. *Their struggle is part of their story*, part of the work He is doing in their lives to mold and shape them into the image of Christ ... not the image I have created in my head and held up as an idol.

You cannot parent your adopted child the same as a child who has never been through loss. It is unfair to them, it is ineffective, and it sets you up for disappointment. But when you look at who your child really is, their unique personality and gifts, struggles and fears, and parent accordingly and with full acceptance of them ... then the beauty emerges, and relationship happens. It may not be perfect or easy, it may mean laughing off what others would say you "should" discipline out of them, but it is right and good and helps them to feel safe with you. That is priceless.

8. *Prayer is my greatest weapon of warfare.* Spiritual warfare is very real and a constant battle in the life of a Christian family in general, and especially intense in the life of an adoptive family. Everything about adoption represents the gospel of Jesus Christ: sacrifice, selfless love, redemption, a new name, restoration. Therefore, it should come as no surprise that the Enemy of our Souls despises everything our families stand for and has determined to fight it tooth and nail. He is nasty and he is relentless in his pursuit of destruction, but he does not have the last word. Praise God for Jesus who bore every bit of brokenness on the cross! Yours, mine, our children's ... all of this struggle and fear is fully understood by our Abba, and He gently reminds me that I have nothing to offer my children if I am not being *daily* filled by the Holy Spirit and diving into the Word of God.

More than anything, I want you to know that God answers

prayers. We have been given authority in Christ to fight on our knees for our babies. Too often I turn to prayer and fasting as a last resort and then I stand back in awe as God snaps into action and beat myself up for not doing it sooner! *God answers prayers.* He loves you. He loves your children. He is writing all of our stories and has woven us all together for such a time as this. Good, bad, easy, and hard … if He has called you then He most certainly has equipped you. Reach out, seek community in the adoption circles around you, find a friend or two whom you can trust with all the difficult details, and fight on your knees together as your raise your kids. No, there are no guarantees … except one.

It will be worth it.

When we stand before God, I pray we are all flanked by every single one of our precious children. I can just see it … Jesus will smile and fix that last jewel on the golden crown before gently placing it on our head and whispering, "Well done." Regardless of the outcome in the lives of our unique, sought-after, fought-for, beloved and priceless children, may He find us, their earthy mamas and daddies, faithful.

Jeanine J. is the grateful mother of five children. Married to her guy for twenty-one years, her days are filled with homeschooling and driving all those kids to their various activities. In her (rare!) free time, she enjoys reading the stack of books on her nightstand and writing at https://alifeofsimplejoys.com. She has facilitated Adoption 101 classes and been a panel speaker for a local adoption agency preparing couples for the unique joys and challenges they will face.

An Infant and a Toddler

The moment when a woman finds out she will be having a child is overwhelming regardless of the circumstances. As a happily married twenty-something, I had already experienced the overwhelming feelings of joy, excitement, relief, wonder, and enthusiasm as two such moments happened about two years apart. A healthy baby girl grew in my belly and a big, healthy boy took up residence in the same womb a couple of years later. Our little family of four was perfect. We had a girl and a boy, and we were comfortable. But we had more love to give. God had blessed us with so much and we felt compelled to share it. With that heart, God opened the door to international adoption.

When we brought home two "older" children from Ghana, Africa, we really didn't know what to expect. We had taken the classes, read the books and blogs, and talked to others who had taken similar journeys to grow their families. But, ultimately, we had no idea how our story would go.

I remember when my biological son was born the midwife said, "Wow! This is a big boy." He was just shy of ten pounds and he had a huge amount of dark hair covering his head.

As I looked at him, I honestly thought, "I just gave birth to a toddler!"

The reality was that he was coming home to a "big" sister who was the actual toddler and they were about the same size (only a slight exaggeration).

There were plenty of wonderful moments as a mother to an infant and a toddler. There were times when I felt perfectly content snuggling one or both of my kids and reading them a book, singing them a song, or taking a nap. Times when they would play together and make each other laugh. Times when I had one in the baby carrier and one in the stroller and we could enjoy a walk outside on a nice day. I love all those memories. But, even in the happiest moments, it was hard. It was constant. It was exhausting. I think any new mom with young children can relate.

When we brought home a ten-year-old and a five-year-old from Ghana it felt very similar to those days years ago, except this time I *instantly* had a new infant and a toddler. They were much bigger than the average infant and toddler, but my feelings and actions were almost identical. The "infant" liked to be held all the time. She wanted to be snuggled and rocked and babied. She thought the world revolved around her and needed to learn that it actually doesn't. We also needed to make up for some lost time, so reverting to baby tendencies was expected and somewhat healthy. The "toddler" wanted to do everything by himself and yet didn't have a great grasp on obedience and consequences. He thought he knew everything but obviously had so much to learn. He was accustomed to getting his own way since he had already lived independently for some of his life. A temper tantrum was not uncommon, as he wanted his way all the time. Unfortunately, a ten-year-old "toddler's" temper tantrums are a little more difficult to manage. It was hard.

Regardless of the circumstances, it is exhausting and challenging to parent an infant and toddler. As I think back to those early days with both sets of kids, I remember the exhaustion and challenges, but mostly I realize God's faithfulness in providing the strength, wisdom, patience, and endurance needed to get through each day.

As the five-year-old "infant" grew, it became apparent that the struggles would be ongoing. Healthy attachment was a challenge, and any new person willing to provide attention became a magnet to our little girl who was so desperate for love and attention. We limited our outside interactions and tried to set healthy boundaries as we intentionally established and defined the concentric rings of relationships. We wanted her to learn that our immediate family was different from aunts, uncles, grandparents, and cousins. Those people were also safe but not the first circle. The next circle was our friends and neighbors and teachers. Next were acquaintances from church and school. Finally, there were strangers.

She has known many loving, wonderful white people who served and lived at her orphanage. They held her, fed her, and cared for her needs, but one day they left. It might have been after a few weeks or months or maybe even years. Her little mind did not know the difference between me and all those other nice white people she had met. This was going to take some serious time and consistency. It was not a bond that would happen very easily.

As attachment became more secure, we learned that this growing girl still required constant reassurance. She asks repetitive questions with simple answers that she already knows. I am definitely not a therapist, but my research has taught me that she is insecure and desperate for security. Even three years into our journey, there are days when I wonder if she will ever trust my answers and stop asking the same things over and over again. These redundant questions and irrational fears become frustrating when they come on a day-to-day basis, and yet I know she needs my constant love, patience, and compassion to break the cycle. The problem is I am a human, and I get tired.

Two years after bringing her home from Ghana, I began to resent this little girl who was constantly demanding my approval and attention. The minute things began going well she would sabotage the happiness. Someone explained it to me as her effort to be in control and keep things "normal." The first five years of her life consisted of a very difficult "normal," so the minute things started going well her little subconscious told her to make it hard, make it sad, make it painful. I honestly didn't want to be around her. I didn't want to create happy moments because she would just make them unhappy. Why bother? I felt guilty for feeling that way. I talked to other moms who had similar feelings toward their children and it helped to know I was not alone.

Yet, my love became conditional. When her behavior was good, and her face was smiling and her responses were healthy, I showed her kindness. When she shut down, demanded attention, asked a bazillion useless questions, freaked out over a tiny kitten, elbowed me in the chest while trying to cuddle, intentionally dropped the hair clips to make the job more difficult for me, or shuffled her feet and walked slowly to avoid a fun walk together, I became annoyed and agitated and withheld my affection. It was terrible.

During that season in our life, I prayed God would restore my love for my daughter. I prayed that He would revive the parts of my heart that had died. I prayed that I would be like a tree planted by streams of water. It was, and is, my prayer to bear good fruit.

"How blessed is the man who does not walk in the counsel of the wicked, nor stand in the path of sinners, nor sit in the seat of scoffers! But his delight is in the law of the Lord, and in His law he meditates day and night. He will be like a tree firmly planted by streams of water, Which yields its fruit in its season and its leaf does not wither; And in whatever he does, he prospers" (Psalm 1:1–

3, NASB).

I felt like I was trying really hard and the fruit that I was bearing looked really good on the outside but when it was cut open it was not good at all. I was mothering four kids, packing, unpacking, decorating, organizing, shuttling kids, planning events, and mostly keeping it all running smoothly. The fruit looked good. But inside the core was rotten and the pits were dried up.

Then, I figured out the problem.

I am not the producer of good fruit, only the bearer. I cannot bear good fruit unless I am attached to the vine.

"Remain in me, as I also remain in you. No branch can bear fruit by itself; it must remain in the vine. Neither can you bear fruit unless you remain in me. I am the vine; you are the branches. If you remain in me and I in you, you will bear much fruit; apart from me you can do nothing." (John 15:4–5, NIV).

The love I have for my youngest child is not an easy love for me. She is precious. She is beautiful, kind, helpful, and loving. She is also so desperate for approval, affection, and attention. It is exhausting. Every day I wake up with a resolve to "do better." I commit myself to try and be more patient, loving, encouraging ... I fail *every day*. Sometimes I fail within five minutes of waking up. I go to bed praying, "Please God help me do a better job tomorrow. Help me love her better, be more patient, give her what she needs."

God has spoken a truth to my heart. "You can do nothing apart from Me. When it comes to loving this little girl, you will never be able to love her enough to "fix" her. Even your best love is not enough for her. You are only called to point her to Me. My mercies are new every morning. Stop praying for perfect love for her. Your love for her will never be perfect but Mine already is. Abide in me. That means spend time with Me, talk to Me all day, fill your mind with My words. I will take care of the rest."

"If you do not remain in me, you are like a branch that is thrown away and withers; such branches are picked up, thrown into the fire and burned. If you remain in me and my words remain in you, ask whatever you wish, and it will be done for you. This is to my Father's glory, that you bear much fruit, showing yourselves to be my disciples." (John 15:6–8, NIV).

I know God is not a genie in a bottle. "Whatever you wish will be given to you" is a promise but it has the condition attached, *"If you remain in Me and My words remain in you."* This is my most important job today. Yours too. Yes, the kids need to get to school or practice or lessons. They need to learn to read. They need clean clothes and they need food on the table. Yes, some emails need to be returned and some bills need to be paid and some calls need to be made. But all of this is secondary to remaining in Christ and having His words remain in us.

Lord, I want to bear *Your* fruit. The good and best kind. I want to be used by you, so you get all the glory not me. Please love that little girl (and the others) in your perfect way. Transform her heart and mind so she knows her true value in you. I will do my best to keep pointing her to you.

For now, I am going to find a juicy orange and share it with my sweet little girl who will soak up every second of my attention.

Jill T. is married to her high school sweetheart and the mother of four beautiful children ... two were born from her belly and two were born in her heart and Ghana. She currently lives in Florida and desires to bear good fruit and help her children do the same. Additionally, she faithfully serves families facing the loss of a parent from terminal illness through Inheritance of Hope. (www.inheritanceofhope.org).

We Know the Way to Hell and Back

Between 1993 and 2008, my husband Joe and I welcomed nine healthy children into the world.

In 2010, I gave birth to a little girl with Down syndrome and a severe heart defect who opened wide our hearts to the world of disability. *Verity.*

In 2011, Joe and I brought an impossibly tiny and gaunt nine-and-a-half-year-old girl with Down syndrome home from a crib on the top floor of a baby house in Pleven, Bulgaria, where she had been severely neglected since her birth. She was the first child adopted from the top floor of her orphanage. She has had multiple medical, physical, cognitive, emotional, behavioral, attachment, and sensory problems due to her years of acute institutional neglect. She weighed only ten-and-a-half pounds the day we picked her up from the orphanage. She blossomed into a beautiful, healthy and happy girl at lightning speed. *Sophie.*

In 2012, the corrupt former director of Sophie's orphanage was replaced with a conscientious powerhouse of a woman who immediately began instituting drastic changes for the better in the orphanage. Other families came forward to adopt the other older children in her orphanage who had also suffered criminal neglect. Today, around seventy older children with special needs from the Pleven orphanage are home with loving families in the United States and Canada. That fall, we began the process of adopting a severely disabled older boy with a million-dollar smile from the same orphanage. *Tommy.*

In 2013, I gave birth to a healthy little boy. *Benjamin.*

Five weeks later, in June of 2013, we traveled to Bulgaria to bring Tommy home. Not too many weeks after his homecoming, we were plunged into a year of increasingly unbearable levels of stress on every level of life.

In 2014, our son Tommy died in our home in a devastating, traumatic accident for which I blamed myself.

In 2015, a young adult woman who needed a place to live moved in with our family. *Emily.* Later the same year, we became the legal guardians of a young woman with cerebral palsy who had previously been adopted from China. *Joanna.*

In 2016, I gave birth to our youngest, another healthy little boy. *Nathaniel.*

As I write this, it's a gorgeous, sunny day in April 2017. We aren't currently in the trenches. We have margin in life now, even as a household of sixteen, which includes several with extra needs. We're living at normal levels of supersized-family busyness. Not survival mode.

We haven't been in true survival mode since Tommy was in our family.

My heart was pulled toward Tommy early in Sophie's adoption process after seeing a brief video of his brilliant smile flashing up from his orphanage crib. What did the child have to smile about? Seeing his smile in those surroundings was as much a miracle as finding a diamond in a cesspool.

I first met Tommy five months later while visiting Sophie in the orphanage, and again three months after, when Joe and I picked up Sophie from her orphanage. Sophie's needs turned out to be so simple to manage it wasn't long before we felt we could do it again.

We could handle another child like Sophie. Just as during Sophie's adoption, God moved a few good-sized mountains to enable us to bring Tommy home. For one thing, rather than the four-year-old he appeared to be, Tommy was going to turn sixteen-years-old several months after we officially committed to adopt him. We squeaked in under the wire, just weeks before his sixteenth birthday, after which it would have been too late to adopt him into the United States.

Tommy and his million-dollar smile.

He was doing so much better than Sophie had been when we brought her home. Since the new director of his orphanage had been instated, Tommy had responded well to the improved conditions she had brought to pass. Unlike Sophie, Tommy had learned to eat mashed foods by spoon and eagerly accepted each bite the caregivers gave him. He enjoyed holding a toy in his hand, was happy to be held, moved and touched, gave amazing eye contact and responded affectionately to personal attention, eagerly met each new friend and new adventure; and he had a rare, untouched, sweet, gentle, shining spirit. He had no active medical issues. He did, however, possess an ear-piercing "happy pterodactyl" screech when he reached the point of sensory overload. This was our only real concern before we brought him home, as our daughter Verity would melt down at sudden loud noises that were much less intense than Tommy's screech.

We had integrated Sophie and her needs into our household almost effortlessly. We possessed the gift of a stable, happy, family culture that we were eager to share with another child. We could picture caring for Sophie and Tommy side by side. We understood and accepted the impact that profound, lifelong neglect has on children with innate developmental delays. Sophie was around an eighteen-month-old developmental level and Tommy was evaluated to be six to eleven months developmentally. We believed our experience with Sophie was great preparation for Tommy. We knew life was going to be super full during Tommy's transition into our family, but we worked hard to be ready for him.

We knew bringing any child home involved risk, but we had every confidence in God to undertake for us.

Tommy wasn't home a whole month before it all began to unravel.

Tommy's needs with no outside help would have consumed the life of a mom with no other children to care for. Bringing him home was like bringing home five or six children at once.

There were: the months of life-altering, explosive, blow-out diarrhea any hour of the day or night that no diaper could contain and no doctor could explain. His increasing reluctance and eventual refusal to take food by mouth. The hospitalizations for fluids, nutrition, testing, and feeding tube. A stomach that couldn't readily tolerate any formula we tried. The detested tube feedings that had to be given slowly enough and spaced far enough apart to avoid vomiting; to fit them all into twenty-four hours required restraining him eight hours a day to prevent dislodging his feeding tube. The nighttime feeds that often resulted in tube fails or vomiting episodes necessitating entire clean-ups in the wee hours. The lists of meds given at various times in various dosages. The periodic IV treatments to increase his bone density—more dull hours spent being restrained. His mouthful of foul-smelling, decaying teeth that couldn't be removed until his bones grew stronger. The hated attempts at weight-bearing to increase his bone density. The stain and stink of diarrhea, formula, and vomit, and the putrid drool of rotting teeth that permeated our carpets, furniture, and home. Being confined to home or appointments and the resultant increasing isolation from loved friends, family, and church. The financial strain of months of survival living with no end in sight. Our inability for the whole first year to access public health care due to delays in Tommy's paperwork; then, not one moment available to devote to the large amounts of paperwork, phone calls, and emails it took to set up the necessary supports. The constant rock and hard place of balancing Tommy's various conflicting needs, then balancing his continuous needs with my responsibility to the rest of the household. The overwhelming mountains of urgent, ongoing needs in every direction, waiting for me to address them. The severe, long-term sleep deprivation, three to four hours each night for many months, with resultant exhaustion and brain fog, making it nearly impossible to manage the thousands of details I was responsible for. Bullying myself along to stay awake and to do everything as perfectly as possible.

And always, always, the feeling of failure when I didn't meet my own high expectations.

I felt like a failure when we had to enroll Tommy and Sophie in public school to provide stimulation and activity for them, which I couldn't manage to provide at home, and also to obtain some desperately-needed respite. I felt like a failure when we had to pursue government help, felt like a failure when I couldn't help Tommy eat by mouth, felt like a failure when I had to give him formula rather than real blended food, felt like a failure when I couldn't provide the one-to-one time I wanted to give all my children, felt like a failure at the many times I was forced to be an absentee mom. The list of failures was endless and stared me down accusingly no matter which direction I looked.

Our marriage. If we could have rated its strength on a scale of one to ten, it might have stood at a six or seven most of the time, acceptable for a normal pace of life but insufficient for the relentless, off-the-charts stress we were experiencing day after day, week after week, month after month. We were absolutely committed to our marriage ... and we were struggling painfully.

Our other children. How painful for a mother who had always upheld high standards for education and training to watch it fall apart. Some days I would tell our four middle boys, ages five to eight, to listen to a book on tape and play with Legos because all my time was swallowed up in cleaning diarrhea and/or vomit off of Tommy and everything around him, giving meds and tube feedings, troubleshooting equipment failures, handling time-consuming phone calls, paperwork, emails, and appointments. The behavior of the four boys plummeted, but I felt helpless to address it, as I was being forced to parent from a distance, on the fly. It tore me up inside to watch three-year-old Verity regress and sink into autistic-like behavior after a truly bright beginning. I watched a couple of our older children pull away and give in to sullenness and resentment. Even my hungry baby would regularly have to cry and wait for an hour or more to nurse while I dealt with one urgent need after another. This went on for month after month.

"God, what are You doing?"

I tried hard to hold onto truth and a sense of humor. I remember leaning over the bathtub scrubbing diarrhea off my little teenaged son and thinking, "Save me, O God, for the poopy has come up to my neck!" However, I allowed the perspective of our detractors to be the loudest voice in my ears and looking around me at how painfully "not working" it was in our family, privately agreed with our critics that we had gone way too far past our limits.

During the darkest months of that dark winter, when Tommy spent a lot of his time uncomfortable and crying, I began to grieve. I grieved for Tommy's misery. I grieved the loss of the family we used to be and didn't like the family we had become. Many things that were important to me were now out of reach with no end in sight. I was killing myself to meet the needs of these children I loved so dearly, and it wasn't enough. My life had become a blur that turned into an out-of-control nightmare of impossible levels of stress, relentless grueling physical and mental demands, a constant sense of failing a test, a very real isolation, grief and depression, and worst of all by far, an underlying feeling of having been abandoned by God. It felt as if we were circling the drain.

I became convinced we must not be trusting God enough, because we had always experienced His provision sustaining us in marvelous ways. For the first time, it seemed He had withdrawn, with little to no desperately-needed help coming in. We had taken this risk as a leap of faith, because we trusted absolutely God would not abandon us. Why couldn't I see Him now? Why was He hiding His face from me? Despite my solid theological understanding of grace, under the intense pressure my foundational assumptions began to be revealed, visceral assumptions I hadn't been aware of during my entire career as a good little girl with standards of excellence.

I have to get it all perfect in order to please God.

He is sovereign, perfect, and cannot make mistakes.

He's withdrawn His approval from us.

It must be our fault. We must have displeased Him.

My spiritual struggle added to my distress. Over and over, I cried out to Him to have mercy on us. Over and over, silence and an increase in the pressures of life.

My sole comfort for months was Jesus' cry, "My God, my God, why have you forsaken me?" (Matt. 27:46b, NIV). Surely I was also permitted to ask Him the same question.

But not guaranteed an answer.

Another glimmer of insight came, this time from another

suffering family … "Ask Me why, and I will not answer that question. Ask Me to show you who I am, and I will always answer that question." I begged Him to show me who He was. Nothing.

"How long, O LORD? Will you forget me forever?

How long will you hide your face from me?

How long shall I take counsel in my soul

and have sorrow in my heart all the day?"

(Psalm 13:1–2a, NASB)

After many months of feeling God was hiding His face from me, one night He granted me a glimmer of a break in the silence.

I'd been trying for weeks to find the time to run to the thrift store ten minutes from our home for some desperately-needed clothes. We had several boys sharing the same size, and with the rate of wear and tear along with the chronic insufficiency of our laundry logistics, we were running out of clothes for them. In addition, the wedding of our oldest son was rapidly approaching, and we were short one pair of dress pants for one of the boys. I arrived at the store on Saturday night, fifteen minutes before closing time, and hurriedly began combing through the children's section for anything suitable. Suddenly, I was stopped short at the sight of one pair of black dress pants. They were the exact size we needed. I broke down, weeping and talking aloud to God. "You're still there. You didn't abandon us after all." On my way to the cash register moments before closing time, a stranger walked in the door and approached me with the offer of a half-off coupon he didn't need. By this point, I was blubbering uncontrollably and could only mumble to him that he had no idea what that meant to me. God still cared about us!

That spring, we finally turned a corner. We had solved the diarrhea mystery and obtained a wheelchair, so Tommy had begun attending school for six hours a day several days a week, whenever a nurse was available. He was now happy a majority of the time, growing from an insecure orphan boy into a relaxed and handsome young man, making strides in his health. He had gained an impressive number of pounds and inches, received leg braces, walked in a walker independently for the first time, and was cleared for dental work. He was bonding with me, reaching out to me for affection and preferring me to others. Most miraculous of all, at seventeen years old he learned his first word, "Mama."

And more help was now on the way, help which would put us into a sustainable situation for the long term. We were just waiting for the nursing agency to call back and set up a day to train some nurses in Tommy's care in order to provide the respite our family needed.

As the pressure eased, a lighthearted sense of well-being, humor, and hope for the future returned to our home. There was a tangible sense of having survived intact, together. One night a minor conflict over something or other seemed to be brewing; Joe memorably broke the tension by declaring, "We know the way to hell and back, and we are not going there tonight."

Then came July 31st, 2014.

We had sent our older kids to a cabin in the mountains for the week as thanks for their sacrifices over the previous year. It was a brilliantly sunny summer day, and there was excitement in the air as I helped the children at home prepare for a fun outing at our favorite creek. After breakfast, they were scurrying about to finish their chores so we wouldn't miss one more minute of fun than we had to. When Tommy's feeding pump beeped to let me know his breakfast feeding was finished, I discovered it had been leaking onto his pajamas, so I stripped him down quickly and popped him into the bathtub to play with toys while I gathered the diaper bags and made sure they were stocked with diapers.

Our then-eight-year-old son tore into the room.

"Mom! Tommy!"

I could hear it in his voice. And ran.

"This is not real ... this can't be real ... I can't believe this is real ... he's gone ... I'm sure he's gone ... he can't be gone ... this can't be real ... please let this not be real ... please make this not real ... oh please please please please ... oh Tom-Tom!"

* * *

"We didn't ... bring him home ... for this!"

The words come out louder than I expected, forced past the choking weight of tears.

I am huddled against the kitchen doorway, watching the emergency medical responders cease their efforts and cover Tommy's still form.

The police officer's face is kind as he steps toward me.

"God already knew this was going to happen," he says.

* * *

After I give my statement to the head emergency medical technician, she stands and asks, "May I give you a hug?"

And hugs me long and tightly through my wrenching sobs.

"Listen to me," she says, stepping back with her hands on my shoulders and looking into my face.

"I've been doing this for a long time, and I've seen a lot. You're going to blame yourself. Don't do that."

"How can I not blame myself?" I choke out.

"Look at me," she says.

"This was not your fault."

* * *

Pastor Mike and his wife Jenny stayed with us throughout that endless afternoon of horror, serving our family with quiet compassion along with several other faithful friends and neighbors. As Mike and Jenny prepare to leave, she leans down toward me where I've been sitting for hours, clutching Sophie on my lap in the big rocking chair.

She cups my face in her hands, forcing me to look up into her eyes. The words come through her strong Chinese accent as clear as day.

"God is sovereign. Do not take responsibility for what He did."

* * *

Nothing they say feels true, they're just trying to make me feel better.

I know God is sovereign, but this feels like a horrible, tragic mistake.

What was this for? What sin was this for?

What is God thinking about me? "You failed the test. You weren't taking good enough care of Tommy, so I brought him home?"

What we managed to give him was so pitiful compared with what we wanted to do for him. We'd hardly gotten started. It was so brief, so pathetic, so pitifully small.

* * *

My assumption based on my knowledge and experience of Tommy's size and his abilities, as well as of the particular bathtub, was that he was at the same risk of death playing there in a few inches of water as he would have been playing in the living room next to a heavy piece of furniture or outside in the yard under a tree.

At the time of Tommy's death, he was the size of a seven-year-old with the ability to sit up and lie down on his back readily. Due to his cognitive limitations, which affected his grasp of cause and effect, he was uninterested in the faucet handle. Even had he made the logical connection and purposefully attempted to turn the water on, due to his significant lack of core strength he would have been unable to turn it on using his hands. The bathtub leaked due to a hole down near the bottom, so even the few inches of water I ran for him to play in had to be replenished periodically. He very much resisted lying on his belly, and in fact was uncooperative with his physical therapist when she attempted to put him into that position. He would immediately flip to his back as soon as he could, as he had spent nearly all his first sixteen years in this position, and it enabled him to move across the floor. At his size, it was impossible for him to drown lying on his back in the bathtub in the amount of water I had run for him to splash in with his toys.

It didn't feel like a risk.

I had never known him to lie down and push the faucet on using his feet, but since he was found lying submerged on his back with his feet facing the faucet and the water running full blast, that is the best theory of what happened. If so, it happened very quickly.

I was immediately pulverized into a million bleeding fragments at the bottom of the blackest pit I have ever known. It would be months before I could sleep without help or wake from sleep, draw a breath, or think a thought without agony. It was eight and a half months before I began to emerge from the pit in bits and pieces.

* * *

Fast-forward to this exquisite spring day almost three years later. Despite our family's regained equilibrium, the fallout from the survival years is real, and we deal with it every day. I am still somewhere in the process of healing, although I have come very far from those early days.

At the same time...

God has changed us and our perspective through the pain He's brought us through. Like a skillful surgeon, He slashed through our lives with His scalpel not simply in order to heal that initial incision, but to accomplish the deep repairs that alone can bring true healing. He unquestionably used Tommy's life and death in our family to reveal major areas that needed to be transformed.

He has begun to repair longstanding problems in our marriage, and we have hope in Him that He will continue to draw us closer in unity. During the most distressing weeks and months, He clearly called our oldest daughter to the mission field; she is now preparing to take the gospel to unreached people groups. He brought Joanna into our family; because of the work He has done and is doing in all of us, we are able to be the parents and family she needs us to be in order to do some hefty emotional healing of her own. Because of our experience of being desperate for help we didn't receive, we are very sensitive to others in that position, and God has allowed me to be a small part of a new ministry to provide respite and support to exhausted parent caregivers.

Back when it looked like our world was disintegrating, I could never have anticipated all God would do in our family by 2017. We are trusting Him to continue His good work no matter what still lies ahead of us, but I confess that I no longer pray intrepid prayers. I do often cry out to Him to have mercy on us and on our children.

My faith is still weak and shaky, but the fact that it is still alive at all is only due to the mercy and grace of God toward me. During the blackest time after Tommy's death, I came perilously close to being convinced I was on the outside of grace—that I was not, and had never been, a child of God. What a horrifying place to be, as close to hell as I ever want to be again.

I am slowly learning how to relate to my heavenly Father in a healthier way than I did before. I am learning to be honest with Him instead of parroting what I know the right answers to be. Rather than feeling that I have to get it all right in order to please Him and receive His love and approval, I approach Him with utterly empty hands, needy, weak, and broken. He has been, He is, so very faithful and good to me. And I am waiting on Him for full healing … and for the return of closeness with Him … and of joy.

Who knows?

Maybe through this journey, God is changing the terrain of my soul in a way He couldn't have if I were untouched by profound spiritual and emotional trauma.

Maybe if He hadn't first destroyed my idea of who He is, I would have remained unable to know Him as He truly is.

Who knows?

Maybe in Tommy's death, and all the aftermath, was the beginning of God's answer to my plea, "Show me who You are."

When through fiery trials thy pathway shall lie,

My grace, all sufficient, shall be thy supply;

The flame shall not hurt thee; I only design

Thy dross to consume, and thy gold to refine.

The soul that on Jesus hath leaned for repose,

I will not, I will not desert to his foes;

That soul, though all hell should endeavor to shake,

I'll never, no, never, no, never forsake!
—From the beloved hymn, "How Firm a Foundation"

Susanna M. has been recording her honest thoughts at www.theblessingofverity.com since early 2011. She and her husband Joe are parents of sixteen, including their oldest son who is married, and two children who preceded them to heaven. They've been young parents, old parents, twin parents, special needs parents, biological parents, legal guardians and adoptive parents, homeschooling parents, and public school special ed parents. It's a good thing they love being parents! All their hopes for this life and the life to come are pinned on Christ. Christ in us, the hope of glory.

What Is Love?

There is something so very natural about the love a mother has for her newborn baby. It is very instinctual—all of the snuzzly, wuzzly kisses and sweet talk and unquestioned devotion just naturally springs up as nine months of labor culminate in that moment when you first hold your wet, wiggly bundle of new life in your arms. For that matter, this love begins even before the baby is born as mommy talks to, caresses, and dreams about the little one growing inside of her. There are few things so intensely powerful as the feelings a mother has for her baby.

Having both biological and adopted children and, in particular, giving birth to a brand-new baby fresh on the heels of the arrival of our first adopted child, has made me realize that as much as my gut reaction is to want to say otherwise, I love my children in different ways.

Before you dismiss me entirely as a terrible mother, follow me through for a moment. The response I have for my biological children is a very natural one, starting even before their birth, and reinforced by all of the natural hormones that naturally produce all sorts of wonderful feelings. My ability to cuddle, soothe, and comfort these little ones serves to further build the wonderful bond we share. In contrast, my love for Nicholai is based on a choice.

While the love I have for Nicholai may not be "natural," it is very real, and growing, and deep, and in many ways intentional in a way that is different from that of my other children. Looking at him and being with him does not elicit the same warm-fuzzy feelings I get from the children who have been mine from their conception.

And I think that last statement holds the biggest clue to where the core of this issue lies. How often do we confuse *love* with *feelings*? Being Nicholai's mother has taught me many things about what it means to love, it has revealed to me many less-than-ideal things about myself, and it is leading me to an ever-deepening understanding of what real love truly is.

* * *

Adoption had been part of my vision for my future as a mother since I was a child. During my elementary years, my parents were foster parents, and it made me aware at an early age of the need for adoptive families for children who did not have the option of growing up with their birth family.

Over the years, my experiences with caring for other children, from helping my mom with in-home day care to my own babysitting and nannying in high school, made me increasingly aware of how much critical, life-shaping development goes on in the first few months of a child's life. I decided there was no way I would adopt a child who was older than eight months old, since so much of who they are has already been determined, and I was afraid of jumping into a situation that someone else had already "messed up."

I was a very young child when I realized my own life was messed up and I needed to surrender control of my life to Jesus. Looking back, I can see how He took that young child and has been working steadily at shaping her ever since. It was becoming a parent itself that God used to strip away my fears of adopting an older child, beginning with our very opinionated firstborn, Seth. As I was pregnant during his second year with Rachel, I was very aware of how, despite our best efforts, we had a "messed up" child on our hands! I found myself in a position where every day was a chance for a new beginning, a chance to take the mistakes of the day before and with the fresh new mercies God supplied, to begin again the work of shaping and tending the young man we had been given to raise.

It was our third child, Isaiah, which God used to erase our fears of adopting a child with special needs. When Isaiah was sixteen months old, he woke from a nap and collapsed back onto his pillow, not breathing and turning blue. Our 9-1-1 call led to a hospitalization and a diagnosis of epilepsy.[2] Becoming, overnight, the mother of a child with special needs was a turning point as I recognized that, first and foremost, *he was just my child*; the "special needs" part was secondary. During that hospital stay, I woke in the middle of one night and it smacked me: I was not afraid to adopt a child with special needs because *I was already the mother of a child with special needs*. Fear. Removed. Just like that.

It was actually my husband, however, about a year and a half later, who became the driving force behind pursuing international special needs adoption. I had told God years earlier that I would know it was His leading, His timing, and not my own emotions when Matt was the one who took the lead in expanding our family through adoption. In the spring of 2012, we learned Isaiah had an ultra-rare chromosomal abnormality. This explained why medication did not control his seizures, as well as explaining many

---

[2] Isaiah was diagnosed with ring (20) chromosome syndrome. The manifestations of this syndrome tend to worsen, not improve, over time. There are approximately 100 people known to have this condition world-wide.

of his developmental delays and behavioral challenges. Soon after, we saw a documentary[3] on the chilling effects of institutionalization on children with even relatively minor needs; and as we compared that with the severity of our Isaiah's condition, it became obvious to us that *we* could be a family for a child who needed one—God had made room in our hearts through Isaiah for another child who would not grow up to be "normal."

Within a few days of watching the documentary, I "happened" to come across a blog written by another adoptive mom[4] who had just brought home a tiny child from an orphanage in Pleven, Bulgaria. That became our trigger to move forward in earnest. As she was posting photos of other children from her daughter's orphanage who were becoming available for adoption, my husband saw a photo of Nicholai and said, "He's our boy."

This orphanage had just undergone a change of director, as the previous one had been criminally neglecting the children. We heard stories of the children spending their entire lives lying in their cribs, only being taken out once a day for a rapid diaper change. We were told they were fed a flour and broth gruel delivered through beer bottles with large holes cut in the nipples. Those who swallowed fast enough lived through their meal; many children aspirated and died. If we were going to do this adoption thing, we weren't going to just scrape the surface of "special needs" and pick a child with some minor, correctable disability; we were going to jump in with both feet and take on a child who had been severely impacted by both his disability and his living conditions.

I had learned years earlier that it is not just food that makes a child grow; a child will not produce the hormones necessary for growth if they do not receive love and affection. Nicholai's medical

---

[3] http://topdocumentaryfilms.com/bulgarias-abandoned-children
[4] http://theblessingofverity.com

diagnoses were cerebral palsy and profound developmental delay. The only way to explain his twenty-two pound weight at eight years old is by a severe lack of nutrition ... and an extreme lack of affection.

While I believe we went into Nicholai's adoption with a very realistic picture of what to expect medically, psychologically, and developmentally, I don't think I fully realized the all-encompassing extent of the impact someone's early life experiences can have on their perceptions of every facet of reality.

Our first week[5] of visiting with Nicholai was very rewarding. Our hearts ached for this poor, tiny, terrified child who was going to become our son legally and had already been our son in our hearts for many months. At our first meeting, we waited in a pristine play room for our son to be brought to us. A staff person roughly shoved the stroller containing Nicholai into the room and left. No introductions, no transitions—it was as though she had just deposited a piece of luggage and gone on to her next task.

The boy was overcome with terror. You could see it in his face, his muscles, his posture of guarding himself by raising his arm and turning his head away. And, oh, the confusion he must have experienced as these two strangers, speaking an unfamiliar language, approached him, crying, trying to be both respectful of his personal space and simultaneously wanting to scoop up and love on this fragile person who had lived a life almost completely devoid of love.

As our week together progressed, it was clear that while Nicholai did not *love* us in return, he was definitely learning to be comfortable with us, relaxing, and even smiling and letting himself laugh a bit with us. Mid-way through the week, we witnessed a

---

[5] Bulgaria requires two trips: one to spend visiting the child before the final adoption request can be submitted, and then a second trip four to six months later to pick up the child.

visit from his "Baba,"[6] and we learned he was absolutely capable of reciprocating affection. He delighted in this woman and soaked up every single bit of her attention. Just the sound of her voice was enough to set him squealing and wriggling with delight. It was beautiful to see he was capable of having this sort of response to another person.

It also reinforced our hopes that this little boy could and *would* grow to love us as his parents. We'd been educated about reactive attachment disorder, and knew a child like Nicholai who had never been given the opportunity to develop a healthy, trusting bond with anyone would be at high risk for RAD. But seeing a variety of appropriate responses from him to different people (sometimes ambivalence, sometimes apprehension, sometimes a relaxed smile, and, for his Baba, intense excitement) led us to believe that somehow he had learned in some capacity to respond appropriately.

We left Bulgaria so sad to be leaving without our son, knowing it would be months before we returned for him, and so eager to have him home with us where we could begin the beautiful task of loving life into him. That was at the end of March.

On August 2, Nicholai Emmanuel was legally declared to be our son. On August 8, we learned I was pregnant.

All of our pre-adoption training had informed us of the significance of the first six months a child has in his new home. We marveled at the timing of our baby's due date, almost exactly six months after Nicholai's homecoming. I was determined to make

---

[6] An NGO was providing funds to pay older women in the community to spend time with some of the children in Nicholai's baby house. Mary (not her real name), had been spending two mornings a week with Nicholai for the last two years. She shared how when he was eight years old and she had first been allowed to take him outside, he had been terrified by everything, but by the end of the summer he was able to go outside with her without fear. This woman became Nicholai's twice-a-week ticket out of his crib.

the most of those six months before I would have a new little person demanding my time and nurturing.

Nicholai's Baba was there to say goodbye to him when we picked him up. Poor little guy started our two-hour drive through the mountains to Sofia sobbing uncontrollably. I don't know how much he was able to understand what was happening, but he seemed truly terrified and heartbroken all wrapped up into one.

Our week in the hotel was rather uneventful. Nicholai was fairly docile and low-key, but he would grind his teeth incessantly at night, and a few times during the week he broke down sobbing again. Cuddling with me was really not his thing, nor was my foreign English language, so I was limited in my ability to soothe him. We learned, too, toward the end of the week that, unlike our first impressions, Nicholai did have some self-stimulating behaviors—most notably we learned where the spot of eczema on his arm came from—he would bite himself. Poor, lonely guy. I was so excited to get him *home* and show him what life would be like surrounded by a family who loved him, and with so many things to do and explore.

We came home and went to work doing what we could to bond with our little boy. Matt and I agreed I would be his primary caregiver, so I was the one who fed him, changed him, touched him, sang to him, and tucked him in for bed every night. We started out trying to have me snuggle and rock with him every night as part of our bedtime routine, but this was very distressing for him. I joked that the quickest way to get him to cry was for me to snuggle him close. Every defensive mechanism he had at his disposal would rise up and fight against the terrifying experience of having Mama hold him.

Most nights after our two youngest were in bed, I would read out loud to Seth and Rachel. We decided this would be a great time to have Nicholai sit with me—he could be close, but since the focus of the time would be on the book, and not on him specifically, we thought he might tolerate it better.

Holding a tiny nine-year-old boy sobbing and rigid, partly due to his cerebral palsy and partly due to him pushing against you with everything he's got, while desperately trying to avoid eye contact, just doesn't elicit the same rush of warm-fuzzy feelings that snuggling a tiny, squishy, floppy, darling newborn baby does. You don't realize until you're in the middle of it how much of what we call "love" is really a mutual reinforcement of good emotions. There was none of that happening here!

Because of Nicholai's physical limitations, he could not (and still cannot) walk or even crawl, but after three short weeks at home, he quickly learned to use his arms to pull himself around the house on his belly at a very efficient pace. We learned that he was drawn to certain unusual objects—he adored anything he could put his hand through, like duct tape, masking tape, linking rings, and elastic bead bracelets. He was content to spend his days on the floor pushing these things around in front of him. We were so glad to let him finally, for the first time in his life, have the freedom to choose for himself where he wanted to go.

Especially in the first few weeks, Nicky would regularly wake a few hours into his night, viciously grinding his teeth, and often crying uncontrollably. Any efforts on our part to comfort him apparently had no effect. The only thing I could do that would sometimes seem to help would be to sing a little song (to the tune of "Are You Sleeping?"):

Mommy loves you,
Mommy loves you,
Every day
Every day.

Nicky has a mommy,
Nicky has a mommy
Every day,
Every day.

And so went our days. He was happiest when left alone. Although diaper changes were definitely a positive thing for him, eating—such a primary nurturing time—was the one regular place he chose to channel all of his distress and anxiety about his new life. Because eating is not exactly an optional activity, especially for a thirty-pound nine-year-old, this meant we had a regular routine of extremely unpleasant interactions. Three times a day, every single day, I made him eat. I'd do what I could to make it more palatable, but still, holding down his blocking arm with one hand and pressing the spoon full of pureed supper against his clenched teeth until he opens up doesn't exactly parallel the intimate snuggling of nursing one's newborn infant.

Eye contact. Nope. Not going to happen. I would make regular attempts throughout the day, gently coaching him, trying to soothe and encourage with my words, but he would have none of it. *Anything* to avoid looking Mom in the eye.

And, in typical RAD fashion, any time we'd have friends over, he would eagerly pull himself across the floor to where they were and do everything he could to get pulled up into their laps. We were grateful to have friends sympathetic to our desire to help teach Nicholai that Mommy and Daddy are the people to snuggle with, not others, but it didn't curb his desire to do so. At the time, I didn't particularly think of RAD. So many of the parenting challenges that are typically associated with RAD were so beyond Nicholai's physical and cognitive capacity it just didn't seem right to put the RAD label on a child who was really quite easy to care for. But there were no apparent signs we were making any progress on bonding during that all-important first six months.

Starting even during those first six months, and continuing after our daughter Phoebe was born, I found myself falling into a pattern of meeting Nicholai's daily needs, changing, feeding, dressing, bathing, even some playing, but not really knowing how to "connect" with him. This was obviously partly due to the fact that with a brand-new nursing baby, there were significant other demands on my time; but it was also largely because he tried so hard to avoid the connection I was pursuing with him. It takes much more mental and physical energy to keep loving and pursuing someone who appears much happier to avoid you than it does with someone who responds positively to even minute displays of affection.

"For if you love those who love you, what reward do you have? Do not even the tax collectors do the same? ... Therefore you must be perfect, as your heavenly Father is perfect" (Matt. 5:46 & 48, NASB).

Far from developing a beautiful connection after our six months of focused "bonding," I found instead that by this time the majority of my interactions with Nicky were spent correcting him ("No, no, Nicky. That is not to play with." "Nicky, don't touch that!") or re-directing him from stimming behaviors ("Nicky, we don't lick the floor." "No, Nicky, fix your finger!") Now this is not to say that I didn't also do many sweet, gentle, kind things for him, but I found myself being easily irritated with his little habits: mouthing the floor, bending his left pinky finger back so far it touched his wrist, things like that.

My irritation did not spring from love for him, but love for myself, and a selfish desire for him to be so satisfied with his life here with us so that he didn't feel the need to revert back to the old stimming behaviors that were his sole occupation for so many lonely years of his life. Didn't it reflect badly on us if he preferred self-stimming to our affection? And inside I knew, too, that many times I felt like I was treating him no differently than the staff at his orphanage—as a task to be completed. There were absolutely times when my redirecting of him was based out of love and concern for him. But there are also many times when my response to these behaviors was not Nicky-motivated, but *Me*-motivated.

Unlike the natural outpouring of loving emotions I feel toward my biological babies, it took a conscious effort to love my Nicholai.

And recognizing that made me realize I did not know what it really meant to love someone. What *is* love anyway?

One night around this time as I was working my way through 1 Corinthians, I just so happened to be reading Chapter 13. What is love?

Love is patient. Patient. Yikes. Why does it have to start with that? Irritation and patience don't really jive.

Love is kind. Kind is such a "ho-hum" sort of word. Nothing dramatic or exciting, nothing extreme or showy. Just "kind." But that's what love is. Love is kind. Love is not a matter of doing something to a person but looking for what I can do *for* that person in the little day-to-day things. At this point, I decided I'd probably read enough to keep me thinking for a good while.

Patience. Kindness. These are not responses that always come "naturally." It's pretty easy to be patient with a sweetly sleeping baby, or a cute-as-a-button toddler, but I'm guessing I'm not the only mother who has been less than patient when her baby is up after only a ten-minute nap, or up for the third time in the night; or when the toddler is standing stubbornly in a puddle on the floor with dirty underpants *right* next to the potty chair she refuses to sit on.

But there's more, too.

"Love ... is not proud ... it is not self-seeking ... it is not easily angered...." (Selections from 1 Cor. 13:4–5, NIV).

As I mulled over this, there was a sudden flip-flop in my mind. I *do* love some of my children better than I do others. And it is Nicholai who I am likely the best at loving, because when I choose patience and kindness with him, when I choose to not be irritated by his deeply ingrained habits, those are choices that are *not* stemming from my self-serving pride-filled estimations of the little human beings I had a role in producing (as adorable as they may be), but rather is coming from something much closer to what love really is.

What is love? Here's another definition:

"This is My commandment, that you love one another, just as I (Jesus) have loved you. Greater love has no one than this, that one lay down his life for his friends." (John 15:12–13, NASB, parenthesis added).

My role is not to achieve good feelings in either me or my children, but to be obedient—to lay down my life for this child of mine. To lay down my natural desire to get a return for the affection I invest in him. To joyfully lay down my time to do the work of the daily tasks. I need to come to terms with the fact that Nicholai may *never* reciprocate my love for him; he may *always* prefer the comfort of his self-stimming behaviors to the gentle comfort of his mother's touch.

That realization is a rather sobering one, and one that leaves me with a lot of room to grow in my love for all of my children. Love is not a matter of feelings, but rather is about action. What I *feel* can ebb and flow, and it is so often rooted in a me-centered view of life. What I *do*, and the inner motivation and attitude with which I do what I do, is the place where real love happens.

Some of my best moments as Nicholai's mother came when he

would wake in the night with a dirty diaper. As I quietly wiped off his tiny bottom and changed him into something clean, I would think about all of the many nights when there was no diaper change for him if he was dirty, and I would be reminded of Jesus words:

"Then the King will say .... 'Come, you who are blessed of My Father, inherit the kingdom prepared for you from the foundation of the world. For I was hungry, and you gave Me something to eat; I was thirsty, and you gave Me something to drink; I was a stranger, and you invited Me in; naked, and you clothed Me; I was sick, and you visited Me; I was in prison, and you came to Me.' Then the righteous will answer Him, 'Lord, when did we see You hungry, and feed You, or thirsty, and give You something to drink?' ... The King will answer and say to them, 'Truly I say to you, to the extent that you did it to one of these brothers of Mine, even the least of them, you did it to Me" (Matt. 25:34–40, NASB).

At those moments, I would be nearly overwhelmed by the awesome privilege it was to be my son's mother. One of the most menial tasks, offered in service to my Savior, my Lord would bring me to my knees. When that is the motivation behind my actions towards any of my children, that is love.

* * *

We have seen many small but good changes in our day-to-day relationship with Nicholai over the three and a half years that he's been our son. His teachers at school report that he smiles excitedly when we come into the classroom. Every now and then Nicholai will even pull himself over to me or Matt when we're sitting on the floor and want to lay across our lap for a while. Just in the last month, he has surprised me with long, smile-laden moments of eye contact, those milk-chocolate eyes gazing into mine with obvious pleasure. Those moments do happen, but they're still not frequent and are coupled with plenty of times when he will go out of his way to push us away. But it does give us hope there is still room for us to grow in closeness. The damage of a decade of neglect and abuse during the most formative years of a person's life is not something that is going to be magically overcome by six months of sweet, snuggly warm-fuzzies, or, apparently, by even a few years in a safe, stable, caring environment.

When he does respond to me now with a smile, or we share those moments of beautiful eye contact, or he scrambles over to me after I've been gone, that is an incredible feeling. But that feeling is not *love*. Love is when I continually lay down my life, my desire for reciprocation; it is my patient care for him when he does not respond to me, or even pushes me away. It is a love that is fueled by the everlasting love of God, and not by the fickle fuel of self-satisfaction that cannot sustain more than a momentary flame.

The thing that comes *naturally* to us is not really love, but is rather a form of self-love, something that only cares about what that little person makes *me* feel, rather than something self-sacrificial that truly puts the other one above myself. Real love, the love Christ models for us, is in fact very unnatural to our fallen human natures and is something that grows in us as we grow in Him. What I know for certain is that love is a choice, and it springs from trust in, obedience to, and complete dependence on the One who *is* love. Being Nicholai's mother has taught me to look at love differently, and it is helping me grow in my ability to love not only him, but all of the others God has put into my life.

Andrea G. lives with her husband, Matt, and their ten children in a house that once belonged to her husband's grandfather, and that she has affectionately named "Motley Garden." Three of their children were adopted from Bulgaria; seven joined the family through biological means, and the crew has a wide range of physical and cognitive … and singing … abilities. Matt and Andrea are never bored! Andrea has kept a blog since shortly after they began their first adoption in late 2012 about their adoption experiences, construction projects (the house has grown and changed since it belonged to Grandpa!), and the way God permeates all aspects of everyday life. You can find her blog at www.roomformore-mn.blogspot.com.

Unexpected Dream

When I was little, I used to take my well-worn toys and build my own house of dreams. With pigtails swaying, I would perform a marriage for me and a future husband, build an amazing house out of blankets and blocks, and fill the house with teddy bear children. First, with my biological children and then with the children I would adopt. I had it all planned out.

Ever since I was young, I knew I wanted to adopt. I dreamed of having a bus full of children from all around the world. The idea of adoption was something I grew up with. I have five siblings with various special needs who joined our family through adoption. One could argue that planning to adopt *is* a family trait.

I believe God plants seeds of desires in our hearts and then waters, tends, and nurtures them until they fully reflect His plan. As God watered the seeds in my heart, He started to tend and nurture this dream in a way I didn't expect.

In 2013, at the age of twenty-six, I felt a stirring that God was calling me to adopt. I was excited but a little unsure. It didn't follow my little girl plans. I never expected that I would adopt before I was married, owned a house, or had any biological children. Yet, I could not deny God had spoken to my heart to trust Him and to take the step to adopt.

It felt risky. So, I did what many have done before … I asked God for a sign. A financial sign. The next day, I went into work and there was a white envelope waiting for me. Not only did it say that I got a raise, but it also had an unexpected check tucked inside. I knew I was ready to obey and start my adoption journey. I gathered myself together and started working towards the greatest adventure in my life thus far.

I knew I wanted to adopt a child from overseas. However, being young and single eliminated a lot of countries for me. I knew that oftentimes girls are adopted more than boys. I decided upon two criteria for my adoption. I wanted to adopt a boy. And I wanted a boy with Down syndrome. Both these factors make a child less desirable for many people, but that is the criteria God placed in my heart. As I researched, it became clear Bulgaria's program suited me best.

I remember the day I got the news in 2014. I was on my break at work and my co-worker came into the staff room to tell me I had a call from an adoption agency. The first thing that came to my mind was "Oh no! They need more paperwork." I went back to my desk and picked up the phone. My social worker was on the other end telling me she was leaving for vacation that afternoon and that someone else would be communicating with me while she was away.

Relieved, I sank into my chair and breathed a prayer of thanks because I didn't need to email another document. Then came news I did not expect to hear. My social worker had received five pictures and two videos of a boy with Down syndrome from my Bulgarian agency.

The usual protocol is to wait until you have the official paperwork to present the information to the family. However, she wanted to make sure I could open the attachments before her holiday. As I was sitting at my desk, I opened the files and saw my son for the first time. It was love at first sight. I called my co-worker over to share the news with her and then called my family. That day I picked his new name and started praying specifically for him by name.

After a mad dash of fundraising and benefit auctions, my sister and I flew to Bulgaria to meet him during a heat wave in July 2014. I would have five days getting to know him.

On July 14, we walked through the doors mid-morning into a new building where we were invited to wait in the main room. Children's artwork decorated the walls in splashes of color and a TV played the news in a language I didn't know. There were children sitting in wheelchairs and on bright yellow pleather couches. I scanned the room to see Sammy but could not locate him.

Finally, the staff went to a chair that was turned away from the entrance. I saw her reach down and wake him up. She put him on his feet and directed him to me, his new "mama." With shaky steps, he toddled over to me and I picked him up. He gave me the firmest and biggest hug and he did not let go. All my sister and I could do was bawl. The joy and relief of meeting Sammy was a sacred time and one that was sealed with tears of love and joy for a child whom I had loved for months without him even knowing it.

I remember our translator was very concerned that I was holding the wrong child. But I saw something the translator didn't see. I saw my son. And he was perfect.

I knew what others saw on the outside. Sammy was a withdrawn, small, almost seven-year-old boy who couldn't walk and couldn't speak. But I got to know a little boy who had the most adorable laugh and loved to be held.

He was very reserved, and I was told he would spend his days sitting on a couch or in his bed. I was able to observe this during my five-day visit. Too soon, we said a tearful goodbye and came back to Canada. The wait for his adoption to be finalized was difficult. It was hard to focus on the present as it felt like my heart was left with a little boy in Bulgaria. Every time I received an email from my agency I was anxious to hear if things were moving forward.

In November, the day finally came. With the sound of the gavel dropping, the courts declared that Sammy was now, officially, my son. I could hardly wait to get him home! But I still needed to wait two more months.

Sammy was seven and a half years old when we walked him out of the institution's grey doors for the last time. After 2,753 days of living in institutions, my son walked out of his past and into a future with his forever family. He was no longer number 1221 in a group of orphans. He now had a name, a family, and a hope. No longer would he be defined by his Roma Gypsy status or labeled as the boy with Down syndrome or the child born into poverty. From now on, he would be known by my family name, and known as my son.

Our first sixteen months at home went as smoothly as a toboggan ride down a hill—incredible joy with a steep and oftentimes high-speed learning curve. We had a lot of trust to gain with Sammy and many obstacles to overcome, but they did not ever feel overwhelming. God's grace was sufficient. I relied heavily on the Lord to guide me and grew a thick skin as many offered their opinions about my methods for raising my son.

Slowly, Sammy overcame the trauma he had around food and eating. He learned to run, jump, and love water. He started to prefer my sister and me over other people. He would come to us for comfort and security. He knew where he was safe. His laughter started to fill our home regularly. Sammy had said "Mama" since before he came home but one day he said "Mom." And it was directed at me and was just not a random word; it had meaning. He knew I was his Mom.

Adoption is such a beautiful thing, but it's not without its darker moments. The road to recovery from the trauma that children face from neglect, and the lack of stimulation and abuse they experienced, is an ongoing process. In Sammy's story, I will likely never know what he encountered before he was my son.

Looking back, I now see that the reserved Sammy was hiding within himself. If he was stressed or overwhelmed, he would withdraw into himself. Picking his fingers, grinding his teeth, rocking and zoning out were all patterns of behavior to express his frustration or stress. Often, he would dig his nails into my shoulders when he was in this state. I held him close while he did, knowing this was one way I could show him that he was safe. He was free to show what he was feeling and to express his emotions to us.

In adoption, the effects of trauma can and, likely will, change most aspects of your family's lives. The top three areas that have been affected for me have been the social, the spiritual, and the financial areas of my life.

Socially: Although I have an amazing family and a small group of close friends, the journey of parenting Sammy is a lonely road. Relationships have changed as I have less time to give to others and more responsibilities with Sammy. If you have not walked the road of parenting a child with trauma, it is hard to understand the array of challenges it brings. Being open and honest about your child's struggles is challenging. All you want to do is protect them and make everything better. I never want anyone to view Sammy in a negative light.

The truth is Sammy can be very aggressive and loud. Social situations are generally stressful for him and me. Not everyone can handle his temperament. It is not easy to have a conversation with someone as your child is biting you or pulling your hair. Apparently, it is a conversation stopper! We continue to work on this, and there is improvement. And yet, I am familiar with loneliness as a result of our unique situation. Having a support system is crucial to survival on the tough days.

Spiritually: I was always very involved in the churches I attended over the years. I have always loved serving my fellow church members. Dynamics have had to change though. Sammy is unable to attend Sunday School without an adult who can help to regulate him. I spent months attending Sunday school with him, hoping someone would come alongside and offer support. I wanted Sammy to have relationships within the church and the Sunday School. I desperately wanted to be fed and encouraged.

I realized my expectations were setting me up for disappointment. So, I changed them. I prioritized and figured out what was most important for Sammy and for me. The top priority was that I could attend service while Sammy was sitting with me. Our unexpected solution involved technology—we found a church where they have a live stream of the service in a family room. It was a total win for us. Sammy can sit with me during service *and* he has the ability to walk around or watch a show. It has been a huge blessing for us.

Financially: When I adopted, I intended to continue to work in my office job at a church once parental leave expired. As Sammy was settling into life and school, I knew I could no longer work a traditional job. I needed to be flexible and be able to bring him to therapies and appointments. I needed to be able to pick him up from school when it was necessary. I needed be available to him.

Finding a job that was flexible and allows me to work from home was the best solution. It also means I work very long hours and it is challenging. However, I can always have Sammy with me, which is essential.

Honestly, we are still in the thick of the trenches and most days are still a struggle. However, there is light at the end of the tunnel. We have more good days now than even six months ago. Even in the depths of his trauma, we see the progress of his trust towards my sister and me. He knows that no matter what happens, we will not leave him and we will keep him safe.

We are working on creating a team that can better support us in helping Sammy to overcome the trauma and neglect he faced as a younger child. God has provided some professionals who understand trauma, which has been a huge source of encouragement.

Looking back on my adoption journey, I would not change a thing. I have no doubt God called me to be Sammy's mom. He gives me the strength each day to love Sammy where he is. I love him more than I knew was possible. It is not an easy road. Adoption is the road less traveled. It is not easy, but it is worth it.

Every day you learn to appreciate the simple things in life and to be thankful. Having a front row seat to the redemption story of a valuable life is the greatest honor and most rewarding role I have had the privilege of doing. Not only am I a mother, which I love, but I am a cheerleader, encourager, and supporter. Sammy laughs more each day and smiles with the brightest smile. He reminds me that the unexpected timing of my journey was ordained by God and in obedience there is great joy.

Above all, Sammy reminds me that God fulfills our dreams even when they look nothing like our plans.

Heather K. is the single mother of Sammy, who was adopted from Bulgaria in 2015. Heather has been working in the disability field for twelve years, supporting children and adults in a variety of capacities. She grew up in a family where they welcomed children into their family through adoption and foster care. Heather has carried on her parents' legacy and is currently a respite provider. She looks forward to fostering and adopting again in the future. She loves her family, Vancouver Island, adoption, chocolate, and country music. One of Heather's friends, Holly W., kindly helped her to put this story into writing.

Standing Firm

I threw myself across the bed and lay there, feeling absolutely trashed and discouraged. Our daughter had been home for three years, and I had felt like a failure the entire three years. I'd buried so many dreams. I have no idea how to parent this child; she has no idea how to be a part of a family. I'm at the end of my rope. I want my family back.

I'd wanted to adopt since I was very young, and I even prayed for my future children around the globe. When my father brought home a foster kid who was kicked out at age eighteen, I was heartbroken at the thought that someone would be without a family.

Now I was grown and married, with several biological children. My husband and I were thinking about fostering and not yet planning to adopt. However, through one circumstance and another, God first led us to begin the adoption process from an Eastern European country and then gave us peace about bringing home a sibling group.

The day we met our children was amazing, like the magical moment when you see your newborn baby for the first time. Two months later, we picked them up from their orphanage. We had three good days together and then everything seemed to fall apart.

Maryska was taken into custody at age five, and at that time she had trouble walking. It was obvious that she didn't get much early stimulation. She spent several years in a decent orphanage setting, and we brought her home at age ten.

Maryska is far behind her peers academically. She has difficulty focusing and is easily distracted, with poor impulse control. When she gets over-stimulated, she gets more and more spastic, loud, and hyper, like a volcano building up.

She has core attachment issues. She parent shops. She doesn't observe appropriate social boundaries with people outside our immediate family but becomes "in your face" obnoxious. At one point, she let us know that she would prefer her aunt to be her mom.

From early on, if I would tell Maryska to do anything she didn't want to do, she would sometimes become catatonic and mute, showing no facial expression for hours. She does things she shouldn't do right in front of me and then says she didn't. She is extremely manipulative. She deliberately needles me often. If I show anything but happiness, she'll smirk and insist that she can't talk to me because I'm mean and might yell at her.

She attempts to create divisions in the family, especially by making negative comments to our younger child about me. I brought some edible wild berries into the house, and later I overheard Maryska talking to the other children. "Mom doesn't know everything. These are probably poison berries."

And oh, the meltdowns! During her meltdowns, she might hit me or throw rocks at me, yelling, "I hate you, take me back to the orphanage, I wanna go back!"

Maryska also has a beautiful side. In fact, it's completely opposite of the junk. She truly has come such a long way. She is kind and thoughtful and concerned about others' feelings. She works hard at school and is a rule follower. She likes things neat and will work hard to make her room look good. She works on being grateful and remembering to thank people. She loves God, loves worship music, and loves church.

I wouldn't have been able to write this chapter six months ago. It was still so hard. I was still shut down emotionally toward the kids. That's a horrible feeling as an adoptive mom.

So, there I was, lying across my bed, feeling like an utter failure, when God got through to me.

He said, "Stand firm in who I am. That's all you need to do."

Just because I'm falling apart, God's not! I need to believe that. He tends to reveal our own brokenness to us using our children, doesn't He? He forces us to look deeper inside of ourselves.

I've learned that my hopes were much more in my children and in my vision of life than I had realized. But you simply cannot focus on your child and pin your hopes on your child changing. There are things that we can't control about our children. We've decided that we can give Maryska what we can give her, point her to Jesus, and let her decide what to do with it.

Our hope is in Jesus alone.

I've also learned that it's vital to remain aware of the devil's traps. I was definitely living in a trap for a while. I can take the bait and believe I'm a failure or take offense at my child's sin. My child's way of coping with her trauma may be to create conflict, but my battle isn't truly with my child. My child is not the enemy.

It wasn't until I laid it down and told God that being trapped isn't what I wanted that I was set free.

I enjoy being with Maryska more now; I enjoy all my children more. This summer, I went to the fair with the children and had fun. I went to the beach with them and had fun. These ordinary events represent major victories. After three and a half years, I finally let God teach me how to enjoy my children.

With all the conflict our trauma-kids can bring into our homes, we can easily feel embattled by their behaviors. But truly "our struggle is not against flesh and blood, but against the rulers, against the authorities, against the powers of this dark world, and against the spiritual forces of evil in the heavenly realms" (Eph. 6:12, NIV).

Victoria S. is currently a mother to eight children in her home, several grown-up kids finding their way in the world, the seven in her heart that never came home, and any others the Lord says are hers. She is grateful for a husband with a valiant heart and a God for whom nothing is impossible.

Treasure in the Brokenness

Adoption has been a part of my life for as far back as I can remember. Perhaps it can be traced back to Cabbage Patch Kids. There was nothing better than when my sisters and I all received a Cabbage Patch doll of our own: opening the birth certificate, reading the wonderful names like *Clea Tessa* and *Dorene Juliana*. Changing those tiny real diapers, spending hours playing "orphanage" with my sisters ... life just couldn't get much better than that. Through play, I knew without a doubt that one day I was going to adopt.

The heart for adoption and orphans continued as my heart for the Lord grew. As I served on international mission trips during the summers, coming in contact with orphans from Ireland, Russia, and Mongolia, my heart broke for the things that broke God's heart. I wanted to somehow scoop them all up and bring them home with me. Not much of a realistic hope for a twenty-something college student still living at home. Yet the desire would remain constant.

I majored in Russian as a college student, dreaming of spending my life as a missionary in Russia, working with orphans. Soon after college graduation, it was clear God had a different plan for this time in my life. I joined the Air Force, met my wonderful husband Josh, got married, and became a stepmom to two amazing kids. Shortly after, I was medically retired from the Air Force and my husband and I then applied for a job with Boys Town in San Antonio, Texas. We got the job as Family Teachers and happily moved to start our new life, loving and parenting twelve broken boys. My husband and I fell in love with those boys and started the process to become certified for adoption, thinking we might end up adopting one or more of our boys. But, the Lord decided to send us a biological son first. We took a step back and got ready to be parents of a newborn son.

Andrew arrived, and from day one, the incredible love we had for him turned our world upside down. Not long after his birth, our world was turning upside down again. We began a seven-year stretch of moving all over the world, with Josh working as a contract firefighter. Two more baby boys graced our lives: Isaac and James. I had always pictured myself as a mom of boys, so I was happy and content.

In 2015, after a year between contract jobs, Josh was hired for a new position. We made a cross-country move to start our life in an entirely new state. We were low on money as he went through a probationary period at work, yet we were satisfied that we were right where God wanted us, trusting Him to fulfill our every need. In July of that year, my two step-kids, Nathan and Emily, were with us, so we took a two-day trip to southwestern Utah. The stunning natural beauty of the area, combined with the joy and contentment in looking at our five beautiful children all together, nearly overwhelmed us.

Then life took a twist we were not expecting.

In a small, wood-paneled 1970s motel in a tiny town in Utah, I opened an email. The email was sent by my mom and the subject was "Peter." I almost chose not to open that email. Somehow, I knew it would invade the sense of contentment I was experiencing. It was a simple email, encouraging her seven children to read the attached link to a blog post—a post about an orphan boy in Ukraine with celiac disease.

I clicked on the link and saw a picture that immediately captured my heart. The blog post was written by Julia Nalle, a well-known advocate for orphans and for Reece's Rainbow.[7] Each picture—each description of him—gripped my heart like nothing had ever done before. I read through the post several times, with tears flowing. Then I showed it to Josh. I could tell right away he wasn't just skimming the post; he was really reading it. He looked up and said, "Let's adopt him."

Just like that. Let's adopt him.

Our peaceful vacation suddenly turned into a torrent of uncertainty, worries, and "what ifs." We agreed to wait a day or two, prayed for wisdom, and discussed the idea with our kids. It was already very clear God was calling us to take a leap of faith bigger than any we had ever done before. We knew that Peter was supposed to be our son.

After a suspenseful two days of expressing our interest in Peter through Reece's Rainbow, waiting to hear if another family had committed to him or not, we received an email with these words: "The other family will not be committing to Peter. You are welcome to move forward. Congratulations!" We collapsed in tears and praised the Lord together. Peter would be part of our family.

Then the reality of what lay ahead crashed into the jubilation. The mounds of paperwork. The wait. The money. We literally did not have the extra $25 to send in with our application to start the process, let alone the money to get the ball rolling on our home study and facilitation fees. As I started to panic, I heard the Lord distinctly say, "Money will not be the issue. You said yes—that is

---

[7] Reece's Rainbow is an amazing advocacy group for orphans with special needs around the world. Please take a few minutes to go to their website, www.reecesrainbow.org, and be amazed by the wonderful work they do.

what I wanted. I'll take care of the rest." And even in the most stressful of moments, those tender words of promise stayed with me.

Like many adoptive families have experienced, unbelievable miracles piled up as we trusted the Lord and stepped out in faith. Every single penny was provided in beautiful ways, often just the very minute we needed it. There are so many people whom we will forever hold dear in our hearts. They supported us, gave sacrificially, went out of their way to help us follow God's call, and loved us well.

That first blog post about Peter ended with the verse Matthew 13:44 (NASB): "The kingdom of heaven is like treasure hidden in the field, which a man found and hid again; and from joy over it he goes and sells all that he has and buys that field." We clung to that verse throughout the adoption process. We were so in love with Peter and the thought of adding him to our family. It seemed like he was the treasure we were seeking. However, when the euphoria waned in the months to come, the Lord reminded us gently that the treasure wasn't a person.

The treasure in Matthew 13:44 is God's Kingdom. And He would show us how seeking His kingdom very often means stepping into brokenness. In Brian Borgman's tremendous book on life after adoption, *After They Are Yours*, he states:

"All adoption stories begin with grief—the brokenness of a natural family. Therefore, all adoption is a ministry of mercy. Adoptive parents are called to step intentionally into brokenness for the purpose of healing. They make boys and girls, whose biological parents cannot raise them, into their own sons and daughters. This is mercy, and it will require a lifetime of ministry."[8]

After going through all the necessary training, studying about children suffering the trauma of losing birth families, we thought we understood things like reactive attachment disorder and post-orphanage behaviors. However, we were unprepared for the brokenness that was suddenly thrust upon us. In all actuality, I don't think anyone can be fully prepared. You just have to embrace it. You have to believe this is a mandate of the King of Kings—to care for orphans. You have to step out in faith, trusting that He will provide the strength to handle it.

In the midst of purchasing a house and moving to southern Utah, we got the call that we were to have our first appointment in Ukraine. We packed up our three small boys and flew across the world to get our newest son. It is difficult to describe the emotions and chaos leading up to seeing your new child for the first time. We had waited for months to meet him; he had waited ten years and nine months to meet his forever family. How can you possibly plan for such a moment?

It was nothing I had expected. Waking at 4:00 a.m. that morning to catch the train to his town, we arrived at the orphanage while he was still at school. We chatted with the director and staff, constantly flitting our eyes to the doorway to catch that first glimpse of him, and suddenly, there he was. Dressed in his formal school uniform, looking tinier than we had expected, no sign of a smile on his face. He approached each of us and did a slight nod of his head as he used the most formal greeting he could: *"Zdravstvuytye,"* (bow to Josh), *"Zdravstvuytye,"* (bow to me). He made very little eye contact with us, and I thought my heart would burst out of my chest! Our sons were smiling from

---

[8] Borgman, Brian. (2014). After They Are Yours. Minneapolis, MN. Cruciform Press. Page 47.

ear to ear and Andrew, our seven-year-old, would occasionally reach out and touch Peter's shoulder, as if he wanted to be sure he was actually meeting his new brother. After a formal meeting where he was introduced to us, he looked at the photo album we prepared and was then asked if he'd like to be adopted by this family. "Of course!" he said. Of course. He knew very little about us, but he had waited so long. He had seen each of his friends be adopted and taken away from him. It was his turn and he was ready.

We loved him right from the beginning. However, we were also a bit stunned. He was very physical and even hurt Andrew a few times while playing roughly. As we watched him play in the Sports Hall, it seemed he had been given a high dose of caffeine. Once I put my hand on his chest and I could feel his heart pounding vigorously. He was like a small bird who had been caged for his whole life. He was now readying himself to break free.

We had our court date exactly five months to the day after we decided to commit to adopt him. Josh returned to the States after the court session, not being able to miss any more work. I stayed in Ukraine with my boys as we waited out the ten-day mandatory wait period. In all honesty, it is hard for me to even let my mind dwell on those days. I was by myself in a foreign country in winter with three small boys who all got sick during the wait period. I wasn't able to see Peter—my own son—since the orphanage had instituted a quarantine to keep their children protected from outside illnesses. After the wait period, we made the last trip to the orphanage to collect Peter. I boarded a night train with four boys, bound for Kiev.

This is when the first thoughts of, "What have we done?" began to gnaw at my heart. It was desperately hard to keep my heart focused on the One who had called us to this. I began to despair.

We were stuck in a small apartment, awaiting Peter's passport and embassy clearance. Peter had never seen an apartment before. He opened every drawer, took food from the fridge constantly and broke a closet door. He pinched and pulled Andrew's hair when he didn't get his way, screamed, raged, and threw fits. And, he complained about *everything*. I might have been able to handle everything else with much more grace, if not for the constant grumbling and complaining. I was shocked. He was free! He had a family! He was getting tucked in at night, seeing some sights in Kiev, eating ice cream and yogurts all day long, and all he could do was complain.

The complaining characterized the next few months. I understood the reasons. I suspected he might have had expectations that weren't met in us, as his new family. I knew he might have been protecting himself from being *too* happy, in case it would all be taken away. I understood these things, yet it did not take away the difficulty of going through it. He focused so much of the time on what he *didn't* have or on the material things he suddenly *did* have. He didn't seem to care one bit about having a mama or a dad or brothers or a *whole new life* in America.

If there is one thing that adoption has done, it has focused us more on who our God is and the deplorable state of our own sinful hearts. You cannot go through adoption as a Christian and not think about the theme of adoption that runs through the Bible. We began to see how we were just like Peter. We were complainers. Just as the Israelites complained incessantly after being set free from four hundred years of bondage in Egypt, so too were our hearts prone to complain in the face of God's goodness. A friend reminded us that when Moses asked Pharaoh to let his people go, God's purpose was so that they could be free "that they may celebrate a feast to Me in the wilderness" (Exod. 5:1, NASB). We think it was so that they could be delivered to the Promised Land, a land flowing with milk and honey. That may have been what the Israelites were focused on, but what God was focused on was the *relationship* with His people. This became so clear (and so humbling) as we watched Peter. He had been rescued from bondage and his new family longed to have a relationship with him—to welcome him wholeheartedly into their arms and hearts. But he was missing it, because he was focused on what he thought he could expect from an American family: an iPad, a phone, a bigger house, more stuff, an endless supply of Legos. This happened again and again: this mirror-image view of our own sinful hearts as we looked at our son. And the constant reminder that despite this, God *still chose us.*

The first few months home were dark ones. I wrote very little in my journal or on the blog during that time, daring not to put into words the chaos and darkness that was looming over my heart and our home. Peter brought darkness and brokenness with him. I saw our sons, especially Andrew, become angrier than they had ever been. I saw my husband's jaw tense and his stress level increase when he heard of Peter's behaviors while he was away at work. We continued to wonder: what had we done? And the answer from the Lord stayed the same: "You obeyed Me." We clung to that. We knew God didn't make mistakes. We came to rely on Him more than we ever had before.

We didn't know it would be so very hard to love. From the moment we saw that first picture of Peter, our hearts had been flooded with love for him. I could hardly sleep at night, thinking about him waiting for a family and not knowing we were coming as fast as we possibly could. Now we looked at this child and felt as though we had an intruder in our home. We felt empty. We provided for his needs. I cooked good meals for him, never letting a night end without kissing him, tucking him in, and praying over him. But I felt as though I was just going through the motions. Josh and I tried to reason with ourselves that God never called us to do anything more than care for orphans. We were caring for his needs. That was enough, right? The ache in my heart and the tears soaking my pillow at night said otherwise. I knew there must be something more ... something more to hope for than just years and years of simply caring for the basic needs of a child who was not born of my flesh.

Then I came to a passage in the wonderful book *Falling Free*, by adoptive mom Shannan Martin. She said that it would have been so much easier if God had just stuck to words like *care for, pray for, love* when He was talking about orphans. But He didn't.

"Instead he just goes for it. *Give. Uphold. Rescue. Deliver.* These are the verbs attached to God's intention for our care of orphans. He tells us to spend ourselves on their behalf, to let our arms grow tired from propping them up. We know all about spending, don't we? Empty our pockets. Bankrupt our time reserves. Pour it out, deplete the coffers, exhaust our limits, *spend.*"[9]

I knew I had not been spending myself on behalf of Peter. To an outsider, it may have looked like it. But in my heart I knew. I prayed for God to change me, to change my heart. I prayed He would allow me to pour myself out, without resentment, on this child who was more like a grumpy old man living in our house. I prayed for eyes to see Peter as Christ saw him. And God answered. While there were still many, many hard days of life in the trenches of post-adoption, there were bits of light, laughter, and love. I made an effort to look at Peter more often, directly in his eyes or

---

[9] Martin, Shannan. *Falling Free: Rescued from the Life I Always Wanted.* (2016). Nashville, TN. Nelson Books. Page 27. (Though adoption is only a small part of how God worked in the Martin family, I highly recommend this beautiful story of learning to live completely sold out to Jesus!)

just while he was playing or drawing. On one of these occasions, Peter noticed that I was watching him. He turned and said, "Mom, I love it when you look at me with love in your eyes." He was seeing the difference, and my heart was so convicted by all the times I had purposely averted my eyes or looked at him with emptiness instead of love.

Peter has now been home with us for over two years, and we are beginning to really settle into our new normal. We've seen tremendous growth. He no longer rages or screams and very rarely complains. He gets along well with his brothers. Aside from normal brother-type arguments, there is very little of the contention we saw in those first few weeks. He's learning to trust that his mom and dad have his best interests at heart and that he is ours *forever*. Early on, we recognized that Peter struggles with the effects of Fetal Alcohol Spectrum Disorder. It is something we weren't expecting and didn't think we'd ever be prepared for. However, God knew we would be the perfect safe place for a boy who often forgets, and who struggles to find his place in a still very confusing world. As we've learned more about his disorder, God has softened our hearts to feel more protective of him. While we still have many "in-the-trenches" kind of days, they are fewer and farther between. Honestly, it will be a lifetime of seeing those healing moments arise, because Peter has almost eleven years of orphanage life to overcome.

Sometimes, I watch Peter and marvel. He loves to be outside with his brothers, climbing trees, jumping on the trampoline, identifying birds, collecting slugs and roly-polies, doing all the things a normal, healthy boy should be doing. Thinking of the alternative (if, perhaps, we had not said "yes" to God) is unbearable. He is meant to live a life of sunshine and love, with the light of Jesus flooding the dark parts of his heart. He is meant to be free and to know what being part of a family is all about. He is meant to feel safe and cheered on, even when he fails. Because of this, and because of Christ's own great love for us, we will continue to uphold, defend, and protect until our arms (and hearts) grow weary with the task. We've discovered there is a treasure that is not only worth seeking, it is worth selling everything we hold dear to pursue. That treasure is indeed God's Kingdom, and it operates in a way that is opposite to the world around us. To find it, you must be willing to seek brokenness. You must be willing to be broken yourself. There is no other way.

Adoption has been a starting point for this kind of brokenness in our lives, and even after only about two years into the journey, we can confidently say it is worth it. We are willing to take on Peter's brokenness, not only so he can begin to heal, but so that we can be refined and be made more Christ-like each day. We have given our lives to a God of redemption—a God who can make beauty from ashes and show us the treasure in the brokenness. I certainly never understood this part of adoption as a little girl changing Cabbage Patch diapers, but I know that when I look at my son, his journey to our family began long before we started the paperwork.

God is faithful. Peter is blossoming into a delightful, content, cheerful boy. The darkness and worries of those early months have been replaced by light and peace in our home. Peter knows where he belongs: right in the middle of a pack of little brothers and in the arms of a mom and dad who love him. God has graciously given us eyes to truly see him as *our* son. We are so grateful the Lord chose us to be Peter's parents, so we can witness the miracle of adoption and be transformed in the midst of the brokenness.

Kameron M. is a follower of Jesus, wife of her firefighting husband Josh, mother to Peter, Andrew, Isaac, and James and stepmom to Nathan and Emily. Their family has traveled and lived in many places around the world, but they have happily settled in southwestern Utah for the time being. Kameron homeschools her four boys and finds much joy in training up her children in the way they should go. She has blogged about their family's adoption journey and is continuing to share her family's post-adoption story and their life with Fetal Alcohol Syndrome. If you would like access to her blog or more information about her family's story, please email Kameron at joshkamandfam@gmail.com. Her heart is for God to use their story to encourage the hearts of other adoptive families and those who are considering adoption.

17

I Am Your Mama

"It has to be a miracle that I made it to this place" ran through my head as I walked into the government-run building in China to meet our son for the first time. The logistics of traveling half a world away are tricky for someone like me. I lived a well-ordered life and never wandered far from home. I liked my routines.

When I was a little girl growing up, I knew I wanted to be a mom. As many little girls do, I pretended to be a mom and homemaker, setting up house with my dolls, mini-furniture, and dishes. I "prepared" meals for them, chatting excitedly about our day while wearing a little apron around my waist. Anytime I was hurting about something, I would pretend my dolly was sad, too, as I did my best to comfort her. I hated seeing anyone sad.

I became a Christian when I was five. For me, this meant I ought to help others know Jesus, so they could know God loves them too. I also believe that God gave me the gift of mercy and a calling to minister to those who are hurting. Those beliefs became some of the biggest driving forces of my life.

In my twenties, I started reading books about China. I often read about the political situation, the one-child-policy, and the children frequently relinquished because of it. This broke my heart. I thought about someday going over to adopt a child, yet the idea of traveling so far away was scary. At the time, I was concentrating on college and hoping I would someday meet the man I would marry. Then I would think about a family.

In 1995, I went to seminary, and also met my future husband, Mike. On our first date we spoke of family and a mutual desire to adopt one day. Mike told me his sister and her family were English teachers in China and had lived there for many years.

In 1999, Mike and I got married; the same year I graduated with my Master of Divinity degree. After moving back to the Twin Cities area in 2004, we began trying for a family. After struggling with infertility for a couple of years, we decided to start the adoption process. China made sense.

Now here we were, halfway around the world in the Jilin Province of China. It was July 2007 and we were finally going to meet our two-year-old son. While I knew it would not be all sunshine and roses, I was not prepared for everything that was to come.

When this tiny sixteen-pound bundle of energy bounded down the hall toward me with outstretched arms and a giant smile, I gasped and fell to my knees. In a hall full of people, he knew who to run to. I was finally able to utter one of the few phrases I had rehearsed in Mandarin dozens of times, "Wo sur, ni da mama," which translated means, "I am your mama." We held each other for a moment of sheer bliss. I was oblivious to everything else during that moment; but this much I knew, I loved him, and I was his mama. But what would that look like? How do I suddenly "be a mom?"

Nian was born with a cleft lip and palate, which we knew from his file. We also knew he was determined and charming, doing whatever he had to do to get attention from the nannies in the orphanage. I was prepared for the physical care the cleft lip and palate would require, and to some extent, the grieving he would go through because of leaving behind everything he knew.

Everything else was trial by fire.

It became clear right away this boy was not going to stop moving his body. He wanted to be held continually, but squirmed all the while. If I put him down, he would cry and bang his head against the floor. I wanted him to know we were his parents and would care for him, so I carried him everywhere. I felt so sad about what he had gone through. My natural inclination to hurt for him allowed me to be present when he most needed it. But this was the beginning of when empathy would be taken to almost pathological levels. I couldn't tolerate the suffering, so I held him until I could barely hold my arms up any longer and was ready to cry myself.

To say he attached to us is an understatement. This was a good thing. In the years that followed after we came home, this connection we shared would carry us through and keep us pushing forward when we were tempted to give up.

Coming home from China with a two-year-old was like coming home to someone else's life. I knew this was our house, and I was Valerie. But I felt like I was living someone else's life at first. *Nothing resembled what it was before and it never would again.*

Nian was hyperactive. He wanted to know the inner workings of everything. He wanted to peel every label off of every pop bottle. If there was paper anywhere, it got ripped. If you gave him a book, he would tear it up. This was likely because he had little in the way of sensory stimulation at the orphanage. So, I did not punish him for these things, but I also had no earthly clue what to do about it. He had to taste everything, including paper and pencils, and other inedible objects. He made as much noise as he could with whatever he could. He would make holes in clothes and rip apart couch cushions. Mini blinds? I cannot tell you how many of those got demolished. Drawer pulls, twisted off. This was extremely difficult for me, because I like order. It drove me mad some days. I couldn't keep up with the number of things becoming broken on a daily basis.

He was like a hurricane. Always climbing, leaping, launching off any high surface he could. He had no fear, in that sense. But in another sense, the constant spinning and rocking might have been an indication that his body was in constant fight-or-flight mode. I didn't know about the possible effects of trauma and hard beginnings on the brain of a little one.

So, there we were. This thirty-something, first-time mama who was used to a quiet, routine existence, and an extremely busy two-year-old trying to figure out where his old life was and exploring his new one; and a forty-something stressed out dad trying to make a living and help his wife who was clearly in over her head.

Those first days back are a blur to me. I was clearly smitten with this charming, loveable boy. I was also overwhelmed and unsure how to handle his continuous movement and the chaos in our home. I did not understand why he did the things he did. I thought perhaps it was simply his way of making up for lost time with so many new sights and sounds. I feared there were other diagnoses we had not been told about. Did all kids from orphanages have the same struggles? I did not know, but in those first couple years I didn't have time to research it because I was shell-shocked and just trying to survive.

I reasoned that since Nian had a tough start in life, he shouldn't have it hard now, so I catered to his every whim. Some of that is good in the initial bonding stage. But as I look back, I see now how I ignored my own well-being a bit too much. I tried to comfort him even though I doubted he understood any of my words. He was only able to utter one word: "Muh." We didn't know what that meant, which added to my frustration.

Nian didn't start speech therapy until many months after we were home. Eventually we enrolled him in part-time daycare, to start socializing him. I felt guilty about that. I had always believed I should be with him full-time. Yet, I was offered my very first chaplain position in a nursing home in 2008. I thought I should take this dream opportunity. I felt guilty all the time I spent away from him. Yet when I was with him, I became exhausted holding him, trying to keep up with him, straightening whatever broke in his wake, and not letting on my "compassion fatigue." I like an orderly house, but didn't clean much. I was always so tired that if Nian went with Mike or to daycare, I often found myself taking a nap. So, housework piled up. I hated the mess around me, but felt powerless to do anything about it. My mom offered to help with cleaning, but I was too embarrassed to accept her offer. Nobody else was aware of what was going on. I didn't want people to think less of me if they knew how out of control I felt and despondent over my "inability to handle it." I wondered what was wrong with me and believed other moms had it all together. I was so overwhelmed. But the boy was my world. I had fallen completely head over heels for him.

Getting out of the house seemed like a good idea, but if I ventured out with Nian to go to a fast food place, I got flustered up at the counter. Nian pressed all the levers at the drink station, ran down the aisles, or climbed displays. I tried to order while I imagined the eyes of angry strangers boring into me as they wondered, "Why can't she control her kid?" It took all of my energy to go anywhere, especially because I wanted to look like a mom in control. But was I in control? Was I even a mom? I felt a bit like an imposter. I felt like a miserable failure at it.

But I wasn't failing at anything, except maybe giving myself grace. *In the ways it mattered, I was there.* Quite literally, I. Was.

There. When he needed nurturing, I had that down. When he needed caretaking, I nailed it. He would come to me to be held, and since he could not say "hold," he would look up at me with those beautiful dark eyes and plead, "Mama hoke?" And I *loved* it. I could never turn him down.

I had read before adopting about "cocooning." The way I understood it, it was like trying to mimic the sensory input adopted little ones missed by being relinquished at only a few days old. I made up games that gave us full body contact. His favorite was simply called "my Nian." We laid down on the carpet together and I held him close. I rolled us back and forth saying "My Nian! My Nian! My Nian!" Sometimes Mike got involved, pretending he was going to steal him away, while he declared, "That's *my* Nian!" Nian would just laugh and laugh.

These seemingly small things were what made the hard things livable. Even while I believed I didn't have a handle on my life at that point, I was so grateful for our connection and for his love of physical touch.

The hard things persisted. Communication was top of the list. I longed to know what was going on Nian's mind. He tried to talk, but they were just sounds. Many times, I was near tears asking him what he wanted. Sometimes I thought if I just spoke "What do you need, Nian?" louder, he would understand and speak clearly. Then I got exasperated. Guilt would follow, so I would hold him and say, "Oh Nian! Mama's not mad at you, Mama just wants to know what you need!"

Mike had his ways of connecting with Nian, too, which gave me some breathing room. Sometimes the two of them got in the truck and did the "train route." He strapped him into his car seat and away they went, all around St. Paul looking for trains. For me, those times were welcome moments of sanity when I did my own thing around the house.

The sensory challenges continued, mostly with the limited types of clothes he would wear as well as his disdain for labels. I kept wondering what was wrong and how to get help if you don't even know what the problem is. We had Nian evaluated when he was four to prepare for school. The testing was incomplete as he could barely understand what they were asking him to do. Ultimately, he received the dual diagnoses of ADHD and Sensory Processing Disorder. I believed there was more to the picture. Instead of using the diagnoses as a place to start, it left me feeling more overwhelmed and frightened for the future. We did not want to do what so many rushed to suggest: use medication. I believed the meds might mask the problem rather than force us to "work through" what the issues were.

We started taking Nian to occupational therapy since he needed help with motor skills in the beginning. This proved vital in seeing the reason behind Nian's actions. It made so much sense to hear that some of the pounding of toys or peeling of things had a biological basis and served a function or filled a need. So, this opened my eyes to the fact that we could fill these needs in healthier ways. This wasn't an overnight answer, but the start of something that over time brought so much improvement.

We had many appointments each week, and I jabbered at him as we drove to each one, hoping he would one day answer me. Familiar rituals like going through the McDonald's drive thru on the way to the appointments were fun, too. Even if in those early days I was anxious or depressed, I tried my best to gut it out, sticking to those important routines and just being there for him. I believe God took those seemingly mundane things and blessed those times for us, weaving our hearts together and crafting our family into a beautiful tapestry, in spite of all the things that weren't ideal. I even got tiny miracles, where I would get some type of confirmation things were going to be okay. One time I was in the living room feeling discouraged. Nian was in his room and all of a sudden I heard his first attempt at a sentence. What a beautiful one it was: "I'm happy me!" Oh how I clung to those words when I needed the encouragement that we were on the right track.

The big, old house we lived in really started to bother me. As the years went by, it was just too much. Built in the eighteen hundreds, it needed so much TLC. We had neither the time nor ability to fix it up, especially after we adopted. As things fell apart, I became more frustrated. Mike was trying to make ends meet and support us and felt fine with the house in the first few years, so I felt stuck.

I was so depressed, I knew I needed help by the end of 2009. At an intake appointment at a local hospital, they recommended I start a two-week treatment program called Partial Hospitalization. This meant attending every weekday for several hours. I was embarrassed, wondering if others would be shocked that a chaplain was struggling with depression. I enjoyed learning new ways to cope with the stress, though. However, you do not get rid of lifelong negative self-talk in a mere two weeks.

The treatment helped a little, but the same stressors remained. I looked for ways to make life easier. I cut my work hours, figuring I would feel more in control with more time to organize things at home. But I continually spun my wheels: "I need to fix this place up! Where do I start? I should organize something. Nian is getting into things. What can I do with him? Guess we'll go to the park. Well that took so much energy now I'm too tired and it's time to make dinner." And so it went. It seemed like we were just trying to make it through each day but with no progress organizing our lives at all. My feelings of hopelessness continued.

Finally, in 2011, I resigned from my job. On one hand, I believed this was best for our family, but on the other hand I hated leaving behind the deep satisfaction ministering to seniors gave me. I cried about that, then felt guilty about missing my job. I felt guilty no matter what I did. I actually felt guilt about my guilt! On top of that, although I had more time to tend to the house, I couldn't make any headway. As soon as I picked up, things got all torn up soon after. Now I truly believed I was just a failure. I figured I had no job, so no excuse not to have things organized.

At this point, my hands would often shake from nervousness. I called my psychiatrist. I was in so much emotional turmoil, I agreed to whatever he recommended. Truth be told, I was already taking an antidepressant, having first been diagnosed with depression at nineteen. The doctor suggested adding "something to help with your nerves." I usually hesitate adding medications or research them first. But I was so desperate I simply acquiesced. If I would have known the prescription was such a powerful sedative, I never would have taken it.

And powerful it was. I took this pill every night and fell into a deep sleep. It was nice to be suddenly oblivious to the mess. I was too tired to care and felt groggy the next day, too. I played movies for Nian and lay there as he climbed on me while I slept. But I forced myself when possible to pay attention and talk to him, for he was now speaking a few words at a time. But I never felt rested and became pretty irritable.

During that time I was sinking deeper and deeper into quicksand. I believed I could do nothing to better our situation. Many things were hard: Being tired, clutter piling up, finances were stressful, trading Nian between the two of us to get breaks, and so on. Before I started the new prescription I felt like I was in the quicksand up to my shoulders and was trying desperately to get out. The pills were the final blow. I buried my head in the sand as well and just went under. But not for long. Soon my mom told me she believed I was on too much medication. I got mad at her, but knew she was right—this was no way to live! I marched back into the same hospital and told them I needed to stop taking these pills. They told me quitting that medicine, in the Benzodiazepine class, would likely cause pretty bad withdrawal and it would be best to wean off it during Partial Hospitalization again. This way, I could reinforce skills during the day and be home at night.

I followed their advice and started the program again, working on positive coping skills. Nian was in school now, so I was able to fully immerse myself in the program. I learned the combination of pills I took probably made my anxiety worse. Each day we focused on different methods to counter the constant barrage of my negative thoughts that had always been with me. Thoughts which, in recent years, became my constant dreadful companions: repetitive, defeating, obsessive. I needed the distraction provided by working on skills as the withdrawal symptoms kicked in—not feeling my arms or hands, a terrible headache, and jittery feeling.

I got through it all in a few weeks, thanks be to God. (I have read recent articles stating that the medicine I was on, depending on dosage, etc., can be tougher to get off than cocaine.) As my body was initially adjusting to being without this sedative, Mike took the lion's share of caring for Nian and my mom graciously brought dinner over and helped with dishes and laundry.

The two weeks went by, but this time I entered the day-treatment phase for several months to continue cementing everything I learned. I found it so valuable to share my feelings with the other group members. Through this sharing, I discovered that my perfectionist tendencies contributed to my depression and anxiety. I realized for the first time just how regimented my thinking was. I believed that there was one right way to do things, including homemaking and motherhood, and that I just couldn't figure out how to do that. Yikes! Breaking those old ideas down gave me a newfound sense of freedom. I was dumbfounded at my discovery that I could make our home how I wanted to, focusing on my gifts and letting go of lesser things. This was big. I began to understand that "becoming a mom" had less to do with finding the one right way, and more about defining it for myself.

Learning to ease up on myself took practice, but I found that I could train myself to think new thoughts. I likened it to the Apostle Paul's admonition in 2 Corinthians 10:5b (NIV), "We take every thought captive to make it obedient to Christ." So instead of just "thinking positive thoughts," I challenged anxious, harmful thoughts by continually asking what God would say is the truth of any situation. So, if I thought, "My life is so messed up and hard that I will never be able to manage it," I countered by thinking this instead: "Life *is* hard, it's part of a fallen world. Yet there are many steps *I can* take to make things better, as God promised He would never leave us, I am not alone..." My thoughts these days are much healthier from years of this practice. But it took lots of hard work.

I also realized the importance of taking time to focus on things that were satisfying to me again: baking, exercising, crafts, and the like. Over time it got easier to leave Nian, and we explained to him that Mama needs time to herself too. Once in a while we got a babysitter, or we left him with Grandma and Grandpa. Those breaks, although rare, were like streams in the desert. They gave us a few hours to revive ourselves.

School was hard initially, but once Nian started first grade at a school closer to our home in 2012, things started slowly turning around. This coincided with my recent treatment as well as living in a smaller house. I was now much healthier and began settling into my role as Nian's mom, realizing how I really did know him best.

I became more adept at figuring out how to help Nian where he needed it, and which things could be overlooked or accepted, along with throwing out typical parenting rule books. We found that water was calming for Nian. So, no matter if it was the middle of the day, I put him in a long, warm bubble bath. It seemed he could frolic in there forever, as long as I watched him. I sat beside the tub enjoying my iced coffee and perusing a book while he played with the bath toys. We stopped caring what other families did and started designing a life that was right for us.

Nian's speech really took off with continued therapy. But even after he learned to physically pronounce words, it was difficult for him to "use his words." It was a daily discipline, encouraging him to tell us his thoughts. It has been a work in progress for him to learn about the give-and-take nature of a conversation.

One of the things that most helped me was a yearly retreat for adoptive moms near Atlanta, Georgia. I first went to Created For Care when Nian was six. There I rubbed shoulders with other adoptive moms … my people. It was healing to know I wasn't alone—this journey is hard. I grieved the hard stuff, letting the tears fall as we worshiped God together. God's Spirit moved in our midst and filled me with the strength I needed to keep going, and with the resolve to parent Nian the best I knew how.

I learned hard things there, too, like the effects of early trauma and about how to talk with Nian about his life before we met him. A big burden was lifted from my shoulders the year I heard "It is not your job to fix everything. Lead them to Jesus, He alone can heal." Of course! I knew this concept from my years of chaplain training. Yet it didn't occur to me as a mom. This is another area I worked intently on. I still regularly talk this through with a therapist, learning when I am being appropriately empathetic and when I am trying to "fix," or being too protective. In 2014, we moved into a townhome, further reducing our clutter. This made life so much more manageable. I have lowered my expectations about how things are "supposed to be." I focus on my strengths: connection, cooking healthy meals, and doing the work that will make our lives run smoother. Much of the nonessential stuff gets let go. Our house isn't perfect, but we have time to spend together doing things we enjoy.

Through many therapies, the interventions we have tried, and even finally medication, we have found little things that helped Nian with the ADHD. I believe the loving connection and safety he found with us was as healing as anything else. Even through the times of "chaos," God was with us and helped Nian along. Nian settled in and started making great gains in all areas. I grew right alongside him, from being a woman once filled with trepidation to learning how to be a mom. Instead of shrinking back at school meetings, I owned the knowledge gained through our experiences. I prepared research papers for Nian's school on the effects of trauma on children from orphanages. I am proud to say I became his fiercest advocate.

Today, Nian is twelve. He loves horses, archery, bowling, swimming, and video games. He talks all the time. He still lets me put my arm around him when I sit beside him. He is very sweet, clever, and kind, and he has a great deal of empathy.

We have learned through the years that diagnoses are just guidelines, not boxes to confine, even as we recently learned Nian is on the autism spectrum. We have become more comfortable with bottles minus their labels. There will be challenges, but we work through them as we go. We know life isn't perfect, and that's okay. We have learned not to compare ourselves with anyone else, but to just be who we are. We have settled into some nice routines.

As I look back, I am so thankful for our journey. I am grateful to God that He brought us through, and for those cherished moments along the way, too. In the midst of the hard, there were always signs of God's provision and faithfulness. I am thankful I can say those words that mean so much to me, Wo Sur Ni Da Mama!

Valerie S. lives in St. Paul, Minnesota with her husband, Mike and their son, Nian. She earned her Master of Divinity Degree from Bethel Seminary. As chaplain and founder/director of E.M.B.R.A.C.E. Seniors Ministry, Valerie provides worship services, Bible studies, and one-to-one companionship in nursing homes in the Twin Cities area. In her spare time, Valerie loves reading, sunny days, cooking healthy meals, and baking some not-so-healthy desserts, crocheting, walking, and dabbling in acrylic painting. She also loves to write. You can follow her journey as a "recovering perfectionist" at Valerie's blog, which can be found at: https://valeriesvoice.wordpress.com.

18

Wherever You Will Call Me

I am sure many of the readers of this chapter are familiar with the lyrics from the popular song "Oceans" by Hillsong. The song's lyrics talk about trusting God wherever He may lead us, and about taking us deeper with Him, so our faith will be stronger. Though I hear the song and these words quite often, they still haven't lost their power to me. God speaks to me through words, written and sung. These beautiful lyrics have provided me with encouragement and strength in so many of life's circumstances, not the least of which is adoption.

A little over a year ago, my husband and I returned from China with our three-and-a-half-year-old son Aaron. The oldest of my three biological children met us at the airport and seeing the two brothers meet brought me to tears. I was so happy to be home—to be on American soil, to sleep in my bed, and to finally have all of our babies together under one roof.

The six-month wait after we were matched with Aaron was hard. I often worried about him, wondered if he was safe and healthy, and experienced angst over whether or not we would actually be united. Once my husband and I finally made it to China, I missed my three little ones at home so much it hurt. All I wanted was for us all to be together, to be a family. I felt that once we were united the rest would fall into place.

I am sure many fellow adoptive parents will laugh out loud

when they read that last line, just as I did when I wrote it. Though I had such wonderful training and guidance, there is no way to truly be prepared for the emotions, challenges, and wonder of adoption.

Our process began on a Sunday morning when, after years of thought and prayer, my husband and I felt confirmation that we were supposed to adopt. God whispered to me through a hymn at church, *Jesus I My Cross Have Taken.* As we sang out, "Go then earthly fame and treasure, Come disaster scorn and pain, in Thy service pain is pleasure, with Thy favor loss is gain." I was confident God was calling us to adopt despite the costs. I knew the sacrifices adoption required, but that didn't change anything. I knew God was not promising it would be an easy road, but it would be worthwhile. My husband felt a similar confirmation during the sermon and we began our application that afternoon.

When we first began our paperwork, we were drawn to a baby girl with minor special needs. We already have two biological sons, one with autism and a repaired cleft palate, and one biological daughter. However, as our eyes were opened to the many little boys on the waiting list who were ready for families, we felt our hearts open as well. We couldn't believe there was no wait for these precious children, and some of them had been on the shared list for years, just waiting for families. As we worked on our home study and application, we decided not to specify a gender and instead remain open to a girl or a boy.

Additionally, during this process God opened our hearts to a much broader spectrum of special needs than we had previously considered. I remember sitting in front of the computer with the daunting list of medical needs on my lap researching each one and finally realizing at the end that we actually were open to many of them. Having a biological son with special needs who was already in need of various therapies and medical interventions, we felt equipped to deal with an array of special needs. Medical appointments, advocacy, therapies, and interventions were already a part of our daily lives. A child with more significant needs would fit into the life we were already living. Would it be hard? Yes. But we serve a God who doesn't always call us to what the world says or believes is easy.

When our home study and application were finalized, our social worker pointed out that if we were open to a boy or a girl we would probably receive a referral for a boy as there is a much greater need for families for boys with special needs. By that point, we were excited about welcoming a third boy into our family and realized that God had completely changed our original plan. Within days, we were contacted and asked to consider reviewing the file of a little boy who seemed like a great match for our family.

Aaron was three years old (older than what we had imagined), had cerebral palsy, and was unable to walk. We requested an update from the orphanage, talked, prayed, and sought advice from doctors. We were trying to make a wise, informed decision, but deep down we knew he was our son. We decided to wait until we received an update on his file, as it was over a year old, before making an official decision, but we knew we would accept the referral regardless of whether or not he could walk. To our shock, a few days later, we received precious pictures and videos of Aaron walking and talking! We knew he would need various therapies and leg braces and would have some developmental and possible cognitive delays, but despite the uncertainties, the update confirmed in our hearts that he was our son.

We met him only ten months after we began the adoption process. Throughout the waiting, I knew God was calling us into deep and uncertain waters where it was not in our human strength to go without His guidance. I also knew this was something we had been called to do and there was no turning back. The Lord filled and blessed me with this confidence and courage in preparation for the road ahead—a road that was full of twists and turns and anything but easy.

From the day we stepped off the plane from China and into the chaos of life with an adopted child, things were hard and all I could do was wonder when they would get better—when he would settle, learn to play, feel safe, stop raging and self-harming. I was drowning. Aaron did not sleep. At all. I was in a thick cloud of depression, with an unhappy, grieving, scared three-year-old. I felt isolated, alone, lonely, and miserable. I missed my old life and time with my biological children. Aaron was suffering as well. Being around him was like constantly walking on eggshells. Anything and everything would set him off into rages, self-harm, and physical violence toward his father and me. When he would hit my biological children, I would become undone. On my darkest days I feared we had made a mistake. Our family had been forever changed and it seemed as though it was not for the better.

For some reason, the one-year mark represented a major victory to me. It was like a distant beacon whose light we would never reach. To me, it held some sort of magic. I believed that at one year things would be improved, we would be a normal family, all of the issues that come with adoption would have drastically improved, and I would be better. But life remained difficult, and at six months I started panicking. We aren't even close to having all of our issues behind us.

At our six-month post placement visit, our sweet social worker looked at me and said, "Do you love him yet?" *Oh no*, I thought, *she can see into my soul. I'm not acting like I love him enough. She knows I am a bad adoptive parent.* These thoughts flashed through my mind as I returned her gaze wide-eyed. She broke the silence. "It's okay if you don't. I have adopted children too, and it takes time." I let out a sigh of relief and my posture relaxed. I love him sometimes, I confessed to her. But some days (most days) it is still really hard. There are times I miss how our family was before. It was all so much easier then. He makes everything so incredibly hard. He hits his brothers and sister and my mama-bear instincts come out. He hits and claws himself and it breaks my heart and makes me angry. I don't know how to get him to stop. Nothing the books say to do seems to work. He is too hypervigilant to sleep, antagonizes his sister, and spends all day whining that everything is unfair. His rage is set off at the drop of a hat, or more literally at the drop of a crayon. When he doesn't get his way, he threatens all of us by saying "I'm going back to China! You are not my family!" By the end of the day I am so spent physically and emotionally, yet I cannot even look forward to a night of sleep because he will be awake, needing us to sleep with him, grabbing for me in desperation if I even stir. Our social worker left with some encouraging words and resources and told me to call her if things did not start improving soon. *What is soon*, I wondered....

Later that week I sat with my neighbor, sweating on her screened-in porch in the July heat. She adopted a little boy four years ago and has been a huge source of encouragement for me. "When will it feel like he is mine?" I asked. "When will it feel the same as my other children?"

"It won't ever be exactly the same," she said in response to my shock. "It will get better than it is now, but it will always feel a little different. Not better or worse, just different. And that doesn't have to be a bad thing. But you *will* feel like he is your child, and he *will* become just as much a part of your family as your other children. It *will* get easier. "One year was a huge accomplishment for us," she said, "a turning point." There was that magic phrase again. One year. Would there really be noticeable change in the next six months?

I continued to worry. What if it never gets better than this? What if the magic anniversary comes and everything is the same? What hope will I have then? I can't live my whole life in this state of anxiety! I was so afraid that my world would crash in around me even more than it already had. But despite this underlying fear, we kept doing the work.

We kept looking in his eyes, telling him we loved him, making him family collages and baby books. We continued singing him songs the attachment counselor taught us, praying with him and for him. We tried to maintain our consistency with discipline and teach him strategies for dealing with his anger. He started school in the fall and with that came a more consistent routine and more people to pour into him and love him.

His sister taught him to play with her and there were moments I would stand in the middle of the house in shock because they would be quietly playing together in her room. This child who had absolutely no idea how to play was now making imaginary voices and playing make-believe.

One day in the fall, when we had been home about nine months, I realized his tone was no longer a constant whine. And the angry outbursts, tantrums, and self-harm, though still there, were not as frequent. We were all making baby steps. The seeds of love were growing in my heart as well, and I began to have more compassion and empathy towards him. I felt less like I was babysitting someone's misbehaving child and more like he was my own.

As Christmas approached, and our one-year anniversary with it, I noticed a shift happening again. But this time it was regression.

After siblings' birthdays and all of the holiday fun and chaos, Christmas Eve was a disaster. He was a mess, I was a mess, and those old feelings and thoughts that he was only making our life harder resurfaced. As many adoptive parents know, the holidays can be a trigger for our little ones and so it was for Aaron. I was sobbing in the bathroom of a cafe during Christmas Eve brunch because he had scratched up his face and tried to choke himself all over a pancake not being cut the way he wanted it.

This is it, I thought, ignoring the truth of how far we had come. *It's always going to be this hard and this awful. We have been home almost a year, and this is still happening.* I eventually composed myself and we went home, missing the Christmas Eve service and laying low for the remainder of the day. After I cooled down and had some time to think, I realized that it was different this time. Though his old patterns triggered old emotions for me, life was not the same as it was eleven months ago when we stepped off that plane.

At some point over the last few months my emotions had evolved. Though I was upset and angry at him at times, I no longer questioned my love for him. He was my son and I loved him like a son. Yes, I felt anger towards him, but in the same way I sometimes feel anger toward all of my children. Though he still had the ability to ruin an entire day, I no longer questioned whether or not we had made a mistake by bringing him into our family.

We have been home for one year, and I can finally say that I love him. I cannot say he is perfect or that his institutional behaviors are gone. I cannot say that I am not still walking on eggshells most days trying to avoid a rage or a tantrum. I cannot tell you when or why my heart shifted toward him. Maybe it was only time. There was not a lightning-bolt moment. Nor was there an instant bond or attachment from the moment we met. I spent the better part of our first year suffering through each long day, considering every sunset a milestone and lying in bed beside him every night hoping that as one night layered upon another it would eventually lead us to mutual love and attachment. I hoped and prayed that every morning waking up next to us, hearing us say we would never leave him, and seeing we were trustworthy would eventually lead him to a sense of security, safety, and confidence. And I prayed it would lead me to a deep love for and attachment to him—something I had no idea would be so hard to come by.

Through these long dark days and nights, God kept reminding me and nudging me toward the story of Peter in the Bible getting out of the boat and walking on the water to Jesus. I had read the verse from my copy of *Jesus Calling* on the plane to China, and then laying on my bed one night, waiting for Aaron to fall asleep, it came back to my mind in a personal way. As I mentioned, I felt like I was sinking in the middle of the stormy waters of my life. But God in his faithfulness reminded me that He never said it would be easy. There was a sweet precious boy hiding underneath a mask of trauma and we had to get to him somehow. Often the oceans seemed to be rising, not quieting, as I was begging for God to do. But though grief and trauma are tormenting, I had to let it happen for Aaron and for myself.

Just like Peter, I had seen Jesus walking towards me on the waters. I had heard His call to adopt loud and clear. I had had no doubts and I had stepped out of the boat in obedience and faith (Matt. 14:28). But once I obeyed and stepped out, I found myself in the stormy seas. I lost my footing and my gaze fell to the ocean's enveloping waves. I stopped focusing on my Savior. I was drowning. But like Peter, Jesus reminded me that I could look up, reach out, grab His hand, and ask "Lord, save me!" (Matt. 14:30b, NASB). And He would.

I reminded myself of this story day in, day out. He was there with me and with Aaron and with our entire family. He was healing our hearts and our fears. Even when the rough waters didn't subside, He was holding me and keeping my head above water. He wasn't going to let us drown. I still feel like I am bobbing in and out of the water some days, but I remember that I have the ultimate source of healing, the Healer himself, by my side. Not only healing my son but healing me as well. Sometimes as adoptive parents we forget that our souls need healing and rest too.

I know we still have a way to go. But I can celebrate that we have come so far. He still hits himself and he still tells me he wants to go back to China. He knows the unhealthy ways to get the attention he so desperately craves. We are still learning and growing as a family of six. There will always be highs and lows in this journey and new triggers in each new season. But I feel less afraid about having the capacity to handle them. I have to remind myself that, yes, he has been with us for one year and that is a wonderful and huge milestone. However, he spent ten months (I assume) with his birth family before abandonment and then two and a half years in an orphanage. One year with us is small in the grand scheme of things, but each anniversary will be one more year that he has been with us, that he has seen we are not going anywhere, that he has gained more security and confidence; and I hope and pray that he believes we are his forever family who will never leave or abandon him.

Just like birth or a major life change, adoption also disrupts the family balance, and as the parents that hold it together, we need help too. It is good and right that we are focused on our precious children who have overcome so much, but to do that well, we need to acknowledge our own pain, fears, anger, and unmet expectations that we face during and after adoption.

Just as our children need us to hold them during this difficult transition, we need someone to hold us, to wipe away our tears, and to remind us that we are doing the best we can. We can come into the arms of Jesus and let Him hold us while we cry and then give us the strength to stand up, keep going, and keep loving the little ones He has entrusted into our care.

Megan R. has been married to her high school sweetheart for eleven years. They have four children ranging from age four to eight, one with Autism Spectrum Disorder and one with cerebral palsy. Their youngest child was adopted from China in 2016. Megan works at home balancing doctor's appointments, therapy sessions, and school schedules for her four kids, and enjoys reading, writing poetry and drinking coffee to decompress. She is also studying for her Masters in Social Work.

19

The Unexpected Gift

After the birth of our third child, my heart was still hoping for more children even though my husband decided his quiver was full. We started later in the parenting journey than most people with me being almost thirty-three and my husband forty-one. So, having three children in the span of just under five years (including a daughter with Down syndrome) didn't just put a period at the end of the proverbial "I'm finished having children" sentence for my husband, it was an exclamation mark!

Still, I continued to pray God would change Jim's mind and my dreams of having a fourth child would be realized. I had pretty much given up on this dream when Jim told me that God had changed his heart about having another child. I was almost forty-five but optimistic about my chances to get pregnant since that was never an issue for us. I remember asking him in that same conversation if having another child could mean adopting, but he said, "No, that isn't what God told me."

I have been a Christian most of my life with the typical peaks and valleys in my spiritual walk. One of those valleys was when I couldn't get pregnant after God gave Jim the green light on having another child. I felt hurt and confused and cried out to God more than a few times asking why? I found myself questioning God's plan for my life and, even worse, wondering whether He truly cared about me. I spent a lot of time in prayer, but honestly it was more begging than worshiping.

I also remembered something God gave me in a very clear word-picture after we decided to try for another child. It was an image of an exquisitely wrapped present with a beautiful bow, and an unknown gift inside. At first, I thought I knew what was ultimately inside the box, even while acknowledging different facets of the hoped-for gift. The reminder that God is still in the business of answering heartfelt prayers was evident in the changing of Jim's heart toward having another child. Another facet was a newfound compassion for friends and other women who experienced infertility, as I could now identify with that ache a little more closely. But still, I figured the main gift wrapped in that amazing box would be a sweet little baby who would enter our family and enrich our lives as we continued on our merry way after the tiny blip of time it takes to get used to a new child.

Fast forward to a year later: I was still not pregnant and thus was guiding more of our fourth-child conversations toward adoption … but with the same result. I continued to pray for this child as I had for so many years until, finally, when I brought up adoption in yet another conversation, Jim said I could get information about the process. What he thought was just allowing me to crack the door on this possibility, was in actuality my pushing the door open with both hands. Thus our whirlwind adoption process began.

Within a few weeks, I had discovered Reece's Rainbow special-needs adoption site and brought up the idea of adopting a baby with Down syndrome from across the ocean. We were already raising a daughter with Down syndrome, so we figured God, in His infinite wisdom, was giving us a chance to bring another child into our family without challenging us much beyond how we had already been stretched raising Jessie.

It took a mere five months from sending our "commitment to adopt" paperwork to bringing home our two-and-a-half-year-old Ukrainian baby doll, Irina. The beautifully-wrapped box was open and, lo and behold, inside was an adorable blue-eyed, bouncing toddler girl. I praised God for this gift and His provisions in getting us to her quickly, so we could now start our new life as a family of six.

Even after I modified my idea of the gift inside the box to include adopting a special-needs little girl, I still could never have predicted or prepared for how my world was about to be turned upside-down physically, emotionally, and mostly spiritually. Oh yes, I certainly gave thought and prayer towards life with another special-needs child in the house; but mostly I was focused on lining up doctors' appointments and therapies, getting her to sleep well (my personal nemesis), and potty-trained and feeding herself … you know, what I thought were the basics. It was all going to be a wonderful "happily ever after" scenario because, of course, that's what happens when you follow God, right?

Other than some of the trademark physical characteristics of Down syndrome that I had grown to accept and love in Jessie, Irina was nothing like anything I had experienced in the twelve years raising Jessie. Her institutional behaviors threw me for a loop— although other adoptive moms had forewarned me about them— and quickly added a layer of stress to all of our lives. I tried mightily to rise above them, but mostly failed on a daily, sometimes hourly, basis.

Mealtimes were a disaster as Irina would scream and throw her head back against her high chair with such violence that I had to hold her on my lap for a lot of feeding times. Even when I had her food ready and poised to literally shove in her mouth, she would scream if the texture was wrong, or if I wasn't feeding her fast enough, or for numerous other reasons I couldn't figure out.

During non-meal times, she had to be constantly supervised because she wasn't safe to herself or others. She would hit or bang her head, pull her hair or someone else's, throw books and toys, or get into non-food items like grass or rocks and stuff them into her mouth. Her needs began to feel insurmountable and I was exhausted.

One of our biggest reasons for adopting Irina was the thought of how nice it would be for Jessie to have a sister to grow older with, as they would both live with us until such time when we could no longer care for them. We spent lots of time excitedly fixing Jessie's room to share with her new sister, as well as talking about all the fun times she and Irina would have once we brought Irina home. However, the beautifully decorated room Jessie was to share with her younger sister became just Irina's room, as Jessie opted to sleep on the couch for almost a year because of Irina's restless sleep patterns. Sisterly time playing together quickly spiraled downward into Jessie's avoidance and occasional hostility towards Irina because Irina's behaviors bothered and at times hurt Jessie. To say I was discouraged by their lack of bonding would be a huge understatement.

It was about three months into having Irina home, which also coincided with the beginning of another homeschool year with my three older kids, when I began to sink into a pit of hopelessness, frustration, and anger about how this child had turned our lives upside down. I wondered quietly and out loud about God's seeming lack of help in my life as I felt depleted and completely unqualified to care for and assimilate this little girl into our family. I wish I could say this is when I dug in deep spiritually and found God's strength in my weakness; but instead I took the wide road of anger, blame, and self-pity. At this point, the gift inside the beautifully-wrapped present was, to me, more of a cruel prank. But instead of asking God what I could learn from this difficult and stressful situation, I focused on the why questions that only served to keep me in a swirl of depression and resentment.

I thought I had hit the lowest time in my spiritual life until another event occurred that would change my world forever. My father died unexpectedly, and with that whatever thin veneer of faith and "holding it together" I had going for me quickly shattered. I had no idea how to cope with my grief and with this child who was so different from what I had expected. I appreciated the support of family and friends, but I continued to feel isolated and alone as I struggled with questions about God that I didn't even want to admit I was asking.

I spent a lot of time praying for God to change Irina as well as asking for strength, patience, and peace, but all I received in response was a heartbreaking silence. I began to fantasize about getting back my pre-Irina life. Then I would feel guilty for having those thoughts. On my worst days, I would remind myself of what Irina's life would be like if she were still languishing in her orphanage crib and that would temporarily give me the motivation to keep going. And although at the time I didn't "feel" a deep love toward Irina, that protective affection for her kept my head and heart in the game so God could continue what He was working together for my good. My prayers for Irina to change, so life would be easier, were about to be answered in a very different way than I had imagined.

I can't emphasize enough how much the prayers and support of friends and family helped along the way. Once I was able to open up to a few trusted adoptive moms about how I was feeling toward Irina and life in general, I realized that this can sometimes be a part of the overall transition with an especially difficult child.

It was in some ways a grieving process for what I had hoped life would be and what my reality was instead, and going through the different stages was healthy and okay, as long as I didn't get stuck in any one phase.

It took almost three years before I started accepting Irina for the person God had made her to be, and it began with God gently whispering things to me like, "Instead of trying to make Irina fit into your world, try seeing the world from her perspective." This was a slow process and continues to this day, but little by little I was able to see some of the causes of her screaming and aggressive behaviors, and in doing so, I gained more compassion and patience in dealing with them. He also reminded me of the verses we put on Jessie's baby dedication plaque many years earlier: "For you created my inmost being; you knit me together in my mother's womb. I praise you because *I am fearfully and wonderfully made*; your works are wonderful, I know that full well" (Psalm 139:13–14, NIV, emphasis mine). God showed me that it didn't matter if Irina ever talked, became potty-trained, or learned even the most functional of behaviors; she is worthy of my love and acceptance simply because she is fearfully and wonderfully made exactly the way her Creator planned.

Knowing and assimilating those truths into my heart have been and continue to be a process, but I can say that now seven years into having Irina home with us, I enjoy her, accept her for who she is, and most importantly love her deeply such that I can't imagine life without her. Irina is still a challenging child with many needs that can still feel like more than I can handle; but God has brought me to a place of peace and strength physically, emotionally, and most importantly spiritually.

Now when I think back to that beautifully decorated box, I know that the real gift God had planned for me all along was a changed heart towards Him and those around me. A heart which is learning to trust God's plan even when I don't understand or necessarily like it. A heart which is learning and living out the truth that even though obedience to God doesn't mean an easier life, it does mean I can count on God being right by my side, cheering me on and giving me strength to persevere when it feels too hard. And most of all, the good gift of a heart which is eternally grateful for the love and patience God generously shows me, so I too can love others better ... even a little Ukrainian girl I never dreamed I could love so much.

"Every good thing given and every perfect gift is from above, coming down from the Father of lights, with whom there is no variation or shifting shadow" (James 1:17, NASB).

Kristin F. has been married to Jim for almost twenty-four years. They have four children ranging in age from ten to twenty-one, including two daughters with DS; one is biological and the other is adopted. In her life before children, Kristin was a high school English teacher and a middle school guidance counselor. Raising children has been one of the greatest joys and challenges of her life, including homeschooling the three older children up until high school. Kristin also enjoys ministry opportunities outside of her home, such as being a small group life coach facilitator, working with the homeless, and more recently working with a group of high school refugee students. Her hobbies include reading, exercising, spending quality time with friends and family, and watching and cheering on her children in sports, including a variety of professional and college teams.

20

The Dream

Have you ever dreamed about something so much it felt real before it even happened? God gave me a dream for a little black boy with a big smile. I literally dreamed about him when I slept once; but almost daily I dreamed about him when I pictured him, wondered what he was doing, prayed for him, planned for him, and loved him. I loved that boy before I even knew his name, and it was a deep love many people don't understand.

Have you ever had your dream come true, only to find out it was nothing like you thought it would be? That was my dream. God gave me the precious little boy I had pictured, but as it turned out—I wasn't who I dreamed I would be. Don't we all dream of being the perfect mama with unconditional love and patience? God has a way of refining us and showing us our hearts in ways we don't expect.

My story started at a young age when I dreamed of a big house with lots of children, and a front porch of course. I have always been drawn to children, and through the years, God refined that love specifically for children who needed families. I pursued a degree in social work and worked as a foster care caseworker after college in an inner city. My passion was clear: loving the kids who needed the most love. During my time doing social work, the majority of the children I worked with were African-American, and God gave me the dream of my son during that time.

After several years of social work, I married a wonderful man. God had planted a seed in him to adopt as well. We knew we would adopt eventually, but we didn't wait long to have biological children and were blessed with three fairly quickly. One sweet afternoon while I was nursing my newborn and watching my two toddlers play, I heard the Lord ask me, "Would you be willing to be done having biological children and start adopting?" In that moment, tears immediately came to my eyes. I didn't know if I could answer with an immediate yes, although I knew deep in my heart God was asking me to surrender my plans and follow Him down a road that required faith. We had a three-year-old, a one-year-old, and a three-month-old. I felt a bit overwhelmed with life as it was. But when God says move, what else can we do but move? I certainly didn't want to miss out on what He was up to.

My husband and I attended an adoption information meeting and prayed a good bit about where to start. We both felt drawn to Ethiopia and began the endless mounds of paperwork to complete our home study and dossier. About nine months later, our paperwork was in Ethiopia and we were set to wait. In all honesty, I was hoping the wait would be later rather than sooner to give our babies time to grow a little bit more.

After our paperwork had been in Ethiopia for four months, we got a call from our caseworker. It was a phone call that would change our lives forever. She explained that a young lady had come into their office to make an adoption plan for her one-year-old little boy, Jeremiah. It would be a domestic adoption and not an Ethiopian one, but our caseworker had prayed about it and had felt led to ask our family if we would be interested. The adoption would be extremely open, with frequent contact, visits, etc. at the birth mother's request. We took the next day or so to get on our knees and ask the Lord for wisdom. It became clear to us that the

Lord had called us to open our home and help a child in need; and despite the surprise to us, He had been planning this all along. We told our caseworker we would be willing to meet the birth mother and see how things went.

It's hard to explain how unprepared we felt walking into this meeting. Complete strangers meeting to talk about a child forever being entrusted to us was overwhelming. We want to be everything she wanted us to be, but what if we weren't? What if she didn't like us? What if we didn't like her? What if we said the wrong thing?

The Lord was quick to remind us that His plans are bigger than one conversation, even if it is a very important one. We were free to be ourselves and rely on His leading us as we met. The moment we walked into the room, I loved this sweet lady, Theresa. Her smile was contagious, and she immediately hugged us both and thanked us for coming. We talked about family, discipline, God, and Jeremiah. It was a holy moment and we all knew it. Just a few minutes after our meeting, she asked us if we would be willing to adopt her son. She said she knew God had brought us to her, and He had brought her to us. With tears in our eyes, we said "Yes!" We planned to meet Jeremiah the next day.

I will never forget the moment of watching Theresa walk into the adoption agency with this little boy, just over a year old, in her arms and seeing my dream come true. Here he was. I was looking at my brown-skinned beautiful baby boy. We spent the next hour with him, and then over the next few weeks he transitioned to our home and my dream was coming true.

At this point in the story, I thought the hard part was over and we could just get on with our perfect life. Little did I know God had different plans and that I was on a journey to be refined in ways I didn't expect.

My expectations were higher than any child could ever meet, especially one who has just been pulled away from the only mama he had ever known. The extreme loss in his life was something I was aware of, but my compassion for what he was going through was very low. We are a great family and I am a great mom, so he should be fine, right? He wasn't. In hindsight, I don't know why I didn't understand. He was grieving and he was unhappy. He didn't like me. He would scream and cry and hit me. He resisted me holding him. Those days were so hard and humbling for me.

I remember at an adoption training class we went to before he was placed with us how an adoptive mom had talked about how she didn't attach immediately to her daughter. I distinctly thought, *That will never be me.* I judged her and even shunned her for her "lack of love" from my perspective. Fast forward a few months and here I was. Jeremiah didn't like me, and I have to admit, I didn't like him either. My love was so small and conditional. I expected a one-year-old to adjust without any problems because this was my dream come true.

The next year was full of exhaustion, anxiety, guilt, and shame for not being who I thought I would be. I was ashamed because I didn't have it all together and that my love for Jeremiah wasn't immediate like it was for my biological kids. I grieved over the loss of my "perfect life" and I was completely overwhelmed with four babies under the age of four.

When he came to us he wasn't in the best health. He was off the charts for his weight and had issues with food. At meal time he would just scream. He would eat more than my husband, who isn't a small man, and still cry when the food was gone. He had multiple problems with his skin, infections, and allergies, and what seemed like never-ending ear infections. Dealing with all of these issues seemed to intensify my frustrations. It's like I knew in my head that those things weren't his fault, but I couldn't stop the negative feelings I was having towards him. It's incredibly humbling to admit these feelings. At their root was a desire to be in control and to maintain my "togetherness." There was so much I got wrong.

On top of my own issues, we were navigating an open adoption, something we hadn't planned for. We loved our son's birth mom, but we also had to figure out what this relationship was going to look like. How involved would she be? Would he be confused when he saw her? Or would seeing her help him? What if she expected something from us that we didn't feel we could give? What if he never loved me and always wanted her? The first year was trial and error and included lots of honest conversations and a lot of doing the best we could. Sometimes the laid-back lifestyle of his birth mom was hard to work with. For instance, we would drive an hour to see her only for her to cancel as we were pulling into the parking lot. Those moments were emotional and frustrating and only added to the stress of Jeremiah's adjustment to our family.

Those moments were emotional for all of us, but eventually we found a new normal. I still didn't get everything right, but as I found myself casting all of my anxieties on the Lord, and confessing to Him my sin of pride and unbelief, I saw the weeds that had grown in my heart and had choked out the true vine of love begin to wither, and love began to grow and flourish.

My love for my son grew and his adjustment, although it was difficult, progressed as he got to know us. Despite the struggle, there is nothing in the world like that little boy with a big smile who I dreamed about for so many years sitting in my lap and laughing with me. He is loud and fun and the life of the party everywhere he goes. I had to realize my love would grow and to be patient with myself and patient with my son. I expected to be perfect and I'm not. God's grace is so sufficient, even when we mess up every day and feel like we have ruined our kids. Adoption is hard. It is beautiful and for many people like me, it is a dream come true. But along the way, we realized that loss and struggle are just as present with the beauty and that is okay. God works in it all and He makes our rough places smooth.

One day, Jeremiah came up to me and out of the blue said "Mommy, I have two mommies and two daddies!" At first my heart sank because he didn't know anything about his birth father at that point because he was so young. But my fears were quickly turned to joy when he said, "You and Miss Theresa are my mommies, and Daddy and God are my daddies!" I was so thankful he understood God was his Father, and also that he was excited about having two mommies. He has come a long way and we still have hard days. He is an absolute joy to us though and we thank God he is part of our family.

Dreams do come true, but I am learning that my expectations should be held loosely. God writes our stories and His ways are perfect!

Lydia W. is mommy to six loud, crazy, and amazing children. She loves to read a good novel during the kids' nap times and drink coffee, and she enjoys opening her home to friends and family. If Lydia had a free day all to herself, she would spend hours on the beach with her toes in the sand.

The Eye of the Storm

Two years ago, in mid-November, I was dreading the imminent return of our twelve-year-old daughter. She was living with friends, after threatening to kill the children and myself.

What a roller coaster our adoption of Amy has been. We had raised two children and had two young ones in the home when I saw Amy's beautiful, sad, and almost defiant look, as she showed her injured limb for the photograph. A large scar crawled down the back of her leg. She seemed furious to be asked to show this evidence of a terribly painful day in her life. My instinct told me this little girl had been through terrors and was fighting back. I showed her photo to my husband, and he said blissfully, "She looks perfect!" That was it. I wrote a letter detailing the care we anticipated she might need, and out of more than fifty families, ours was chosen, because we seemed aware of her pain and brokenness. Little did I know that we were entering a monumental spiritual battle for her life, the life of our marriage, and the life of our whole household.

I point out this is a spiritual battle because that's exactly what it is. Make no mistake: the only way you will make it through a situation like this is with the power, strength, and protection of the Father Almighty, and the grace of His Son and His Spirit. Even then, in your humanity, you will fall short, doubt yourself, wonder why you threw your whole family into chaos, and why you ever thought you could love this child and that they could love you back. Your noble intentions will bring a time of great trial and testing into your lives. You will find out who your real friends are. You will find out what is inside you, what is unhealed. You will have all your weak spots and fractures revealed and it may be very ugly. In addition to helping the child heal, you will have to heal and change, too.

By Amy's sixth year home, I felt that I was chained in prison for life, linked to a person who hated me and who was bent on destroying my life, every bit of my joy, my hope, and my family. While I would never let anyone treat me this way, she was a child, and I saw no way out. If this is your experience right now, I pray the Lord will give me the words that you need to hear—words of encouragement and guidance—and that His life will fill you and His Spirit will speak hope, where there was none before.

Amy was injured in a fire that took the life of her grandfather, who rescued her but died before her eyes. Amy blamed herself. With the death, Amy went to her parents, where she remembers being left alone as they worked. Hungry, little Amy searched for food and wandered the streets, grabbing what she could in the street markets. This angered her father, who abandoned her at four or five years old, after a long train ride to another part of the country. There they spoke a dialect she didn't understand. My little sobbing Amy was taken to the police and then the local orphanage. An older boy took her under his wing and used her sexually. She saw him as a protector and a friend. She felt important and loved by his attention, which set her up to seek that kind of "love" in the future.

When we traveled to adopt Amy at five years old, she was terrified and ran away from us. She was hyper and impulsive, with no boundaries. I was encouraged to be patient, to believe things would get better once we were home, after she had us to depend on. Unfortunately, this did not prove to be the case. Amy had an injury to her heart that time and "love" could not heal. She had a young part of herself, which persisted over the years, and that part believed no one knew what was best for her. No one could keep her safe, but she herself. Adults were useful for food, for a place to stay, for achieving what she wanted and needed, but that was it. She didn't believe she needed parents. After seeing her grandfather die, she wasn't going to be that vulnerable again. If she needed or wanted something, she helped herself and took it. Reasoning like a toddler, "I see it, I want it, it's mine," was and sometimes still is how she functioned.

The early years home were focused on structure and finding therapies to help her heal. We had chore charts and a very regular but simple life, with extremely clear expectations and boundaries. She was in an in-home therapy, which my adult daughters and husband thought was ridiculous. Neuro-reorg focused on helping to heal the brain through movement, and we spent an hour each day, down in our basement, doing that physical therapy. I hired help to run the therapy so that my presence was not a reason to resist. Amy, who had proprioceptive disorder, became more coordinated, had less impulsivity, and had big improvements in tracking, which made reading easier. Raging and tantrums went way down. It was time-consuming, but we saw big jumps in ability and self-calming.

Amy proved to be a charming yet dishonest student, who could also be kind and caring. One year, Amy took an autistic child under her wing and "helped" him with physical tasks he couldn't do for himself. I saw in Amy the potential to be loving. It was encouraging. As the years progressed, it became clear, however, that Amy was unable to feel remorse, and she didn't seem to have a conscience. She often acted out of revenge and hurt our other children. She once confessed, "Mommy, sometimes I am so mad inside, I just want to hurt something." She had been injuring the pets and found some kind of release in the pain of others. She charmed her father, often setting the rest of the family up for his criticism by lying and staging situations to make us look bad. From his perspective, it appeared that we were "ganging up" on Amy.

Gradually, my husband took on the role of her knight in shining armor and her protector. He no longer consulted me or encouraged me, but overruled many of the boundaries I set down with Amy. Roots of division crept into the marriage. I felt great frustration and helplessness. I lost respect for him and resented his freedom to walk away from the difficult situations that faced me daily. He was uninterested in learning more about RAD or in putting her on medications for her behaviors. I later learned that Amy had a fantasy that she would skip down the driveway with her dad and they would go off and make a new life together. She was actively working to make it a reality and felt excited inside when Daddy became angry and yelled at Mommy, because it meant she was closer to her goal.

At school, she would lie to the teachers and say things to family and friends to earn sympathy and to make me look like a harsh parent. In these situations, she was the innocent victim. I had taken on the role of the "enemy" in her eyes. At the time, I really didn't know the depths of her hatred for me. In my eyes, I was the "healer" and the mother and leader of her support team, who would never give up on her. I worked to educate her teachers and principals, to make sure that they understood about RAD, and I frequently checked out things she said about her teachers that seemed off to me. They were normally dishonest misrepresentations, designed to make the other adults look bad and to keep her support team from being united. I faced this head on. This meant Amy had less privacy, but it was in her best interest to be frank.

Amy was charming. She was articulate and attentive to adults and she was also observant. She knew where things of value were left. She listened in on conversations to glean information about future events and to plan how to stop them, in case she didn't want to participate. She would sabotage family outings by deliberately throwing fits or creating fights, so that we would not be able to make it to our destinations. She harbored resentments and lied more often than she told the truth. It seemed to her that everyone else had a better life. They had adoptive parents who gave them more things, which meant that they loved them more. She would injure our other children, if she felt they deserved it, because they seemed to be more loved than she was. These injuries would be done in stealth, out of the view of any adults. She would find a way to make people pay. Of course, it was justified, because she felt she was the victim, and when her father came home, she would run to him, quickly presenting her version of events, so that those she injured would also get a scolding from him. Over time, the strife and division in the household increased. We were all trying to survive in the chaos. My husband began to avoid coming home. Eventually, he took a job in another state, without even consulting me. It is one thing when outside adults do not understand, but when our most intimate relationships are affected, it cuts to the core. Our enemy has a strategy and it is very simple. Divide and conquer. Lie, manipulate, accuse, and deceive.

I worked to care for the children on my own and to prepare for our move to that state, but events delayed the move. Amy began medication to assist with mood disorders and volatility. Things with Amy, during that time, continued to escalate, but there was a very freeing aspect to it, too. I no longer had to deal with triangulating and accusations within the home. I also gained some very valuable sources of support. Our church had life groups, and I met weekly with other adults who began to hold up our family and our children in prayer. A teacher at her school, who had worked with trafficked women and children, kept an eye on Amy for me, and called weekly to support me. He counseled her informally, throughout the school days, when events would occur. Amy was having a very clear-eyed male give her feedback on her behavior. He was a Christian man with loving and appropriate boundaries, and no illusions. He was beyond manipulation.

During that time, Amy and a neighbor stole devices and began talking online with men that clearly were predators. Amy lost all access to any devices. Later, while at a sleepover, Amy hacked into the school's computers to look at the grades of others. She and the other culprits sent letters of apology in the mail to every person whose grades they had seen. The next year, she had no overnight invitations. Family was her main contact outside of school time. When we were close to moving, she found and stole an iPod and used it to go online and have inappropriate contacts. I discovered the device and recovered it, which was the first in a string of thefts of iPods and recoveries, seven in all. She hacked into accounts and ordered iPods, which I intercepted and returned. She opened accounts in my name and ordered an iPod, stealing credit card information to do so. I felt I was in a weird "Catch me if you can" life. I could never let my guard down. The thefts became closer and closer together. She had no remorse, crying, "It's mine!" when protesting with the police, who became regular visitors to our home. She stole a check and was caught on camera forging my signature to buy an iPod; and finally, she stole an iPod from another child, at her youth group one night. Amy was charged with identity theft and forgery. Each iPod purchase was potentially another felony. I hired a lawyer and began the court process.

This was followed by two final violent events. In the first, she attacked the family and ultimately, kicked her six-year-old brother, who flew ten feet in the air and hit a wall. Everyone was very shaken up and in shock. She was led away by the police in handcuffs and taken to the ER, which didn't have a bed for her. They released her back home. Having survived beating us up, she told me she figured she could handle even more than that. This brought my church/school support into our home, for crisis intervention. Ultimately, Amy threatened to kill the family. Amy left our home that night. She stayed with a youth leader and, weeks later, with a family friend. We waited for what seemed to be "the slow arm of the law" to take its course. I had no idea what the future held. At my request, my life group prayed over our family, laying hands on me, asking the Father to bring me a treatment program He endorsed, rather than jail time, which I felt sure would lead to her further abuse. I still loved and cared for her and did not want anyone to hurt her.

The next day, I learned about the Institute for Attachment and Child Development (https://instituteforattachment.org). Forrest Lien knew my story before I spoke it. "Let me guess," he said. "You are calling from a closet, and you've locked all the doors because she listens to everything you say on the phone. Let me tell you about your child...." And he began, in a no-nonsense, no sugar-coating way, to describe her and our life as a family, and even the damage that had been done to our once rock solid marriage. I looked about myself at the clothing on all sides and was astounded. For the first time, someone understood the depths of the situation. The validation and the explanations he gave felt so freeing. I wasn't crazy. I wasn't a cruel or abusive mother. I wasn't the problem. My husband wasn't the problem. We had both been cast into classic RAD parent roles: He was the duped Knight in Shining Armor and I was the Nurturing Enemy.

Court-ordered treatment began, and Amy was there for six and a half months. She lived in a therapeutic home where she had complete safety but no freedom to hurt or manipulate others. She was given the security she missed growing up, as a toddler. She learned that the grownups would keep her safe. They would be in control and that would be good for her. She could finally relax. She had a safe spot, with a basket that contained books, paper, pencils, journals, and things to keep her occupied. After school, she came and stayed in that spot until directed by an adult. Her room contained only a bed and an alarm on the door. She could not leave without adults knowing. No one could come into her room and hurt her. She was safe. There were cameras, so there was no doubt about what was occurring. She was in line of sight always. Her clothing was selected by the parent every morning. Her job was to be a child and learn how to be respectful, responsible, and easy to be around in all environments. She wasn't rescued from her feelings but encouraged to feel and journal about them. She could say anything, if it was truthful, and the adults would not be angry with her. They were calm and unruffled, and she could practice and learn how to be a family kid with them because she had no stake in destroying them. They could not be divided or manipulated. All those old games did not work.

The therapeutic parents had respite once a month. They had support and training and instruction, and they could walk away and were not trapped, as I was. These practice parents taught the little toddler in my child that marriage is a good thing and spouses support and back each other up, that parents can be safe people. We each are responsible for our feelings and actions and we can't blame other people. Our family also received care and training, and I participated in weekly therapy with her. I saw her start to shift before my eyes into a more honest and authentic person. When she apologized or said she loved me, there were tears in her eyes and she actually meant it. The other children began to feel safe once again, and our home felt completely different. Friends noticed a huge feeling of peace when they walked in the door. No longer living in a state of high alert, we worked on recovering from our own PTSD. Later, I learned how to set up a similar safe spot at home, and how to provide the structure she had had at the Institute, so she would be able to come home when discharged.

She is now often fun to be around. She can be genuinely lovable and funny, in a quirky way. She no longer threatens, and when she attempts to manipulate or control, I stop her in her tracks and call her on it. However, she needs high structure and took advantage of the chaos of our move to a new state this summer. While packing, she stole an unused family phone and began corresponding via Wi-Fi with a predator overseas, imagining she was in love and would run away to a new life with him. As a high school student, she is not able to handle the temptations of a phone. She's back to sitting in a safe spot at home. I pick her clothing, and she can't participate in sports or just hang out at school with friends, which is sad. She has weekly therapy with the Institute and respite care one weekend a month. She is having consequences for her actions, but they don't affect the whole family. We are leading normal lives, and the season of chaos is over.

Unfortunately, my husband has been a reluctant, and only occasionally present, participant in all this therapy. He does not view it with the same trust that I do. He feels like the "spark" was taken out of Amy's eyes and her personality has been dulled. He does his best to support me as I carry on the role of the primary parent in her life. Ideally, he would have been able to participate in all the weekly work at the Institute. He could not, and I still struggle to give up my frustration and to forgive him for what he was not able to do for me, which I really needed. We are still working on healing. Little by little things improve, and I am able to trust and forgive.

There is one component to her healing that I haven't woven into this story. Her battle and our battle truly was, and is, a spiritual one. When she walked in our door, angry and destructive forces came with her. The enemy hates us and everything we stand for and believe. We struggled with our own hearts as we dealt with judgment, slander, anger, resentment, division, and finally bare hatred, frustration, depression, and hopelessness. Day by day, the enemy worked very hard to gain ground.

Part of my personal story is that I also was abused as a child, in ways that Amy had been. I had healed and forgiven the perpetrator, but Amy's behavior brought my young self to the fore, and I sought my own counselor to deal with the strong feelings that bubbled up. I knew how some of her behaviors felt from the inside. I knew, ahead of time, some of what she was thinking and much of what she would do. So, the Lord was taking my brokenness and pain, and using it to help me be compassionate and persistent with this child.

I no longer think that any sin is harmless, and I yearn to stay in the Father's presence and with His Spirit. Jesus has removed the spiritual forces of evil from us and He intends us to be free indeed and to walk in the power of His Spirit.

I encourage you to call for help. Do not be shy to share the depth of what you are going through with Christian friends. You need their prayers and their help in this battle. It is impossible to go it alone. If some do not believe you, pray the Lord will send you others who will. Our struggle is not against flesh and blood. The enemy is not your wounded child, or your spouse, or anyone else, but a much more malevolent force is at work for your destruction. Know in your heart that he will not succeed! His plans *will* fall to dust at the Lord's feet. Your God intends you to overcome. The battle is already won, in the heavenly places.

Not one of us can save ourselves. But there are things you can do to help. Get respite care. Get skilled support. Speak to the Institute for Attachment. Join their on-line support group. Find reliable help, and if you are like most of us, you will have to look after your own heart. Release resentment, release anger, release fear ... release all that is holding you captive. Rebuke these overwhelming feelings and ask the Lord to help you with them. They are from the enemy. I know how hard this is and I don't deny you have a right to those feelings, but they will eat you up and hurt you. It is time to let the Lord carry you and wash you clean. The people who are judging you unfairly, who may slander your good name, who are lying, or injuring you, or who are not supporting you, or have abandoned you ... they are flawed and imperfect, like we all are. Go to Him with humility and forgiveness in your heart for them. Let Him be the judge. He is honest, true, and kind.

Jesus was asked, "How often shall my brother sin against me and I forgive him? Up to seven times? Jesus said to him, 'I do not say to you, up to seven times, but up to seventy times seven.'" (Matt. 18:21-22, NASB). If you are patient and forgiving with others, He will be patient and forgiving with you. This journey has most likely brought out an ugliness in you that you shudder to admit. It's okay. You are battle weary and dirty from the fight. If we say we have no sin, we make God a liar. I pray that the blessings of God the Father and His Son, Jesus, our Savior and Redeemer, and the presence of His Holy Spirit will uphold you and be with you, in every step you take. The battle is not over for most of us. I urge you to rest, recoup, and get help, but never give up. Keep going, for the victory is His, and I know it will be sweet!

Grace R. enjoys life with her husband and two corgis, a gaggle of kids, and a box turtle named Murples. She's an avid gardener and designer and loves the Lord with all her heart. Someday, she hopes to travel to Australia and maybe cuddle a koala or race a kangaroo.

In the Middle of the Night
(For Mamas in the Trenches)

Dear mama in the trenches, on your knees, barely crawling, darkness surrounding you ... before we spend a little time together, be sure of this ...

God, the Creator of the universe, sees you. You. He loves you and He desires to be in this journey with you. You are not reading this book by chance. The Great God who calls you beloved has placed this gift of encouragement to remind you that you are not alone. You may walk a lonely path, but you are never alone. Will you open your heart with me as you read? Maybe before you get into this chapter you just need to sit quietly for a time, asking Him to meet you where you are. Close your eyes a minute and picture Jesus. Do you see Him? Maybe right now you don't. For many of you, I know you can hardly see through your tears. Give yourself permission to tell Him that. It's okay. Immanuel. God with us. He is right there with you. Will you let Him breathe new life, new hope in your heart today? Let Him open your eyes to His presence. After all, that's His specialty.

As I pen these words, I imagine you next to me. These words from my heart are from my place of struggle to yours. You see, I am right there in that trench too. Though we don't know each other, and we may never meet this side of Heaven, I know this ...

You want what's best for your child. You love, and love, and love, and yet that love is met with rejection. Rejection that is not about you personally, yet you haven't been able to convince your heart of that. You are exhausted. Heart weary. Battle worn. Lonely at times. Tired of reaching out for help only to be judged or criticized. Hurt from the relationships you've lost. Guarded with your words because many don't believe you, but crying out on the inside. Afraid to trust God because it feels like He doesn't hear you. You have called out in desperation over and over and the answer is still wait. Or, not yet. Or no.

You love Jesus, yet deep down inside you wonder if He really gets your struggle. How this has affected your marriage and family. Your lives. Maybe you're afraid to voice your most vulnerable heartache and questions to Him.

And one of the deepest aches in the most hidden place of your heart is this ... you feel like the wrong mom.

I write this chapter in the middle of the battle. I am not on the other side with a story all tied up with a beautiful bow. I'm in the middle of broken pieces around me too. My own, my child's, my family's. I too am in the middle of night, holding onto Jesus as we wait for morning. I share as a fellow trench traveler, covered in mud with skinned-up knees, as we run, walk, and often crawl Home. I write not to offer answers, because by now you've been schooled that there aren't any. But I can offer you my story of hope—of Jesus, and my honest struggles of learning to hold on when the seasons of night and battles are long.

As so many adoption stories go, God had different plans for our family than we did. Our plan of adopting one turned into adopting two. A projected one-year journey of bringing them home became three. An adoption agency we thought we could lean on, only to find out they were committing fraud. Then the homecoming and the hopes and dreams of embracing our adopted children into our family took a very different turn.

Reactive attachment disorder and other heart-wrenching words became part of our vocabulary. One child responded to the attachment techniques we learned, and one did not. Suddenly we learned that love is not always enough. We went to all the conferences, read all the books. Joined the online support groups, listened to the webinars. Changed parenting techniques. Weekly attachment therapy with an expert in the field. Skype calls with other experts. And yet, we still sit in a very broken place. If you're a mama in the trenches of trauma and RAD, then I don't have to go into details. But know we are in the teen years working through this, which has meant help from professionals, both in health care and law. I'll be completely honest with you—as I write this, our child with the stronger attachment struggles isn't living in our home. He hasn't been able to for some time.

For us, it has been five and a half years of struggle. Intense struggle that has affected our whole family, including each of our five other kids. We are still in the middle of the night.

During this journey we've faced other heartaches outside of this, as I'm sure you have too. One of our children is facing cancer, and there are financial hardships, and the loss of relationships.

So, know the words I write are not trite—they are the desperate understanding of a girl longing to learn how to hold onto Jesus when the hard just keeps on coming.

I remember being in the hospital room with my daughter while she was getting chemo, already weary from the attachment struggles back at home. It was the middle of the night, and I had a very honest conversation with Jesus. I had a choice to make. I was either going to run full speed to Him, with all my hurt, questions, and fears and find Him in a way I never had, or I was going to run the other direction.

I chose to run to Him. However, in order to do that, I had to work through a few things. I loved Jesus with all my heart, but I was tired of church answers. I wanted authentic faith. I wanted to honor Him no matter what. But there seemed to be this separation in the Christian culture of being able to really struggle and yet continue to honor Him in it. Especially when that struggle was long. Where were the voices of Christ followers in the middle of their long roads of struggle? Where was lament in the church? I was determined to search the Scriptures and find my way to a more authentic, intimate place with Jesus.

I found David in the Psalms, with a raw faith, pouring out his heart over and over in lament. He faced a lot of night. I noticed this pattern as he laments:

A cry for help and rescue. Asking hard questions of God.

A pouring out of all of his heart thoughts and feelings. Nothing held back.

Adoration and praise to God. A reminding to his heart of who God is and what He has done.

It was a model of intimacy with Jesus in the middle of the night season. A blueprint to move truths from my head to my heart. From David, I learned one way to honor Jesus is to be my authentic self. Not to stuff my feelings or fears, but to take them to Him. Because it is in my going to Him that I put Him in the place of honor—I'm saying: God, You are the only one who can help me through this. God, I honor You by being honest with You, by saying You are big enough, good enough, and I want to trust You with all that is in my heart and not stuff or ignore it. I am letting my pride go, my fears go; showing my neediness of Him.

There's a passage in 2 Chronicles 20:1–29 (NLT) that I want to spend some time in. This story is a beautiful, practical example of how to face the battles of life. It's the story of three major armies declaring war on King Jehoshaphat and the Israelites.

The armies were on their way and Jehoshaphat was terrified by this news, so he begged God for guidance. He knew they would not survive a battle against three armies. He went straight to the only true source of help. He ordered those he was leading to seek God by fasting. Then, Jehoshaphat gives a heartfelt prayer, adoring God and recalling His faithfulness. He declares truth in the midst of feeling terrified, saying "We can cry out to you to save us, and you will hear us and rescue us" (2 Chron. 20:9b).

He lamented to God and cried out, "O our God, won't You stop them? We are powerless against this mighty army that is about to attack us. We do not know what to do, but we are looking to You for help" (v. 12).

Let's stop here for a minute. Do you feel this? Do you wake up in the morning, walking on eggshells, powerless about what you know you will have to face? Not because you have a bad child, but because trauma changes behavior. Your situation feels hopeless and never-ending because you are desperate to help your hurting child, but you have run out of options. You don't know what to do. As you (and I) wait for help, and we see night all around us, we train ourselves to fix our eyes on Jesus.

I don't know what that will look like for you, but for me it's taken different forms.

On what felt like a day from the story of *Alexander and the Horrible, no Good, Very Bad Day*, I decided to celebrate the truth that God is with us, even at times if it didn't feel like it. So, I went and bought a chocolate cake and ice cream. That night, my family and I celebrated God's faithfulness to us in the past, and the truth that in His time, He would rescue and redeem the situations in our life that are so broken.

Another time, I went and bought a plain rug and painted the

name of Jesus on it. It was to be a visual reminder right when I got out of bed to fix my eyes and stand on the firm foundation of Jesus. (A little cheesy maybe, but it works as a tangible, daily reminder to me.)

I encourage you to ask God to give you and your family ideas of ways to tangibly hold onto Him in the middle of the night. When you feel you can't see Him, ask Him to open your eyes to see places where He is there. Then be willing to look for it. He will help you fix your eyes on truth.

The next part of the story for the Israelites is a word from the Lord, spoken by Jahaziel, one of the men of Judah. "Do not be afraid! Do not be discouraged by this mighty army, for the battle is not yours, but God's" (2 Chron. 20:15b).

I want to make a distinction here, God never shames His people. Convicts, yes. But shames, no. In this verse, God acknowledges that we feel fear. It's not a dismissal of our feelings, but a desire to take them from us and turn them into faith. This can't happen unless we recognize them and give them to Him. He wants us to know that it's not our battle to worry about—He has taken it upon Himself! I can almost hear Him saying, *Oh my child, I know you are afraid, I know you are discouraged, but look to Me. Look to Me, and I will show you how you don't have to fear. How I will lift your head and eyes from the heaviness of discouragement. Release it to me, because I am trustworthy. You don't have to fight this. Give it to me and I will fight for you. I will carry this battle. You can come to Me and find rest.*

Often in the Christian culture, we push feelings away. I have done this for years because I equated feelings like fear, anger, and discouragement with being less spiritual. This kept me from a truly authentic relationship with Jesus. Once I was able to release this belief, I found a faith and freedom like I had never known. I found the only way I can cast off those feelings of fear and discouragement is to face them and give them to Jesus. Ignoring them does nothing. Giving them to God is my act of faith. I am telling God I trust Him with all of me. Vulnerability always involves risk, but I know from experience that God honors wholehearted faith.

Next, God tells His people to march out in faith. To take their positions, but they will not need to fight. He tells them to stand still and watch the Lord's victory. Again, He reminds them they don't need to be afraid or discouraged because the Lord is with them. After this, Jehoshaphat and the people of Judah and Jerusalem bowed low, worshipping God. The next morning, the army of Judah went forth, appointing singers to walk ahead of them, praising God. This is their song:

"Give thanks to the Lord; his faithful love endures forever!" (2 Chron. 20:21b).

They are giving God His worthy praise, but also reminding their hearts of who God is. They are fixing their eyes on Him.

My favorite part of this story is found in verse twenty-two: "At the very moment they began to sing and give praise, the Lord caused the armies of Ammon, Moab, and Mount Seir to start fighting among themselves" (2 Chron. 20:22). Did you catch that? As they were praising God, acknowledging His sovereignty, He was at work, but they couldn't see it yet.

Dear sister, can I invite you to hang on with me? Can we, in our struggle, work to train our hearts and eyes to praise Him? Can we praise Him for who He is? Because by praising Him, He builds our faith to believe and trust that He is at work even when we can't see it. Our journey might be one long hard walk or it may include battles coming at us from all sides. Can we link arms, singing our praise to tutor our hearts? And one day—maybe here on earth, or not until we see Him face to face—our battle will be over.

The rest of the story is about how those armies fought amongst themselves, and when the army of Judah arrived, the armies had completely destroyed each other. "Not a single one of the enemy had escaped" (2 Chron. 20:24b). King Jehoshaphat and his men then went to gather the valuables left behind by the armies. There was so much to collect, it took them three whole days to gather it all. God not only rescued them but gave them abundant blessing.

The next day, the people gathered in the valley. They named it the Valley of Blessing because they thanked and praised the Lord there. They returned to Jerusalem celebrating the victory with instruments. "So Jehoshaphat's kingdom was at peace, for his God had given him rest on every side" (2 Chron. 20:30).

I know you long for rest on every side. Goodness, you'll take rest on one side! One hour would be great! But the rest we're talking about is a heart rest. God is telling us to teach our hearts to rest by focusing our eyes on who He is—through the act of adoration and praise. It's in knowing that God is with you every step of the way and letting Him fight your battles. Ask Him to give you ideas about how to do that in a practical way.

One practice I've been doing when I'm in a season like this one now, where we have specific problems that need solving, is to ask the Lord, "Jesus, what does being still look like in this situation today?" I have my Bible and a notebook in front of me and I sit and listen and write down what I hear. Some days it means taking a specific action, other days it means waiting and praying, fasting, or another act of worship. It's a practice of me giving God the control and not just tackling the issue but seeking Him first on it.

Sweet sister, I pray you can find another warrior mama to journey with. I wish I could give you a hug to let you know you're not alone. (And I would tuck a little dark chocolate in your pocket for emergencies.) But most of all, I want you to remember that He sees you. He cups your chin in His hands, wipes your tears, looks into your eyes and says, *My daughter, I see you. I see every holy gift of love you offer Me as you love on a hurting child. You are just the right mama for your child. I designed you that way. And your places of need and struggle and mess ups don't make you less than. They give you opportunity to need Me and know Me in a deeper way. I see your brokenness right along with your child's. And it's okay. Will you come, fix your eyes on Me and find rest for your heart? When you are ready to give up, when you cannot go on anymore, when you are in the middle of impossible, will you look to Me—call to Me with your honest faith? You see, I came for those in need. Let this impossible struggle you face cause you to run to Me. To find in Me a refuge you have never known. Leave the outcome of your child's future, your family's future, your future to Me. I can be trusted. You are My beloved and I am proud of you because you are Mine.*

Tammi D. has a passion to come alongside other women and help them find freedom through deeper intimacy with Christ. Her favorite place to be is watching the sunset with her husband and six kids. She spends time as a photographer, bringing beauty to the home and heart. You can find her on Instagram as avenue17designs.tammi and online at tammidryden.com.

When God Breaks Out of the Box

My desire to adopt has always been there. I can't pinpoint a certain person or event that brought it to my mind. It has just always been part of who I was from an early age. It was simply there.

When our first biological child was about six weeks old, I heard a radio segment about international adoption. My heart was quickened, and I called and ordered some information. I poured over the pictures of waiting children. My heart was broken reading bios and I went crying to my husband asking if we can adopt. I knew nothing about costs, home studies, clearances, or trauma. I just simply knew I had to.

His short answer was "no." The longer answer included all the reasons why. Over the next few years (twelve to be exact) I would read articles on adoptions and would cry and bring them to him. He would take them from me and just give me that look. The "You are crazy, but I will humor you" look. Little did I know, he had a file he put them all in.

God was gracious to me during this time to place me in close contact with an international adoptive family of six children. Through their friendship, I learned what saying yes to adoption really meant. What brokenness, abandonment, and trauma can create in a child's heart. I slowly began to take off some rose-colored glasses and leave behind romantic notions of "rescuing" a child. Of course, you never really know until you are in it.

Greg continued to say no with the reasons of finances and honestly wondering if he could really love another child as his own. I remember standing in the kitchen crying to him, saying I knew we had another child out there and I just didn't know who he or she was or where they were. He chuckled and said he loved my passion, but he just wasn't ready.

A trip to Zambia changed all that. He felt a clear call from God to go, and while serving in a squatter's village, his heart was changed by a precious little girl, Selita. I received an email with a picture and only the words "This girl has stolen my heart." I knew then that God was working. I was more than ready!

Greg came home, and three months later we were in contact with an adoptive agency for Ethiopia. I was excited and ready to go full steam ahead. However, I put God in many boxes, which I required Him to work in. I was not traveling on my own. I'm too scared. I was not meeting any birth family. I'm too emotional. I am not adopting over age three. I'm not equipped.

God busted out of all those boxes. Every single one, and I am so glad He did. If He hadn't, I would have missed out on our first son (who was almost six when we adopted him) and a beautiful relationship with his birth family. We learned so much from his adoption and what trauma really looked like and how all our lives were changing. It took quite a while for the six of us to find our new normal and learn to be a family together.

Two years later we began the process of another adoption in Ethiopia. This time there was a much different process. The wait was longer, and the process had changed a great deal. The adoption of Kaleb is what led our hearts to begin to work in the Sidama region of Ethiopia. Without his adoption this might not have ever happened, and many lives would not have been changed. God had a greater purpose than we knew at that time.

Had we not said yes, had we not let Him bust out of our manmade boxes, we would have missed out on so much. Did we experience much heartache? Yes, and honestly, we still do. Parenting children of trauma is hard on many levels. I was somewhat prepared to bring a child home with a lot of emotional and physical "baggage." What I didn't expect was how hard it would be for me with all my own hurts, wounds, and baggage. Holding a five-year-old as he wept for his mother and his country without any way to communicate with him ripped my heart out. It also opened deep wounds in my own heart. As my husband said, "All of our U-Hauls of baggage collided." We had to learn to navigate through all of it and love each other through our own wounds and despite each other's behaviors. It's a journey we are still navigating a lot of days.

I read and devoured any article or book I could find on childhood trauma. These not only helped my relationship with my son but also with my other children and myself, and even my relations with other people. We live in a world full of wounded people. Learning to understand and recognize reactions and behaviors that result from past hurts is key to loving others.

Having another person you can call when you are frustrated and lay it all out to (and not worry about them judging your child or you) and listening to them remind you of all that helps is a tremendous comfort. Most times they are repeating back to you what you already know, but you still need reminding of it while in the height of emotions. I went to conferences on trauma and would text pictures back to my husband from slideshows saying, "This is us!" It was such a relief to hear that I wasn't imagining things and there were others in the same place. At one point, I didn't realize how much trauma a child can have from being adopted as an infant. I was seeing it and living it though and trying to make sense of it all. Having professionals and other moms validate my experience and my son's emotions gave me solidarity and strength. I learned how so many reactions are really at this point just automatic responses for them from the pain they experienced. They learned to survive and cope as small children using these responses. This helped to foster compassion in my heart even more.

Do I still make mistakes? All the time. I admit them to my sons and even try to share my own pains and hurts. We sit and talk about why I react sometimes the way I do and then why they do. It's helpful for them to see others struggling with their own pasts as well. We remind ourselves of God's grace and how each day is a new start. I remind them that they are my sons. I love them. Nothing changes that—it doesn't matter how much they misbehave or how frustrated I may get—I always love them in the midst of it.

Is there healing from the Lord? Yes. He redeems all things. But there are still some sensitive areas that get pushed on at times that still cause pain—in them and me. As we enter the teen years with one, different issues and emotions become stirred up. But we continue to press in, continue learning to love one another, and continue to heal.

Through our adoptions, God brought another purpose to our lives. While in Ethiopia for our first adoption, we visited a government orphanage. I was already emotionally raw from the previous couple of days. I stood over cribs of children with vacant expressions and wept. A man with our group told me, "Charisa, God loves these children." I responded with "It's not fair. It's not right" and continued to weep. I decided at that moment I was going to do something. Anything. I had to.

Once home, I looked for ways to help. In the beginning, it was sharing our story and the need with our circle. I then volunteered and worked with our agency organizing donations to make sure families brought over what was actually needed. It felt good to be a part of helping the children, no matter how small it was.

We then adopted Kaleb from a different region in Ethiopia. Adoptions were basically shut down in that area soon after he came home. We knew of several kids in his orphanage who were essentially "stuck" in the process. It broke our hearts thinking of the ones still there. We also knew that because agencies were pulling out of the region, funds were dwindling and there was a great need to take care of these children.

Greg and I talked about doing something and were moved to action by a Francis Chan quote: "Our greatest fear should not be of failure but of succeeding at things in life that don't really matter."

Our goal at first was just to make sure our son's "crib-mates" were taken care of. We contacted some other adoptive parents who gave to our dream through finances, prayers, and encouragement. They also funded a vision trip for us to meet with the orphanage staff to create a plan. The first thirteen children were sponsored within weeks. We then added other initiatives, and one by one they were funded, and people were put into positions to make it all happen.

Hawassa Hope was started as simply an initiative to make sure the children left at the orphanage had their most basic needs met, but it turned into something we had only dreamed of. In fact, our dreams were not even this big!

The children's home is still supported, and its main goal is now local adoption and reunification when possible. It also is a loving home to children with special needs. We have a community sponsorship program with over 200 families. We are now funding our ninth clean water project. An initiative just started supporting vulnerable women in pregnancy to ensure they and their children have every hope for life. We have funded businesses for women across the region. I am blown away with what God did with our "yes."

Directing Hawassa Hope can leave me weeping many days from heartache. It keeps me up at night concerned for our families and those we have come to love. It's not an easy path.

However, if we had not said yes, we would have missed out watching God move in the hearts of others. We would not have witnessed the miracles we have. We would not have experienced redemption, not only in others' lives but in our own.

Is it hard?

Yes. But God didn't call us to easy.

Charisa K. lives in the beautiful Shenandoah Valley with her husband, Greg. She is a mom to five children—two adopted from Ethiopia. She is a lover of grace and tries to always be ready to give an answer for the hope that she has. She is also a lover of justice, which ignites her passion to be involved in her local community and to be Executive Director for Hawassa Hope. She blogs at www.forsuchasthese.com.

24

Whole in Heaven—Hope on Earth

"How many children do you have?" A polite question and a great conversation starter. I still wonder what the best answer is. To some, I answer five. To others, six. At times I even volunteer that one of the six is already in Heaven.

John and I met in college, married after college, and dreamed of moving overseas to serve in medical missions.

After granting us three healthy babies in less than four years, God used a boy, a book, and a deployment to turn our hearts toward adoption. The boy led us to Reece's Rainbow, an advocacy site for orphans with special needs. The book led us to a specific diagnosis, one which we as medical professionals could wrap our heads around (and therefore did not cower at the prognosis, nor believe the stigma). John's deployment led us to deep and determined prayer. *God* led us to Mandy.

God is still writing our story with Mandy. She has been home for over five years, and the struggles are intense. The effects of alcohol exposure in utero have been significant. Bonding and attachment have not been ideal (an understatement); and psychological illness, cognitive compromise, and language disabilities have created a life we never would have imagined. How deeply the trauma cuts—both in her life and in the lives of her parents and siblings. The cleft palate and chronic immunodeficiency that are a part of her life, along with the associated therapies, medications, and surgeries, are nothing compared to the hurdles in her brain and soul.

When we find ourselves questioning whether we are the right family for Mandy, we remember the miracle, and submit to the One who made it possible. The miracle? As we were in route to Moscow for her official adoption in 2012, Russia closed its doors to families from the United States. God, in His mercy, allowed our case—and our case only—to be seen that week. He changed the heart of the government prosecutor who had been sent to shut our adoption down. She ended up advising the judge to approve our adoption of Mandy, and a little over a month later, we brought her home.

Mandy is a precious child of God. She was nonverbal and meek in Russia and is now loud and bold after five years in our imperfect family. She is rarely able to grasp abstract ideas, but the year after her little sister Bekah went to Heaven, she grasped the vital truth with eternal consequences—salvation. For this we are grateful. We continually ask God for His eternal perspective when considering Mandy's life and our lives now that she is our daughter. Without looking ahead to Heaven, where we will sit at His feet and *finally rest*, we would not be able to continue walking this path. We would fall on our faces and never rise.

Since Mandy came home—in the thick of the challenges, the weakness, the emotional turmoil, and the bright spots God always brings (we see them if we are looking for them), He brought two more children into our family. Bekah, our little firecracker, and Benjamin, the strong tank of a boy who has been home only about a year.

Here is our story, specifically Bekah's story, as told in journal format from my point of view. Keep in mind, Mandy had just come home in 2012.

* * *

We'll call her BJ (February 2013).

It all began with the photo of a little boy, with severe congenital heart defects, whom we called TJ. TJ's huge eyes caused our older four-year-old son to ask, "What is he looking for?" To which I answered, "A mommy and a daddy." Without missing a beat, our boy exclaimed, "We could be his family. Mommy, let's ask Daddy ... and Jesus!"

Not long after, I noticed a little girl who also had the ominous label of complex congenital heart disease (CHD). A rather exciting list of acronyms, all of which I understood and felt the weight of, followed her name. DORV. CAVC. PS. Common AV valve insufficiency. The kid was essentially living with a one-chambered heart. (My profession and one of my passions before my babies were born was caring for children with CHD as an RN.) We nicknamed her BJ. I had no idea I would ever look at this little girl's picture again.

Over the next few weeks, John and I talked and prayed. Before we got far in prayer, TJ was matched with a family in Europe. That was a nice, clear answer.

When John says he will pray, I can count on it. After days of quietly thinking and praying, he told me the only concerns he had about adopting BJ just exposed a lack of faith. Me too. Since before we met, we have dreamed of moving overseas to work among people who haven't had the chance to hear about Jesus and who don't have access to good medical care. Is this dream possible while caring for a child with a chronic disease? It didn't stop us from adopting the first time (Mandy). God made it clear He would use our obedience in adoption *now* to guide us *later*. The current health issues in our family will narrow down where we can move, but it still appears to our limited eyes that it can work.

But what about a child with chronic *cardiac* disease? Major defects that can only be modified, but never truly fixed? A little girl who perhaps may not be able to live at altitude (never mind that we live at approximately 4,500 feet)? One with so many *potential* quality of life issues? Could she be listed for transplant if her "repairs" don't "work"? Ethically, would this even be appropriate? Our minds whipped all this out as we read her medical report.

Over the years, our vision of overseas work has changed. It's not up to us. Our job is to be obedient moment by moment, and while we may have a long-term vision, we can't cling to our vision if it means disobeying now. One of the first questions asked of us when we shared the news of this second adoption was, "What about your plans to move overseas? Certainly, you wouldn't take a child with her condition ... somewhere like that? Would you?"

About this time, we watched a movie woven through with the idea of *generational vision*. "Generational vision" means our actions now set the stage for the future. What we do *now* could prime our kids for great things in God's Kingdom, things we can't even imagine. Really, once we heard this idea, we realized we had no reason *not* to step out and pursue the adoption of precious little BJ, who, at around one-and-a-half-years-old, had a bluish tint around her big black eyes, on her sweet face.

In addition, we saw a clip about Dr. Tom Little and the documentary about his life. I was struck by something Dr. Little said:

"If your life doesn't really challenge people to ask anything, then you ought to consider your life."

Every time an acquaintance shakes their head, or a friend can't conceive how we can *possibly* care for another one, a *sick* one ... we remember Tom Little's statement. We serve the same God that

Dr. Little did. He gave his life in humble service to Jesus. We want to as well.

One of our main goals as parents is to teach our children about Jesus, to provide a loving environment in which to learn to obey and serve Him, and to act as broken vessels striving to set the best example possible as imperfect parents. A huge part of this is to *make it clear to our children through our words and actions, that every person is valuable and precious in God's sight and in ours.* They will learn it is more important to care for children and live simply than to avoid welcoming orphans (because it *will* make family vacations more complicated, and it *can* get in the way of the convenience that comes once all the kids can ride bikes or swim in the lake or sit still in airplanes). They will personalize their walks with Jesus, because this life is difficult, and without Him they will not come out strong and faithful and true.

The words, "It is poverty that a child must die so that you may live as you wish," are attributed to Mother Theresa. This "poverty" isn't limited to a lifestyle that leads to the death of a child. It is the neglect of a child: the decision not to adopt or participate in some form of orphan care for the sole purpose of preserving our first-world dreams and aspirations.

What started in August 2011 as a quick glance at a boy on the other side of the world has become another huge step in our dependence on God, our reliance on His eternal perspective, and our faith that He will provide all we need ... especially emotionally.

* * *

After we committed to adopt BJ, we learned she was being cared for in China by an organization called Love Without Boundaries. Through advocacy and fundraising, this organization had raised enough money to fund a palliative cardiac surgery for BJ. This surgery was done before the orphanage knew BJ had a family coming for her, so it was done to provide her with the best quality of life for the next two to three years. It was deemed unwise to do the first of a series of repairs that would have resulted in a more permanent "fix."

Bekah Julie, "BJ," came home in December 2013. BJ had fully recovered from her surgery and got along well with oxygen saturations in the low 80s (normal is mid-to-high 90s). She forgot to read the adoption books that say she is supposed to struggle with the transition—a huge answer to prayer, as we are *still* in the thick of this with big sister Mandy. Bekah neglected the fact that low blood oxygen levels her entire life (50s and 60s before surgery) should have compromised her brain function and development. She loved her family, was terrified of dogs, and made a lasting impression on those blessed to meet her. She was known for her wit in both English and Mandarin: "I eat doctors for breakfast." "Are you kidding me? You betcha!" and "Oh, honk you, man! So much, man!" (Her way of saying, "thank you very much.")

In August 2014, Bekah was strong and relatively healthy—the best condition to be in for a heart surgery of the magnitude required to keep her alive long-term. We moved to Denver to be closer to the hospital, both for this cardiac repair, which included reversing the palliative repair done in China, and for two or three subsequent valve replacements in coming years.

We then spent three weeks sitting by her bedside in the cardiac ICU, watching as nearly everything went wrong inside her once-strong body despite interventions, machines, and an amazing medical/surgical team.

* * *

Bekah's third birthday and Bethany's gift of hope (early September 2014).

Today started with quite a few tears on the home front. We worked on cards for the birthday girl and wished we could be together as a family on Bekah's third birthday. Only four visitors were allowed in Bekah's room at a time—and no children, due to early flu precautions.

We also shared a bit about Bekah's devastating neurological injury with the kids and explained what it could mean for the future: wheelchair, tube feedings, dialysis, ventilator ... a sister who is totally, completely asleep (aka "in a coma").

Then my daughter, Bethany, got an idea, and my outlook on the *whole situation* changed.

I didn't realize while I was *responsibly* thinking through what Bekah's code status should be based on the news we had received (and her continuing unstable condition) that I was starting to drift away from future victories. Then Bethany came up with *Bekah's Watermelon Fun Run*. Yes, we're going to fight like crazy and dream big dreams for Bekah and for our family.

Bethany described this "fun run" as:

- Every year on or near Bekah's birthday
- A time for people to get together to honor Bekah and pray for Chinese orphans
- A fundraiser for Love Without Boundaries
- A place for people who can run, who have strollers, and who use wheelchairs to enjoy God's creation and have fun together
- An opportunity for little kids to play lots of games with watermelons (clearly Bekah's favorite)

What started as an event in Bekah's honor became an event in her memory.

* * *

Whole in Heaven (September 6, 2014).

Yesterday John was with Bekah at the hospital and I was with the other four kids at school. John called me during school. "Please come," he said. We were out of there in five minutes. Grandma took the kids home, and I went to John and Bekah. We agreed she had to go to the operating room to see if anything could be done, but implored the surgeon, "If it's bad ... if it's everywhere ... clean her up, give her morphine, and give her to us." Everyone so tenderly honored our requests. The caring doctors and nurses walked us through and kept her comfortable.

* * *

We have been praying for His will to be done in Bekah's life—to His greatest glory in His eternal Kingdom. Quite truthfully we have been clinging to Romans 8:26–28, not knowing how to pray, but confident that the Holy Spirit communicates for us.

Bekah had a very difficult medical course following surgery three weeks ago. She baffled intensivists and frustrated surgeons. She was in fact a very, sick, little girl from the moment she was born. Looking back on her life, we see miracles. God's loving hand allowed her to survive for over a year with an unrepaired heart. It was a miracle her orphanage advocated for her, got her to Love Without Boundaries, and provided palliative surgery for her in January 2013. Then God allowed her to come to our family, as undeserving as we were.

Truly, her ability to experience and love life—to speak two languages, to bond to her family, to crack hilarious jokes, to pray, "Dear no thank you Jesus, thank you for (long list of people who love her)," and to enjoy camping. Rarely does someone with her medical history have that kind of life. We celebrate all these incredible works of God in her life and therefore in ours.

On August 14, she went to sleep on the operating room table, smiling and asking if a fellow patient she had named "Big Guy" was feeling okay. As far as we know, she never fully regained consciousness. Her kidneys, liver, brain, and finally her intestines did not receive the blood flow they needed to maintain her earthly body.

Early this morning, September 6, God fully and faithfully answered our heartfelt pleas to care for her in His perfect way ... whatever that meant. She is whole in Heaven. According to Scripture, we receive the gift of eternal life by believing Jesus died for us (Romans 10:9). Study of the Word reveals His special love for little ones. For this reason, we know with confidence, when Bekah drew her last breath, she was welcomed as a princess of the King, who has swept her up in His arms, wiped her tears away, healed all her many, many owies into glittering crowns, and has given her eternal delight in Him.

As a tangible result of this hope, when we cuddled her this morning, we were able to say, "See you soon." Not "goodbye." When the breadth of eternity is considered, our remaining years in these broken bodies are but a moment.

* * *

Now, in 2017, we are gearing up for the third annual Bekah's Run*Walk*Roll. Hundreds of people have been impacted by Bekah's life, and God has used this event to provide nearly $50,000 for the care of other "little Bekahs" in China via Love Without Boundaries. We are humbled to know of two children who chose to believe in Jesus because of Bekah's life and death.

As for our family, we miss Bekah daily and deeply. Thinking of her brings laughter to our hearts and tears to our eyes. We share stories, tell jokes, and routinely sigh and say, "That little punk." For a while, the kids were worried about *her*. She was an orphan and had only had her family for eight months. *"She really loved us, and then she had to leave."* I explained it to them this way: "Imagine Daddy is taking Bekah to the park. She loves Daddy, she loves the park, and she is excited. She loves Mommy and her brothers and sisters too, but she is not sad to leave them because 1) she loves where she's going and who she's with, and 2) she knows the rest of us will join her soon." She is in Heaven with her Creator, whom she loves above all others, and she isn't sad about being separated from us because she knows we are coming soon to join her.

We have learned over the past five years (since our first adoption) that keeping ourselves (dad, mom, and other kids in the home) emotionally healthy is vital to keeping the family intact. This has been a greater challenge for us than the grief that flowed from Bekah's earthly death. We are still digging out of a hole of emotional turmoil, not as much from Bekah's death as from the daily challenges that come with loving our other two adopted children. We are still digging because we have pushed through the past five years without adequately evaluating how we can care for ourselves and each other. I can only pour out to others in a healthy way when my cup is full. God is so good, however, and we are grateful for all He has taught us through these adoptions.

Last year, God brought us back to the Heart Institute at Bekah's hospital. Benjamin, our sixth child, was born in China with complex CHD and has two or three more open-heart surgeries ahead of him. Someday we will sit in the same cardiac ICU, waiting for him to wake up. We pray he does—after all, he has two languages, three careers, and one special future wife in mind.

"...In paths they do not know I will guide them. I will make darkness into light before them and rugged places into plains. These are the things I will do, and I will not leave them undone" (Isa. 42:16, NASB).

Elizabeth L. is a Colorado mountain girl at heart, married to the most even-keeled man on earth. She has loved Jesus since she was eighteen and appreciates His great patience and grace with her as she cares for her five children and remembers her sixth little one in Heaven. Before having children, Elizabeth worked as an RN at three different children's hospitals, caring for children hospitalized with cardiac defects/disease, cardiac transplants, and liver transplants. Erin and her oldest daughter pour their hearts into caring for orphans via their annual memorial Bekah's Watermelon Run*Walk*Roll (bekahsrun5k.org).

The Last Two

We went into marriage knowing we might not be able to have biological children, and knowing if that was the case, we would try to adopt. So, after a couple years of marriage, and after trying some fertility procedures, we began to adopt.

This was a little complicated by the fact that we were missionaries in Europe. The country we were living in was notoriously difficult to adopt from, with long wait times even for older, waiting children. We found an American adoption agency that was willing to work with Americans living overseas, flew a social worker to our house for the home study, and were matched a couple of months later with a birth mother who was about a month away from giving birth. When she had the baby, we flew to America and picked him up (he was eight days old) and went back overseas to begin our life as a family of three.

The adoption and transition to family life went so well, we did not wait long before beginning the process to adopt again. We brought home our second son, age five months, from Cambodia, when the eldest was a few days shy of turning fifteen months old.

Again, the adoption and transition went very smoothly, and about a year later we started the process again, this time from South Africa. Our little girl's adoption took a few months, and then we were able to bring home our adorable, just-turned, one-year-old.

We adopted again, from Ghana this time, a lovely little fourteen-month-old girl. We tried to adopt from Ghana again in 2008, but that adoption fell through at the eleventh hour, after I had spent three weeks with the little girl and was just waiting for the final adoption decree.

The failed adoption was the most devastating thing that had happened in my life up to that point. We had invested a year of our hearts, prayers, and money (much of it donated) to bring her home, and then we couldn't. It took us a couple of years to recover, both financially and emotionally. And in the meantime, Ghana became much more difficult to adopt from. So, we decided to adopt one more time, from Ethiopia, and try to get a brother/sister sibling group.

This time, we thought, we could handle slightly older children. Our youngest was four years old at the time, and so we said we would take children who were under age five.

Of course, we talked about the decision with our children. The boys, now aged about ten and eleven, were eager to get another boy in the house after the last two female adoptions ("We'll play with him all the time!" they said), and the four-year-old was impatient to get a couple of playmates near her own age.

We were eventually matched with a twenty-one-month-old girl and her five-year-old brother. To be sure, the boy did look older than five (we could see from pictures that he had adult teeth in front), but he was the same size as our four-year-old and we reasoned that he probably wasn't older than six anyway.

And then the adoption process in Ethiopia got even slower. There was an official slowdown, but there were also numerous delays because of mistakes made by officials and dilatory document-producers. (For example, it took six months to obtain the birthmother's death certificate, even though she had died at the orphanage's clinic.) Our slowest adoption up to this point had been the failed one, but this one took over a year and a half *after* we had been matched. Because the previous adoption had failed, and because the process was moving so slowly, I had a hard time believing this adoption would go through. I purposely did not do much planning for the new kids, or even thinking about them, because the endless waiting might be in vain after all, and I felt like I couldn't bear another heartbreak.

All through the waiting, the children in our home were growing older. As the time finally came near for the new children to come home, the boys began to say, "What's this kid going to be like? He won't be loud or anything, will he? Or mess up our stuff?" I assured them that he wouldn't.

Of course, having been in the adoption world for twelve years at that point, I had heard of reactive attachment disorder, but I thought it was only found in children who had been neglected as babies or young children. I knew our Ethiopian children had at least attached to their birthmother. In addition, we met several families who had adopted older children from Ethiopia and elsewhere in Africa, and none of their children had had any major transition problems. I didn't anticipate any big challenges.

Finally, we got word we could go to Ethiopia for the court hearing and meet our new children. By now the boy was supposedly seven and his sister was three. They were somewhat shy and didn't speak any English, and I didn't feel a gush of love or emotion for them like I had with the others—probably because I had been protecting my heart a little too well. But that first half-hour meeting with them in an empty room at the orphanage went off all right. The next day we came back and spent another hour or so with them. We promised to come back one more day before we had to leave, but when it came time for the visit, our driver said it was too late in the afternoon and he couldn't drive us. We tried to hire a taxi or anyone else to take us, but we couldn't find anyone. I found out a couple years later that the orphanage had the children all dressed and ready to see us, but we never showed. The other kids said to ours, "Well, I guess they didn't like you and don't want you now." It was probably for that reason that the little girl, Sarah, decided that she didn't like us either. The boy, David, was just hurt and confused.

We expected to go back and pick them up in about three weeks, but due to a delayed medical test no one had told us about, it was four months before we could bring them home. This time, I went alone and my husband stayed with the other children.

I have often been glad no one filmed that meeting when I showed up at the orphanage as the children's official new mother. Sarah took one look at me and started screaming. She ran away and would not let me touch her at all. David was standing there rigidly; he allowed me to hug him but made no move to hug me back. We couldn't leave the orphanage right away; I had to go to the clinic with them and get their medicines and instructions. I chatted with one of the orphanage workers while I waited. "So, you're adopting her?" he said, pointing to Sarah. "She has a very strong personality. She's always bossing the bigger kids around— telling them what to do."

While we were waiting, Sarah was surrounded by people she knew, and she played with them and calmed down. But when it came time to leave, she kicked and screamed and tried to get out of the car. Thank goodness she knew and loved her brother, because she allowed him to hold her and talk to her (in Amharic, of course), and eventually she stopped crying. However, for the rest of the week in Ethiopia, she really wanted nothing to do with me.

David was helpful, polite, and sweet. We couldn't communicate much, but I was so very thankful for his help with Sarah. I figured that after about a week, we would all be recovered from our adventure and we could go back to our regular homeschooling routine with all six children.

And then the storm broke.

I had been right: the children did not have reactive attachment disorder. What they did have was trauma—the trauma of being taken out of the orphanage environment (the only place Sarah could remember) and thrust into a life with people they couldn't understand, food they disliked, totally new smells, animals that were new (Sarah was absolutely terrified of our cats), and not a single thing, besides each other, that was familiar. And they didn't even know each other all that well; they had been at the same orphanage but had slept and eaten and spent their days in different parts of the complex, so they had only seen each other for an hour or so each day. They lost their language; with no one to speak Amharic to except each other, and surrounded by English, they quickly forgot the language they had always spoken. Of course, they (and especially David) did not become *fluent* in English for a long, long time. So, there were many months when he was essentially without a language, even for his own thoughts.

It is not surprising, then, that David would have tantrums. Loud, long tantrums. He threw things, he screamed, he kicked. He ran out the door and down the road. He used whatever English words he knew to try to hurt me. He called me all kinds of things in Amharic. He told lies. We never knew what would set him off. He ruined Christmas Day by happily opening all his presents, and then throwing a fit so huge that I spent hours in a bedroom trying to deal with him while the rest of the family finally ate Christmas dinner without us. We figured out he was probably at least two years older than we had been told, although we never pursued finding out exactly how old he was. He certainly was mentally and emotionally about age seven when he came home.

Sarah had decided, after a couple weeks with us, that I was all right. So all right, in fact, she wasn't going to lose me the way she had lost everything else. Which meant I could not be out of her sight at any time, including the middle of the night. Getting her to fall asleep alone in her bed was impossible. It took me about an hour every night, holding her hand and singing to her, for her to fall asleep (and then the neat trick of removing my hand from hers without waking her up!). I had never done that for any of my other children—I popped them into bed with a cheery "goodnight" and they drifted off to sleep.

After I got Sarah to sleep, I had to get David to sleep. Even though he was older than she, I had to sit or lay down beside him for him to be able to fall asleep. Sometimes he didn't sleep until eleven or so.

And after they were both in bed, I spent time with my older children, who were aghast at the change to our lovely little family. They resented these foreign, odd-smelling, tantrum-throwing newcomers who were hurting their mother and wrecking stuff. It wasn't anything like what they had bargained for. They also were forced to think about adoption, and particularly their own adoptions—something they hadn't really thought much about before, since they had been so young when they came home. It stirred up all kinds of feelings within them.

Finally, I would go to bed myself, only to be awakened by Sarah an hour or two later, who would cry for me until I came. If I managed to get her back to sleep and then returned to my own bed, she would wake up an hour later and do the same thing. She had a toddler bed, which was too small for me to share with her, so eventually I just began sleeping the rest of the night on the floor. I was exhausted.

And the orphanage worker who said that Sarah had a very strong personality? He wasn't kidding. She desired dictatorship. Thank heavens no one was inclined to obey her, because it would have only reinforced the behavior. As it was, everyone ignored her commands, which frustrated her enormously and usually resulted in wails and tears.

There were glimmers of hope through all of this. When he wasn't having a tantrum, David was a sweet kid. He was generous and helpful, and asked a lot of questions about spiritual things. When he did run away, he would make sure I was following him, and he always said he was sorry after a tantrum.

Then there was what I was learning. Someone wrote to me just before we brought them home and said, "I pray that those children understand how very deeply they are loved. All the work, grief, frustration, exhaustion, and expense that you have endured to bring them home. It is a beautiful illustration of your love for them." And after they came home, the thought also came to me: "I hope someday they appreciate all we have gone through for them."

But as time went on, I understood. They won't get it. I know they won't. They might get to the point where they acknowledge that bringing them into our family was difficult, and they may even be grateful we made the sacrifice. But there is no way they will be able to comprehend just how hard it has been.

And I am thankful for this fact, because it gives me a tiny glimpse into God's love for me. Just like my children, I did not "deserve" to be adopted into His family (I had done nothing to earn His favor). He has given me so much—physical, tangible blessings galore, not to mention the spiritual, eternal blessings that far outweigh them—and I am often patently ungrateful for them. Like my son who looked at all the things he had been given (he used to have *nothing*) and then whined because he didn't have the same McDonald's toy as his sister, I look at other people's lives and whine when they have something I don't have.

Just like my son's lack of English and knowledge made him misperceive situations and get angry over what he thought was an injustice to himself (*you're lucky* was heard as *you're yucky*), I get frustrated when I don't understand God's ways and think He is being unfair to me.

It cost us a lot to bring these children home; it cost money, stress, time, effort, and frustration. Some days I felt like it cost me my mental health. It cost God far more to bring me home: His Son. I cannot fathom—really, I have no idea—what that felt like. And the price Jesus paid to redeem me was so high that no human could ever have paid for it. Not only do I not comprehend it, I forget to be grateful for it. And now I know what God feels like. Just a little bit.

The children have been home now for four and a half years. David's tantrums gradually grew fewer and farther between. At first, he had one nearly every day. Then a few times a week. Then once a week, once every other week, once a month … and so on. His last tantrum was over a year and a half ago. He barely remembers being so angry and can't understand why he acted that way.

Sarah finally learned to go to sleep on her own, after about six months. She stopped waking up at night and crying after Daddy became the one to go to her. Evidently, he wasn't worth waking up for, in her opinion, because she stopped doing it. She still has a strong personality, and we found out in the past year that she has learning difficulties that probably contribute to her frustration. We are working on the character issues, as well as the neurodevelopmental issues, but she is an energetic and usually happy child.

All is not roses, of course; some of the older children still struggle with resentment toward David, for how he disrupted their lives so unexpectedly, and with Sarah for being so noisy and easily angered. They are beginning to grapple with their own attitudes and issues, and I am thankful that these circumstances have allowed them to see what is going on in their own hearts. I pray continually that they will all learn to love all their siblings, no matter what the history between them is.

When people talk about adopting as taking a leap of faith, they usually think of the initial process of bringing the child home. I always thought the most difficult part was the months leading up to finally being able to put the child to bed in our home. I have since learned, however, that whatever leap of faith started the journey, it is the walk of faith that sustains you through the rest of the adventure. I have been humbled by my own weakness and amazed at the grace and power of God. The story of our family is not really a story about our family; it is the story of how God uses circumstances and people and all kinds of things in order to show His greatness and His character. We do not know everything God is doing, or will do in and through our lives, or in our children's lives, but we are privileged to be able to see even a part of it now. For the rest, we will wait till eternity.

Barbara C. is a missionary wife and homeschooling mom to six adopted children. Her hobbies are writing, reading, cooking, and answering questions like "So, where do your children come from?" She and her family live in Ireland, surrounded by medieval castles, picturesque flocks of sheep, and ancient stone monuments. These things are unappreciated by her children, who are more impressed by traffic jams, skyscrapers, and hot weather. Barbara is the author of Wisdom from Proverbs: Devotions for Homeschooling Moms, and Ned: Barnardo Boy (children's historical fiction about international adoption).

Blessings in the Midst of Chaos

My husband and I were married sixteen years before we decided to go into foster care. We lost our first son when I was twenty-nine weeks pregnant. Three years later, after another complicated pregnancy, I gave birth to our son Seth. He was born with a heart defect, which required open heart surgery when he was two. I became pregnant again and gave birth to our daughter Diana. When she was nine months old, I had my first of two major surgeries. We went through some real tough trials in the first five years of our parenting journey. There was undeniable chaos at times. We experienced a great loss and had many fears. Thanks to God, we had the ability to find joy in our hard moments. The blessings throughout our parenting journey has continued to outweigh the chaos.

It came completely natural for us to do foster care. We simply wanted to make a difference in the lives of children in our community. We knew our lives would be changed by the many children who entered our home and our hearts. What we didn't know was God's plan was much different than our own.

Parenting is difficult no matter what. There will be many blessings mixed within the chaos of life as you are raising your children. While raising adopted children from the foster care system, the chaos you experience will be a whole different kind. It may even leave you at times searching for that blessing. Don't stop looking. The blessing is there. Look for it amid your fears, through every struggle and in your darkest hours. And if you need to, pray for your blessing to be revealed, because it could become lost in all the chaos.

It is my sincere desire that as you read our adoption stories you receive a renewed sense of hope in your own. Hope is a gift freely given through the grace of our Lord and Savior. There is hope for every one of God's children. I pray you can cling to that throughout your journey. I believe it is the key to all successful adoptions. You need to believe and trust that "in all things God works for the good of those who love him, who have been called according to his purpose" (Rom. 8:28, NIV). It is a special calling to adopt. I am pretty confident you'll have moments when you will be questioning this calling and your ability to continue. But guess what? That's okay. He doesn't promise any kind of parenting will be easy. But He does give us encouragement in His Word. So, cling to His Word often and remind yourself in times of trouble that He will guide you in parenting your children, if you allow Him.

In every storm, remember why you chose to adopt. Embrace your journey and let God work. God can bring peace in the hard times and clear away your doubts. Learn to trust Him in all of it. There is no question your adoption journey will strengthen your walk with the Lord. I pray you will seek the Lord for His wisdom, as you parent your precious gift.

My husband Kent and I have three adoption stories and each of them is unique. In an eleven-year-period, we have been given the sacred privilege of fostering over twenty-five children.

These children share many of the same attributes. All have come to us afraid, experiencing separation and loss. They have each exhibited trust issues and have each had some form of specific need. In addition, each child was in the midst of some type of hurdle (big or small), or would be in the times ahead. All of them have needed help to heal emotionally. Some children have required us to seek additional resources to parent them adequately. It is certain, they've all needed a safe and loving home.

* * *

Ryan

Ryan was our first placement call. When I answered the phone, it was immediately different than what I had expected. This child would not be able to return home and would be available for adoption. We knew immediately, God was in all of it.

We felt pretty confident about fostering prior to that first call. Our confidence was shaken several times in the years to follow. Our plans initially were to help one child at a time and work towards reunification with their parents. But, God's plan for us is often different than our own.

My mind was racing even more than my heart on the drive to Social Services to meet Ryan for the first time. We were casually introduced. He was two years old and sat on the floor of a quiet room. He held onto a small toy and looked up to see who had entered the room. No matter how I have tried, I cannot find the words to describe how I felt when I looked at his sweet, expressionless face and our eyes locked for the first time. I instantly experienced something within me. It was as if God birthed him deeply into my heart. I longed to hold him close and never let him go. I knew then, without a bit of uncertainty, God was giving us another one of His precious gifts. God has reminded me of that moment many times in the midst of life's chaos.

We took Ryan home and began our first adoption journey. The circumstances around his removal were horrific and hard to grasp. He was frail, did not speak, emotionless, under-nourished, and labeled a "failure to thrive" child. We made a conscious decision to not see the obvious. We chose to see a content fighter, a valued and cherished child of God.

Ryan was terrified of water, loud noises, and bright lights. He also became over stimulated very easily. He would overeat because he hadn't learned what it felt like to have a full belly. This would often make him sick. Yet, he was happy, loving, and such a carefree little guy. We utilized all available resources to help him catch up with so much that he had lost prior to his removal. A speech therapist came into our home three times a week and worked with his speech and communication. He only had the ability to make one sound. They taught us how to communicate with him through sign language to meet his needs and continue to grow his vocabulary.

One of my sweetest memories is waking up in the early morning and hearing him cooing and babbling for the first time from his crib at two and a half. I didn't want to disturb him, so I lay in my bed and listened. Then, I heard him repeating "Ma-ma." I laid there and listened to that precious word over and over again. I cried, and I prayed. In that very moment, God revealed to me that, no matter what amount of chaos was ahead, there would be many additional blessings to follow.

Ryan overcame hurdles fast. We set goals for him with the help of a team and worked together to meet his needs. It was a group effort. It was time consuming and difficult, but our efforts were not in vain.

His adoption story did not include visitations with the biological parents at any time throughout the process. Termination of rights came somewhat quickly and the court hearings moved along smoothly. This is not always normal for the adoption process through Social Services. We later learned how easy this adoption was, after we experienced the great turmoil, hurt, and loss that came with our next.

With Ryan's adoption came a lot of "firsts" with working alongside Social Services. It was very difficult at times to navigate through all the guidelines that are in place for foster care children. Learning about Medicaid, finding specific doctors, and not having any family medical history were hard things to manage at times. For the first few years, Social Services supplied us with WIC checks (used for basic food items at the grocery store), and using these checks caused some embarrassing moments for me at the checkout. Living in a small town where I thought he would be snatched up or confronted by a biological family member kept me fearful at times. Having only approved persons allowed to care for him when we needed childcare was a bit chaotic. We are grateful for a dear friend of ours who became approved and provided wonderful childcare for Ryan and other children who came into our home through foster care.

With each new challenge we faced, a parenting one, or some legality, we continued to pray for His wisdom and guidance. We prayed even harder when some harder "firsts" started happening. Court hearings were always challenging. Meeting his biological mother and then later meeting his biological father each brought on different emotions. We hadn't prepared ourselves for the feelings that came along with any of these moments. We also had a harder time finding the blessings in some of them.

My heart literally ached for his mother who was unable to care for him. I had a deep compassion for her, because she was unable to mentally grasp what was taking place with her son. Meeting her helped bring some closure to my mind, but my heart took much longer to heal. We are forever grateful she gave birth and chose life, and to God for later entrusting him to us.

We have had lots of questions asked about "his story." We have always tried to give appropriate answers that would not hurt Ryan. I have made the mistake with sharing too much before and realized quickly that the details just do not matter. So, the details are only given when it is evident that they will somehow help him. His story is just that, his.

Some of the fears we had along the way came and went until his adoption was final. It was only ten months after his removal when his name was changed to ours. Today, at the age of thirteen he is does extremely well. He makes friends easily and carries himself in a calm manner. He is pleasant, compassionate, and helpful. He has a love for the Lord and is active in his youth group. He loves football, cross-country, and music, and often makes us laugh and smile. The blessings are everywhere with him around.

* * *

Ella

Our fourth gift. Two months after Ryan's adoption was final, we received a call to foster a sibling group of three girls. The girls were two, four, and nine years old. From the day they arrived in our home, until the day Ella's adoption was final, nearly two and a half years later, it was a whirlwind of chaos. There were days I felt alone, misunderstood, and even misguided by Social Services. Being a parent to six kids with three of them having additional special needs was emotionally draining. I reminded myself often why we chose to go into foster care to give me the boost I needed to continue.

On top of meeting their specific needs, there was a significant amount of additional appointments, meetings, therapy sessions, and court hearings. I am convinced we could not have done it without the grace of God and through His strength. I spent lots of nights cradling the children and praying over them. I also spent many nights on my knees praying that the Lord would speak to the hearts of those making decisions on their behalf.

There were circumstances with their case that caused the department havoc in trying to move forward with the best resolution for them. The hardest part about the proceedings taking so long was the fact that the girls were court-ordered to have visitations with their biological parents during the entire time of waiting. Visitations lasted almost two and a half years. This was a traumatic time for all of us. Having these visitations only prolonged the girls' healing process. With every visit came new pain, anxiety, and frustration, and a few destructive behaviors. It continued to cause them additional hurt and loss. It broke my heart repeatedly as they begged not to go each time. I sat on the side of the highway many times before or after their visits dealing with sick stomachs and throw up. Their nerves were shot and so were mine.

The visits began supervised and then briefly moved to unsupervised. Then the decision was made to see if the parents were capable of an overnight with them. This was their last opportunity to see if they could follow basic rules mandated by the court while the children were in their care. This decision concluded that the parents were not able to follow the basic perimeters set for them. Shortly after, termination of their parental rights finally occurred. Visitations remained for a short period of time after and then stopped forever. The healing began.

I would love to say that when the parental rights were terminated we were relieved and had peace. This would be far from the truth. We were extremely torn and frustrated with the decisions the social workers, therapist, lawyers, and judge were making regarding what they felt was in the best interest of the girls. We had discussed adopting all three girls if their case ended in adoption. However, the court ruled it was in their best "individual interest" to be separated. At the time, we just couldn't wrap our heads, or our hearts, around that decision. It's awful hard to trust God when you are experiencing great pain.

Each of the girls had significant needs and they each went through a long process of testing and assessments. Ella's sister, I will call "the middle child," had the least of all issues and seemed to adjust the best in most situations. She had a beautiful carefree spirit and a funny sense of humor and loved people. It didn't take us long to see that she didn't have any attachment disorders that would prevent her from doing well in a forever home without her siblings.

The middle child's transition started first. We had no idea then how beautiful her transition would be for all of us today. She was adopted by our close friends. This helped in some ways, but emotionally it was still very difficult. It was complicated and full of chaos at times. But over the years, we have been reminded of God's faithfulness often. There really are wonderful blessings that can come out of our greatest pains.

We didn't try to understand God's plan in separating the girls, we just chose to fully put our trust in Him. We couldn't see how our hearts would ever mend. And it wasn't our hearts that were our focus. We thought that the loss the girls were going to encounter would be too much for them to heal from. But our God is still in the healing business and He was working in all of it. He has proven to us repeatedly that He is in control.

We didn't understand just how precious it was when she chose to refer to us as "Aunt Sue and Uncle Kent" when she transitioned out. She has remained a beautiful piece of our life who has given us great joy. We loved her for less than a year in our home and we've continued loving her for another nine years. We will always love her. We have continued to experience the goodness of God, as the years have unfolded. The two sisters see each other almost weekly, attend the same church, have sleepovers and spend holidays and special events together.

Ella's oldest sister was diagnosed with several disorders and had many struggles. Because of the environment she was raised in, and the guilt and confusion it gave her, she suffered from ambivalent-attachment. This caused her to remain more attached to her parents than to anyone else. Her attachment disorder gave her a feeling of obligation to her parents even though she had been neglected by them. The court determined that the parents could provide care for one but not all.

We knew how difficult this transition was going to be when we learned this time we would be transitioning a child for reunification with her parents. The unknowns to how this was going to work kept me up at night. At times, it made me question everything about the system we supported. But, it was up to us to make the best of every moment we had with her. We made a conscious effort to plant seeds and to give her lifetime experiences she would never forget. We poured into her as much of God's Word as possible and taught her that she was a child of God. We wanted her to know that her parents and others may fail her, but God would never fail her. She accepted Christ while in our home. She was active in church and in kids' choir and she loved every minute with our extended family.

God's strength alone was the only way we were able to make her transition happen as it did. It was nineteen months after entering our home when Kent and I took her to be reunified with her biological parents. We unpacked her things in their small apartment and helped her set up her room. We prayed over the family in their living room before we left. The thirty-minute drive home was one of the hardest drives we have ever had to take together. No words were needed. Our hearts were connected. Instead of sharing words, we shared tears. They continued to fall as our hearts healed. We still pray for her today. We pray the seeds we have planted continue to be watered.

Ella was the youngest and the frailest. Although she was two years old, she only weighed seventeen lbs. and wore size nine-month clothing. She had already had her tonsils and adenoids removed and had suffered from a bowel blockage. She was so tiny it scared me to hold her too tightly. She did not speak when she came. Most of her basic needs were quickly met by her oldest sister who had been her primary caretaker.

We didn't sleep much because she didn't know how to stay asleep. She never learned to self-comfort as an infant. We tried all kinds of techniques to help her to sleep all night and to teach her how to comfort herself when she woke up. It has been an ongoing hurdle for many years. In the chaos of so many sleepless nights, I was somehow able to still find the blessing. I was reminded often of how precious it was that God had chosen us to be the ones to bring Ella comfort. The magnitude of that blessing has always stuck with me. After all, God is our comfort. We know we can go to Him any time and He will be there to bring us the comfort we desire from Him. Ella relied on Kent and me for that same type of comfort. God gave us strength with very little sleep to comfort her during the night for many years. I don't know how we functioned on some days. Somehow God gave both Kent and me the energy needed to continue to meet not only Ella's needs, but all our children's needs and to continue in our ministries. He has continued to amaze us. We thank Him often for His goodness and we give Him all the glory for what He does through us.

One of Ella's biggest struggles has been her speech. She has an impairment that causes her to stammer and stutter often. Her speech therapy started when she was two years old, and she is still in it today. She continues to hold onto the hope of a complete healing. She has such a positive attitude despite the social impact it has made in most areas of her life. She connects best with those who are patient with her. She overcame a slight hearing impairment after having four sets of tubes in her ears.

She has always been a helpful, kind-spirited child who likes to make people happy. She has spent several years in and out of therapy to help her with anxiety, separation, and loss. Her beautiful heart is full of forgiveness and love. It has helped her to move out of her past and step into the future God has for her. She wants to be a pediatrician or work with children someday. With her ability to persevere, her positive attitude and the way she relies on God in all things, I can see her doing just that someday.

Adoption doesn't solve all the problems or hurts a child has encountered from his or her circumstances. Adoption does give a child hope. It gives them a sense of value and it helps them move forward in the healing process.

Adoption can make your heart ache and your head spin, and it can turn things in your family upside down for a while. But the blessings do outweigh the chaos. They even manage to outweigh every struggle and disappointment too. Remember you are not alone in this endeavor. There are many others who have been or are in the trenches with you. And God will never leave your side. Even when you think you are failing and do not see Him working, remember He is always working on your behalf. So, keep keeping on despite the chaos you may endure and love fiercely as He loves you.

* * *

James

James was fifteen when we discovered him and learned he had been searching for a forever home. He had given his life to the Lord at a camp he attended. Not only did he know he needed a Christian home, but he also wanted someone who would allow him to continue a relationship with his sick grandmother. He also wished to stay in the school he was attending. It would be the first time he finished school where he had started. When God brought us together, He worked out the details for him to get his heart's desire. He was able to spend time with his grandmother before she passed away. I petitioned the city school board to allow him to stay in the school where he had started even though we were out of the city limits. And he got his Christian home.

James's initial removal occurred as an infant. He was placed with another family member before being removed again and entering the foster care system where he endured several placements and two failed adoptions. It was a terrible repeated loss that James had to go through. And it caused him, as it would anyone, great pain. He was later placed in a group home in the community in which we lived.

How we met him was almost as unique as James is. I was helping in a local Heart Gallery. The Heart Gallery is an event held to showcase the many teens who have already had parental rights terminated and are available for adoption. Their pictures were hung around the gallery and their displays included a short written biography. I went to help staff the event and my heart was immediately drawn to James's picture and his biography. I became emotional and questioned why on earth God was tugging on my heart to know more about him. I called Kent and asked him to come to the event. I never said a word about James. He began to move around the room reading all the teens' biographies. When he got to James's, he stopped and stood in the same place I did. He even had the same type of reaction as I'd had. He walked out of the event with a heavy heart for him.

Printouts were made of all the teens who were represented at the Heart Gallery, and I took one home. That evening we spoke to Seth (now seventeen) and Diana (fifteen) about the possibility of giving a teen a forever home. We never told them how our hearts were drawn to James. We asked them both to pray about it and to let us know if the Lord laid anyone on their hearts. They both wanted to learn more about James.

We knew James had dealt with lots of separation and loss. We also knew he had a verbal processing disorder that can prevent him from understanding things correctly or be able to repeat things accurately. We later learned he adapts well to change because he has had to live in so many different scenarios. If he doesn't think he will fit in, he tends to change so he doesn't stand out. He is fun to be around, friendly, and liked by everyone.

Our family enjoyed our first meeting with him. He was shy and apprehensive, but that was expected. We experienced a few more times together in our home shortly after our first visit. I then got an approval from his social worker and the group home where he lived and began to pick him up on Wednesday nights for youth group. We were building a relationship and slowly moving forward without knowing exactly how God was going to work.

After several great visits over the next couple of months, James became terrified and withdrew all contact. We were all thinking he would be spending his upcoming birthday with us or at least Christmas. Two months slowly crept by with no contact from him. It was hard to not take it personally. I knew it was something greater that was keeping him from what he was longing for. We knew he was full of fear—fear of rejection and fear of disappointment again. We prayed for God to take all his fear away.

Christmas and the New Year passed, and one day James's social worker called. She said, "I have someone with me who wants to know if he can have a second chance." She asked if she could bring him over to the house. Of course, he was invited into our home with open arms. We promised him on that day we would never leave him.

He transitioned into our home, and the very next day Kent was able to share in a wonderful blessing. He baptized James at our church surrounded by our church family and friends. James had shared with us that he wanted to do it right away.

It was a different kind of transition than our other adoptions. We all accepted the differences in moving forward, and it was an understandably difficult time. He was in therapy to help with his transitioning. I ended up going to sessions with him. We tried to work out some of the hurts he had experienced in his past from the "mother figures" in his life who had failed him. We worked hard on building a relationship. We both agreed to accept what would be "our normal," and we worked on moving forward. We knew we both had love for one another and we both agreed it was difficult. How I mothered him didn't always function well. The difficulties with a lot of those things were not his fault.

Not having James at an early age came with different kinds of challenges than with our other adoptions. Teaching him simple things about belonging in a family came with some trials. He is a survivor and has amazing determination. He lived a life of surviving day to day through his loss and pain. It has been a beautiful thing to watch as he has allowed the Lord to heal things from his past and work in his life. He may not always make the best decisions, but he is continuously learning. He does know God is with him always and he trusts Him.

James moved into our home with less than perfect grades. He had no desire to do school work. It took months of consistency, a few nights a week at a learning enrichment center, and lots of frustrated times completing homework before bed, before he began to see the fruits of his labor. As he became more organized and allowed us to parent him, he began to improve his grades rapidly. He ended his senior year in high school with all A's. He was the first in his biological family to graduate and take college classes.

We tried to fill James with as many experiences as our other children had, so that we could all have a common ground for conversations and memories. He went to Disneyland to celebrate his adoption becoming final, and he spent two weeks in Michigan with my parents and my brother's family to help with extended family bonding. He has attended youth camps, youth retreats, concerts, beach trips, college for the weekends, and many other things that have given him some wonderful things to hold onto.

He has always struggled with asking advice, seeking our counsel, and wanting guidance in decision-making. He hadn't had that luxury for fifteen years. He recognizes the gift he was given by having parents, but it remains difficult for him to rely on us. When he graduated, it became harder for him to understand there were still rules and consequences to his actions in our home. He didn't believe we were making decisions that were in his best interest. This can be difficult for any young adult to grasp. But for him, it was even more difficult to grasp, and for a while he placed a wedge between us. He acknowledges us as his parents but doesn't always allow us to have a parental role in his life. With God's grace and timing, that wedge will be completely removed one day. If not, we will continue as we are, loving him unconditionally and being there for him.

Everyone loves James and enjoys his company. But no one really knows him like we do. He has such a kind soul and a heart of gold. Others see those things and his silly sense of humor and things seem okay. We see all those wonderful things about him too. We also have embraced a hurt boy trying to overcome so much that has occurred in his life. He tends to be guarded and rightfully so. His fear of failing us and others tends to create secrets and sometimes lies. These things are truly not intentional, and we have worked through many of them by today.

He knew how to hurt me the most with his words and with his actions. He will tell you today, it wasn't really me that he was taking his anger out on. I knew that all along. I loved him through the tough times, just as much as I do the fun times. I forgave him long ago for not knowing how to express his love for me. I have prayed he would forgive me for not knowing how to help him or respond to him in those hard times. Kent has been able connect with him much better than I have. They have bonded differently, and I have always tried to find the answers on what to do, or not to do, to better our relationship. We continue to accept our love the way it is. It gives me great joy to talk with him and to have him near us.

James moved out and sought out some of his biological family when he was a freshman in college. Things didn't unfold the way we thought they would. We have felt hurt, confusion, and sadness. When we walk away from God, He never leaves us. He waits patiently, waiting for our return. We try to love James like God loves us. So, patiently we waited.

James moved back home after a year of wandering. The time away was hard on him and has caused him to see life differently again. I wish I could have spared him from experiencing more pain. All along, we knew in our hearts he would return. We accepted there were things James had to learn and to figure out on his own. We are thankful for the Lord's protection while he was away. Today, he is working hard to be responsible and is cherishing the moments with his family. We will always be here for him in whatever capacity he is able to allow. God never stops working on our behalf. He continuously mends and works on all our hearts. He has always proven faithful.

Parents never stop parenting. They never stop learning and growing either. I couldn't have written this without embracing the uniqueness of our family's dynamics. It is important to teach your children to embrace their stories. Always be open and honest with your adoptive children regarding their past. Answer questions that are age appropriate for them to understand. Remind them we all have stories God can use to help others and to bring Him glory.

I discussed the decision of writing this chapter with the kids, and they each agreed their stories could be shared with you. They too wanted to help other adoptive parents and encourage them on their journeys. To me, this was just another blessing. Our lives will always have some chaos. But we can all learn to find the blessing in the midst of it all.

Susan W. belongs to Jesus Christ. She married Kent twenty-eight years ago. He is a Care Pastor through the Church of God and she serves others alongside him. She is a mother to five beautiful gifts, a mother-in-law to two special people, and a Mimi to one little princess. She has been living out her passion as a foster/adopt parent for twelve years, and trained, recruited and mentored many others through her local Department of Social Services. She has led a small group for women who share her passion for hurting children for nine years. She supports and works with Royal Family Kids Camp (a camp for children in foster care). She loves to laugh often. Most importantly, she is extremely thankful every day for God's Amazing Grace. She writes often at www.truthloveservice.com and at www.facebook.com/FosterAdoptParentsSharingCaring/.

27

Lessons I Learned as an Adopted Daughter

"God plucked you out of that orphanage for a reason, Sasha."

I remember my dad telling me this, from the time I was a little girl with pigtails, round-rimmed glasses, and thin legs in orthopedic braces. Today, I am a junior at Bucknell University, where I double major in Creative Writing and Russian Studies with academic honors.

I was seventeen months old when I came home from Ulyanovsk, Russia. My parents thought they were adopting a healthy baby girl. However, I have a mild form of cerebral palsy. This is a brain injury that can have a wide range of effects on a child's walking and motor development. In my case, it affected the right side of my body. I had to wear leg braces and have eye surgery.

Doctors in Russia and the United States told my parents I would never walk and would always need special-needs classes in school. Today, unless you know me well, my CP isn't noticeable. My CP also did not affect my cognitive development at all. In fact, I started speaking complete sentences in English just two weeks after coming home. Countless times, I have heard the story of the day my mom stood in court, telling the Russian judge, "I will pour my life into her." That is exactly what she did. Little did my parents know where one orphan from Russia would lead the rest of their lives.

Today, I am the oldest of six sisters, soon to be eight. It was my adoption in 1998 that opened my parents' hearts to special-needs adoption. After me, there was Angela from Taiwan, who has cerebral palsy and epilepsy, and who is profoundly deaf with a cochlear implant. She may not walk, but she can do handstands and swing on the bars in her gymnastics class. Then there is Grace from the Philippines. When we were in Manilla with her, she had a urinary catheter as a feeding tube, club feet, cerebral palsy, and scoliosis. She also has the thickest, bounciest black curls! In 2012, we brought home my sister Violeta from Bulgaria. When she came home in June, she weighed twelve pounds at five and a half years old. Today, she is almost walking by herself.

Next come my two sisters from Ukraine. We traveled to Kyiv in 2014 amidst the Maidan protests. Victoria has a mild form of spina bifida and severe failure to thrive. At nine and a half, she was the size of a six-month-old infant with large eyes the color of a puddle after fresh rain. Anna, now affectionately known as Stretch after she grew fifteen inches in two years after coming home, has severe brain injury. Finally, most recently, my mom and I traveled to China to bring home my teenage sister, Abigail, only hours before she would have aged out of the system and become unadoptable. She has a moderate form of cerebral palsy, which affects her limbs and speech. Abigail is super smart—she can speak and read a King James Bible in Chinese and she understands almost everything you say in English. Her hearty laugh and grin are infectious.

My background is central to who I am, as an adopted child and as a young Christian woman. I believe my parents have taught me differently than most adoptive parents. I want to share a few of the most important lessons I have learned.

Don't Read All the Books

If my mom had read all the books and advice about fetal

alcohol syndrome and the physical and emotional issues that come along with it, I would not be where I am today. If she had believed the doctors who insisted I would never walk, then chances are, I wouldn't be walking. There is a line in the Christian film *Facing the Giants* that says, "Your actions will always follow your beliefs."

If my parents had believed I would never walk, they would not have pushed me, day after day. I would have been content with wearing braces or using a wheelchair because I would have been raised to believe that is all I could achieve.

Today I can recall the hours of frustration every day when my parents would follow my every step saying "Sasha, put your foot down. Put your foot down. Heel toe. Put your foot down." I remember crying over the fact that I struggled to read an analog clock and didn't understand the multiplication table in the third grade, when it seemed all my friends were getting it. My parents kept pushing me, through all the tears and attitude. They saw me as the honors student I am today, even when others shook their heads.

I strongly encourage you—don't let the words that come along with adoption frighten you. Post-traumatic stress disorder. Reactive attachment disorder. Fetal alcohol syndrome. Aging out teenager. God's Word tells us we were not given a "spirit of fear and timidity, but of power, love, and self-discipline" (2 Tim. 1:7, NLT). Fear is not from the Lord. It is a tool from the enemy to keep us from carrying out what God's Word so clearly instructs: "to look after orphans and widows in their distress and to keep oneself from being polluted by the world" (Jas. 1:27, NIV).

As I write this, my sister Grace comes to mind. She has spastic quadriplegia, scoliosis, and severe brain injuries. She looks so fragile that many people are afraid to hold her. If my parents had let this scare them away, they would never have known what a sweet smile or a deep belly giggle Grace has to offer. Most importantly, Grace's adoption from the Philippines was the start of my family's non-profit organization Ting Ministries.[10] Starting with simply providing formula to Grace's orphanage, today Ting Ministries sponsors families and pastors in multiple countries.

Thirty-four Filipino street children and counting have found a home with a local pastor because of Grace. Ting Ministries also sponsors aunties for the special-needs children in her orphanage, along with Vacation Bible School, clothing outreaches, and more in a predominantly Muslim tribal region. Grace's story is proof of what the Lord can do, if we trust Him and do not give into fear or the discouragement from others.

The Sacrifice of Adoption

People often ask what it is like to have six younger sisters with special-needs. I would not change a thing about my family. There are days when it is hard. Orphan care is not picture perfect. Providing 24/7 care to children who can give nothing back is very challenging. Parenting kids with the baggage of sixteen years in an orphanage is not something adoptive families do for "fun" or "just because we want to."

It is a command.

James 1:27. Psalm 68:5–6. Proverbs 31:8–9. The Bible makes it clear Christians are to care for the orphan. Nineteen years ago, my parents made the decision to bring me home from Russia and pour their lives into their new daughter. It's one thing to talk about sacrifice. It's another to live it, day in and day out. Yet when Christ called His disciples, He said "Whoever wants to be my disciple must deny themselves and take up their cross and follow me"

---

[10] Ting Ministries is a non-profit 501(c)3 organization that provides help to aging-out and special-needs orphans and that supports adoptive families around the world. Ting Ministries is on Facebook, Instagram, and Twitter and at www.tingministries.com.

(Mark 8:34, NIV).

Caring for the *least of these* means carrying the Cross with you every single day. If you have to carry the Cross with you, that means other things in your life have to be moved ... or left behind. Maybe we don't want to make that uncomfortable commitment.

This is a hard realization. Are we okay if the children we pour our lives into never achieve anything in the eyes of the world? If the daughter you love never calls you "Mom" or appears to love you back? It is easy to fall into discouragement. To blame God for giving you a child with such difficulties, especially when Facebook or blogs show the happy times of other families. I urge you—do not be discouraged! The Lord is not surprised by our struggles. I admit there are times when I have gotten angry at the Lord. When I met one of my sisters in-country, I was so unprepared for her needs, my immediate thought in the moment was: I want to take her back to the orphanage. Today, I can't imagine our family without her.

Does this mean that now, with hindsight, everything is perfect and easy? No. It means I have made the decision to trust God's plan in putting our family together. Even on the days when the last thing I want to do is to love my sisters or sacrifice my time to care for their needs with no compensation, I remind myself that every child deserves a family. When I find myself angry at the orphanages who caused and lied about the severity of my sisters' needs, I think to myself: If it were me, wouldn't I want a family?

In his book, *Adoption and the Gospel*, our friend Gerald Clark from the Home for Good Foundation, writes about how orphans don't choose their circumstances. They don't want to be orphans. As Christians, who have been adopted into the family of God, it is our responsibility to adopt (Eph. 1:5).

How great a sacrifice was Christ's death on the cross? Yet this suffering is what allows us to be God's sons and daughters. When we accept Christ and His death on the cross, we take on His name. We no longer are by ourselves. We are Christians. Our citizenship has changed from this world to Heaven. This is exactly what physical adoption is. When my parents adopted me, I took on their last name. This name is what gives me the privileges of an American citizen. The parallels between physical and spiritual adoption have deepened my own faith, because not only have I been adopted by Christ—I have literally been saved by adoption on this Earth.

I don't think adoption is guaranteed to be easy. Rather, my encouragement lies in the fact that adoption is what the Lord calls us to and if we are following His commands, we can rest assured.

Not an Orphan Anymore

I need to get over it. This is by far the most important lesson I have learned as an adopted child. I believe it is key to why I do not struggle with issues of identity and loss as so many other adopted kids do.

When I was younger, I struggled with many of these same questions. Why didn't my mom want me? What would my life have been like in Russia? When I was nine years old, stepping into a Russian Baptist church one Sunday, memories I didn't even know were buried in my mind resurrected. Unexpectedly, I started to sob. Years later, I traveled to Bulgaria—my first adoption trip to an Eastern European country since I left my orphanage in 1998. Tears automatically started to well up in my eyes when I entered the orphanage. While my reaction wasn't as severe as when I was nine (since I knew where the feelings were coming from), they were still there.

The bad memories are real. Yet, my parents raised me differently than how many adopted children are, in the way they dealt with the memories and the pain. We acknowledged it. We prayed about it. Then we moved on. My parents never allowed me to wallow in self-pity or use my past as an excuse for misery or attitude towards others.

It comes down to identity. If my identity is in my past as an orphan, I am going to continue to carry around all that pain, the questions, and the loss. However, if my identity is first in Christ, then He fills the void created by orphanhood. He satisfies that longing and is the Answer to *all* those questions.

This is a hard lesson. Not necessarily because it is difficult to understand or to do. It is hard because it requires that I change my behavior. I can no longer use my past as an orphan as an excuse. For example, when orphans in Eastern Europe "graduate" from their orphanage, most have no idea how to take care of themselves. Someone else has always done everything for them. Even if these children end up in safe homes, where they can go to school and learn job skills, they don't want to. They have been raised with the mentality "I'm just an orphan. Why should I bother? The government will take care of me." This mindset has been so ingrained in children, that even when they are adopted, it is difficult to get rid of it. Even with all the opportunities in front of them, they prefer to hold onto what they know and their learned helplessness.

Why wouldn't anyone want to be free of this pain? It may be because their identity is still rooted in their pasts; they cannot get over their identity as an orphan. As an adopted child, this is a decision I had to make for myself. My parents could teach me and listen, but it was ultimately up to me. Once a child makes this decision and puts Christ first in their life, it is the beginning of freedom. And once an orphan is truly free, the Lord can use them in mighty ways. If more orphans were able to find the kind of joy and contentment in Christ that I have, imagine how the Lord could use us! Remember, earthly adoption is a reflection of salvation. If more adoptees are armed with this understanding and a passion for Christ, I believe we can create real change (Mark 16:15).

Natalya "Sasha" C. was adopted from Russia with a mild form of cerebral palsy. Natalya is passionate about sharing the plight of orphans, particularly the aging-out orphan crisis. She is currently attending Bucknell University, where she double majors in Creative Writing and Russian Studies. You can find her blog at www.natalyawriting.blogspot.com where she writes about orphan and disability advocacy, and more.

28

Always Raised

Years ago, I saw the life I longed for in the movie *Inn of the Sixth Happiness*, starring Ingrid Bergman. Based on a true story, the movie chronicles the adventures of Gladys Aylward, a British maid who scrimped and saved shillings until she could purchase a one-way ticket on the trans-Siberian railroad to China to serve as a missionary. Set in the Sino-Japanese War, she eventually saves the lives of one hundred abandoned Chinese children—abandoned by their own parents who had fled the Japanese onslaught. Gladys determined to walk those children across deep and dangerous valleys, through a formidable mountain range, and into safe territory during the Chinese-Japanese War; it is harder than she could imagine, and longer than she can endure. At times on her journey, darkness and fear overwhelm her, tempting her to quit. Yet, in the end, she and one hundred children walk across the final mountain top into safety singing, as her impossible dream comes true.

I believe that our adoption stories are most typically stories of impossible dreams that do not really differ from hers—we walk up steep mountains, hike along precipitous ridges, and trudge through dark valleys; but we also have times when we feel we are living in the middle of some Rockwell or Monet painting, surrounded by mischievous joy or blossoming sublimity.

So here are snippets of how I believe God is making our

family's impossible dream come true. It is the story of death working backwards, repeatedly, in and through our family of thirteen, to bring a hundredfold reward (Mark 10:29). It is the story of how God used our worst nightmare—the death of the promised son—to accomplish my wildest dream of many abandoned children coming into loving families.

First, through "Five Resurrections," hope displaces grief to help equip me, as a mother who had lost her firstborn son, to love children who had lost their parents. I learn there are no secrets hidden from God; God has good purposes, unbreakable promises, supernatural deliverances, and shocking surprises in store; and God allows heartbreaking deaths, followed by victorious resurrections, multiplied in and through us again and again. Now, this is the longest section of our story, because I believe many of you dear readers have experienced a "death" so to speak—a kind of loss that feels akin at times to a death. I believe the Lord wishes to give you the same life-infusing miraculous hope He gave me. Next, in "Eight Adoptions," God turns death for one into life for eight, as we learn together what it means to be a family. Finally, in "Words for Life," two decades worth of adoptive-parenting lessons open the secrets of loving and of legacy.

"I pray that the eyes of your heart may be enlightened in order that you may know ... his incomparably great power for us who believe. That power is the same as the mighty strength he exerted when he raised Christ from the dead..." (Eph. 1:18–20, NIV).

* * *

Five Resurrections
It was nearly lunchtime that Tuesday by the time I made my way across town to my office under the bright Carolina blue sky. My

thoughts turned with excitement to all the plans we'd made for celebrating the next day, September 20.

"Lord, thank You for tomorrow, we will celebrate ten years for the gift of having Jonny as our son, years we came so very close, so many times, to not having him; you know I am afraid that this might be the year we lose him. As we get ready to celebrate his birthday tomorrow, I ask you to prolong his life. If this is the year that he has to have the heart transplant, somehow Lord I trust you will be faithful to bring us through. You are powerful, an expert in miracles, and nothing is difficult nor impossible for you. Keep us thankful for each day that we have the joy of being parents."

After work, my three kids and I (eleven-year-old Lorane, nine-year-old Jonny, and three-year-old Wise) hopped on our bikes (or in the burley) to head to the grocery store. As we approached, Jonny suddenly began to cross the street and in the blink of an eye, the front and back tires of an old forest green car, which seemed to have appeared silently out of nowhere, rolled right over our precious little boy. Shortly after we arrived at the hospital, the doctors gave us the heartbreaking news every parent fears. Brian and I wept as we said goodbye to our son of promise, and I found myself praying:

"The Lord gives and the Lord takes away; blessed be the name of the Lord. Lord you say that You give your angels charge over us to keep us from stumbling yet I feel like you didn't do this with Jonny ... Lord there will be a terrible emptiness; fill us with Yourself as You alone can do."

What I didn't realize was that Jonny's one death would multiply to become *The Five Deaths* ... the death of my son, the death of my marriage, the death of my family, the death of my God, and the death of me. The death of my marriage, as my husband and best friend Brian, for the first time ever, was emotionally, spiritually, and practically ... absent. I vacillated like a rubber band, stretching on most days between anger and compassion. The death of my family because the empty chair and the empty bed and the empty spot in the car left a somber dark cloud. The death of my God, as I felt betrayed by both the Lord and by His people: the One who supposedly loved me best had determined that the worst that could happen, would; and His own often avoided me, leaving me on my own with my saga of sadness. And the death of me, as instead of the friendly, cheerful, compassionate, fun-loving, affectionate, diligent person I was before—I had become a person I disliked ... withdrawn, somber, aloof, boring, cold, unmotivated, and angry. In sum, I myself had become and behaved like, an orphan.

Please stop here, and reread that last paragraph, reflecting on this: "Have I, or has someone I love, including my child, experienced serious loss or disappointment that has left open and unhealed wounds?" While most of you will not identify with losing a child and the depth of deaths multiplied, most will in fact identify with unanticipated loss or unfulfilled longings in one or more of these areas—maybe it was when you, or that person you have in mind, had a massive change through fostering, adoption, or moving, or maybe you faced infertility or lost someone in your family; maybe it was when someone you love became chronically ill or when the one you most trusted betrayed you; or perhaps it was the unanticipated consequence of pursuing a dream that led to nowhere, or of chasing idols like success, accomplishment, attachment, missional living, or even ministry, which have left your soul bereft. Recognizing this in your own story or in your child's story will add meaning and open up prayer channels for what comes next. Because the word "testimony" means "do it again," I invite you to stop and pray as you read the *Five*

Resurrection stories that God will "do it again" for you or for those you love.

The first death God attended to was the first that had occurred. After the accident, my daily trip into work required I pass the very spot of the accident, unavoidably seeing the mental video clip on "repeat" of the green car crushing my little boy—few knew the daily despair this sight poured into me, as I re-lived the trauma over and over again. After two months like this, I found myself at the Metropolitan Art Museum in New York City, standing before a painting of three angels picking up a young dead boy off the road and carrying him up to heaven. When I returned to Atlanta, I saw in my mind's eye on the day of that first dreaded drive back to work, not the familiar clip of death, but rather the three angels taking the young boy to heaven, and the young boy was Jonny. The Lord had placed into my mind His video of life; since that day, I do not recall ever seeing that video of death again. It was, simply, erased and overwritten. Healed by the new true narrative. *Resurrection #1.*

Though I came to believe that for Jonny "to be absent from the body is to be present with the Lord," my own mother's heart was open, raw, and aching—with the exception of scattered patches of conjugal numbness replacing sections where marital intimacy had previously lodged. After I poured out my sorrow over the distance between Brian and me with a dear friend, she gifted me a book by a Jewish couple who had also lost a ten-year-old son. The authors' analogy held refreshing revelation: If a husband and wife were paralyzed in an automobile accident, the wife would never consider asking her husband to help feed her—you see, his paralysis is visible from the outside. But after the death of a child, an emotional "hidden paralysis" ensues, gripping each parent in its invisible cloak. Once I realized Brian had suffered his own emotional "paralysis," my path of grief led me to seek help from close friends for a season, meeting for coffee or lunch, or to share and pray. Brian's path, on the other hand, led him towards solitude —journaling, counseling, spending time alone in the Lord's presence, writing letters to Jonny, and silent retreats to the nearby Monastery of the Holy Spirit. We also chose to start dating each other again, getting babysitters so we could go out for some plain old fun and recreation. The marriage that for a time felt like a terminal disease to be endured, began to show signs of progressively vibrant, restorative, transforming, and joyful life. Laughter and friendship returned to our marriage. *Resurrection #2*.

But what about our family? The morning of Jonny's birthday, I found Lorane sitting cross-legged on her antique white canopy bed in pensive thought ... "Mommy, our family will never be right with only two kids ... Can we please adopt?"

Shocked and worried, I began, "Honey, you can never replace your brother." "Mommy, I understand all that. I don't feel I am trying to replace Jonny. Will you and Daddy just pray about it?"

So, in the twinkle of an eye, our eleven-year-old had talked me into praying about adopting. I soon came to understand that as a mother who had lost her child, I was equipped in a special way to love children who had lost their parents. Though Brian's confidence would come later, he, too, felt that providing love and a family to a child in need would leave a legacy he would someday look back at and feel thankful for. After the year of endless document prep, Brian, Lorane, Wise, and I were on our way across the Atlantic to frigid Russia to bring our new kids, Michael and Rose, ages seven and eight, into our warm home, which would soon again teem with noise and life.

In the wake of their trauma of abandonment and ours of losing our son, simple tasks of daily life as a family gave us a chance to walk together, little by little, towards the healing we all needed. Like the nondescript fall day when Brian was raking the back yard and found a little dead bird buried beneath the brittle brown leaves. Without thought, he picked it up and tossed it over the fence. Rose, suddenly hysterical, screamed at the top of her lungs in Russian, "Daddy threw away the baby! Daddy threw away the baby!" So, Brian came, took Rose by the hand, and led her inside. He then sat on the couch after placing her facing him, perched on his lap. He looked her squarely in the eye and, with his father's love, spoke softly yet with authority. "Rose, let me tell you how much I love you. I love you so much that I got in a big airplane and went all the way over to Russia, and then I went and found you and brought you home. I will always be your daddy and you will always be my little girl. I will never leave you and I will do all I can to make sure no danger ever hurts you. Do you want to go on a walk?" By the time he finished, Rose was calm and seemed to have recovered from the reminder that the little dead bird's fate could have become hers. In this season, we were once again living as a family who together savored life in spite of each of our previous encounters with death. In God's irony, one son's death had unlocked life—life of the body, soul, and spirit for Rose and Michael. And in unlocking life for them, He had unlocked life for our family as well. *Resurrection #3.*

But where was the key that could once again resurrect in me a sense of God's closeness? Prayer was dry, distant, falling on deaf ears. Scriptures were silent. The vacuum of our visible tragedy felt bigger than hope in an invisible God. One evening when I had taken one of my escape-from-the-pain-of-life-drives, I returned to an unfamiliar blue Honda parked in our driveway. When I went inside, Brian explained that Susan, a woman from church whom I barely knew, was waiting in the living room. Reluctantly, I went into the living room, dreading a superficial conversation.

"So, what brings you here?"

"Well, I know you and your family have been through a lot," Susan explained. *"I was praying for you and felt the Lord show me that I should come over and visit and pray for you.* I know we don't know each other very well, but I'd like to talk for a little while and then pray for you if that would be okay."

My eyes filled with tears as Susan came over and sat beside me and hugged me. Imagine for a moment what it was like, living in a desert for four months without water and then having living proof that the long-awaited oasis of spiritual encouragement and restoration that has finally appeared is not in fact a mirage. Hot tears burned my eyes and a lump lodged in my throat. And that was the first night of the return of a prodigal heart to a loving Father, all brought about by the arms of love that put on "hands of service."

From that evening on, she came every week, several times a week, for several years. If the kitchen floor was dirty, she swept; if I had not thawed anything for dinner, she cooked; if the laundry was in piles, she washed it; if Wise was whiny, she sat on the floor and played; if Lorane wanted to go out for ice cream, Susan took her. And always there would be a time for her to find out how I was, and how to pray. Susan's friendship was like oxygen tubing, a simple conduit for the endless supply of Christ's unfailing love, which in its constant supply, reversed death's onslaught against faith. *Resurrection #4.*

But could anything bring back the old me? I found out a little over a year after the accident, when I was again on a work trip to New York City. Pondering in my hotel room whether I would always be stuck in the self I disliked, I sensed the Holy Spirit say out of the blue, *"I raised Jesus from the dead and right now I am going to raise the part of your heart that died with Jonny."* The voice was not audible, but it was every bit as real as the most audible voice I have ever heard. The voice was simply a strong and unavoidable sentence engraved into my mind by the Holy Spirit. And at once, the person I used to be, the person I had always been before Jonny died, was totally back. For me this miracle was as dramatic as if someone had had a leg severed in an accident and suddenly, one year later, the leg was simply, in the span of one minute, back again complete and unscarred, with no sign of its former trauma. No person could ever have done for me what God did for me that night. The "other self" of my split personality had disappeared and I returned to Atlanta as Susan, the Susan God had made me to be, healed, restored, and at long last, resurrected. *Resurrection #5.*

* * *

Eight Adoptions

After God had done for me what no other person could have done by accomplishing all these resurrections, I longed with all my heart to love Him extravagantly in return. So, one Tuesday evening as I sat around our kitchen table in prayer with three friends, I stretched out my hands and with an earnest heart said "Lord, you know I love you and I will follow You anywhere you lead me. If you just help me understand Your will for my life, I promise You that I will obey you."

The following weekend I went to a nearby retreat center in Conyers, Georgia, the Monastery of the Holy Spirit. I expected a weekend of solitude and reflection, of enjoying the Lord's Presence, so I was stunned when the Hispanic monk standing in front of the reception desk issued me my room keys and then barked this abrupt command while tapping his index finger on his wristwatch over and over, like the Mad Hatter: "I have taken a vow of solitude, but God has me here waiting for you. I am supposed to pray for you. Come with me quickly now so I can pray for you, because I only have five minutes before vespers begins."

I felt shocked, a little scared, and initially hesitant, but I felt I had no choice but to comply when he issued a demanding order, "follow me quickly." So, I followed him into a library-like room, where he said "sit down here" and pointed to a nondescript armchair. I sat, and he laid his hands gently on my shoulders and began to speak.

"Don't feel my hands but the Hands of the Lord Jesus on you; don't hear my voice but the voice of the Lord Jesus to you; I will use these hands to bless children; I will use you to provide a home and a haven for children who have been abandoned; you will work together with your husband in this place, and its name shall be the House of the Godly Child ... Always lay your hands on sick children and the Lord will heal them."

I felt startled by this totally unexpected encounter with someone I had never met, someone who could not know that just six months earlier we had done precisely what he had prayed—we had "provided a home and a haven for children who had been abandoned" by adopting our first two Russian children, Rose and Michael. He wouldn't have known of my recent prayer, promising to obey God's call on my life.

Within several months, Rose began to cry often around bedtime. When I asked, "Why are you crying?" her answer was always the same: "I really miss my sister Joy."

You see, Joy was Rose's best friend at the orphanage, and the two of them had held hands at the orphanage across their two beds, side by side, every night from ages four to eight years. After several years of prayer, it was clear to Brian and me that the Lord was leading us to adopt Joy.

When I went to Russia to visit Joy, I was surprised that the orphanage director had two boys in her office, alongside Joy.

"Who are these boys?" I asked.

"Why, they are her brothers, Luke, aged fourteen, and her little brother Isaac, aged seven."

Having seen the heartbreak when my own children Lorane and Wise were separated from their brother Jonny, I knew I could not separate siblings. So, Brian and I ended up expecting one and receiving three. These three treasures were gentle, kind, and peaceful.

Only two months after we got home with Joy, Luke, and Isaac, our first adopted son, Michael, came home from school one day with a startling statement.

"Mommy, today I asked my friends to pray I can go back to Russia and find my other three sisters and adopt them."

Shocked, again, I explained, "Honey, you have a very tender heart, but sometimes tender hearts get broken. God sometimes answers no and sometimes yes and sometimes wait. I love you and don't think this is possible, and I don't want your heart to get broken."

"Mommy, I am going to keep praying, but could you try to find out if anyone knows where my three biologic sisters are?"

So, I sent an email asking a friend in Russia named Sasha to try to find out. One week later, I got a call from this friend in Russia—the same dear friend who helped us and so many others with our adoptions. He said, "Susan, I have some news for you. I have found the three girls, and they are in an orphanage very close to St. Petersburg. In fact, when you come next week to visit, you can meet them."

When I met Shelley, Grace, and Kristin, again ages seven, ten, and fourteen, I felt like I was meeting my own children whom I had known for many years—for they looked and acted just like Rose and Michael. Within a short time, we knew the Lord was calling us to adopt them as well.

So, now it is twenty years later. Our ten children are all grown—and we are contented empty nesters, with friends and family always coming and going. Six of our kids are married, and we have five granddaughters, with the sixth granddaughter and the first grandson on the way.

We have children who have been valedictorians, missionaries, Young Life staff, state wrestling champs, sculptors, and employees-of-the-month. We have also had children who have been in jail, faced addictions, and been pregnant out of wedlock, as well as one with reactive attachment disorder and even a daughter trafficked at age nineteen. But what is important to me is that through all this, each of our children has had a good relationship with us— they know we are *for them* and on their side, even when we are *against their choices*. And more importantly even than this, to me, is that each of them has some measure of personal faith and relationship with our Lord.

* * *

Words of Life

After twenty years of adoption parenting, speaking at many conferences, and writing many blog posts, there are several principles I call "words of life," which at some point transformed me and my approach to parenting. I share them here and pray the Lord will use them to equip you to walk in joy and faith, with an unshakable contentment that can be the norm for those of us who are promised membership in Jesus' "kingdom which cannot be shaken" (Heb. 12:28, NASB).

• *Reflect Him, not them.* There were times when my children were defiant, disrespectful, dishonoring—and I felt anger or frustration. I absolutely love Ezekiel 20 in *The Message* and have often prayed the Lord would help me respond to them out of who God is and *not* out of how I feel. I actually pretend I have a hidden mirror placed vertically in my mind, pointing straight up toward my Lord in heaven—and I am intentionally raising the eyes of my mind and heart, seeking to *reflect Him to them*—as He is kind, merciful, slow to anger, and abounding in lovingkindness. This is much better than having my internal mirror sitting horizontally in my mind and pointing at them, which would *reflect them to them*, when they are angry or defiant.

• *Change to love, not Love to change.* During one of our times of sadness and anxiety about our trafficked daughter, I was praying in desperation, "Lord, show me how to help her." Then I stopped, waiting to see if the Lord showed me any clear path forward. And He did, in four words, "That's not your job." So, I asked the Lord, "Then what is my job?" Two words clearly impressed on my mind: "Love her." I realized at that moment that my desire to "help" her was really a desire to change her. The Lord wanted to change *me* in order for me to love her well, rather than for me to love her in order to change her. This makes so much sense—Do you like it when someone tries to change you? Most of us don't. And guess what? When I asked the Holy Spirit to fill me with His love for her, and He changed my focus to loving her rather than changing her, *she changed*!

• *Live the "Copy-Jesus" life.* When we think about what most motivates us to draw closer to Jesus, it is being around people whose lives of intimacy with the Lord inspire us to want the same. I remember when one of our daughters went through a very painful time in high school and had tirades of screaming "I hate you! You are nothing to me! Nothing! I am going to tear up those *$-ing adoption papers because you are *not* my mom!" My heart was broken. I couldn't sleep that night, so got up around two a.m. and opened my Bible, asking the Lord to speak to me, and the Lord gave me such amazing comfort. But back to the point, about five years later, one night after church, we started talking about who we copy. That same daughter said, "Mommy, I just try to copy you—you are the only one I copy. I know I said so many things that hurt you when I was growing up, but I was a teenager and was hurting myself. Mommy, do you think I am like you?" What I have learned is that if we copy Jesus—the resurrected, glorified, at-the-right-hand-of-the-Father-Jesus, then, eventually, they will copy us.

Jesus Arises for You

"Arise, shine; for your light has come, and the glory of the Lord has risen upon you. For behold, darkness will cover the earth and deep darkness the peoples; but the Lord will rise upon you and His glory will appear upon you"(Isa. 60:1–2, NASB).

For you, dear treasure, I pray you see that with every storm that arises, Jesus rises higher (Matt. 8:24–26), replacing them with His calm. And I pray you are encouraged by Jesus' words to you as His disciple, "I will not leave you as orphans; I will come to you" (John 14:18 NASB). And as He comes, He always comes with His love that fills us, and in so doing, equips us to love the literal and figurative child or children who need this same love. May we remember often that "Whoever welcomes this little child in my name welcomes me" (Luke 9:48, NIV).

Dr. Susan H.'s life has been intersected, by God, through personal, ministry, and professional roads at the global orphan crossroads. Personally, God led Susan and her family to adopt eight more children, ages seven to fourteen. From a ministry perspective (Hope at Home), God's call is to speak His hope of changing the world by transforming every orphan and vulnerable child into a beloved son or daughter. Professionally, Susan has worked in North America, South America, Eastern Europe, Asia, and Africa; she is a highly published scientist and is a senior advisor for global health at the Centers for Disease Control and Prevention. She is dedicated to using the best of science to forge broad governmental, civil society, and private partnerships that protect children and young people from violence and its enduring consequences.